Planning London

D1345742

Planning London

EDITED BY
James Simmie
Bartlett School of Planning
University College London

UCL
PRESS

First published in 1994 by UCL Press.

UCL Press Limited
University College London
Gower Street
London WC1E 6BT

The name of University College London (UCL) is a registered
trade mark used by UCL Press with the consent of the owner.

ISBN:
1-85728-057-1 HB
1-85728-058-X PB

British Library Cataloguing in Publication Data
A catalogue record for this book is available from the British Library.

Typeset in Baskerville.
Printed and bound by
Biddles Ltd, Guildford and King's Lynn, England

Contents

CONTENTS

This book is dedicated to
the memory of my father
W.S.S.

Preface

This book has been written by the staff in the Bartlett School of Planning at University College London. It emerged from the need to introduce first-year undergraduates to planning for the first time. It was felt that the best way to do this was to introduce them not only to planning in the abstract but to use the rich variety of issues, problems and examples that abound more or lesson the doorstep of University College. So the decision was taken to use case study material drawn from the London region to illustrate to students what planning in large cities in Britain is all about.

This proved to be easier said than done. Once half-a-dozen staff had produced what each of them considered to be the absolutely basic minimum reading lists necessary to introduce students to planning in London, the list was so long and distributed among so many different sources that it could have taken up the better part of a four-year degree course on its own.

Planning London has been written to overcome this problem. It is basically an introductory review of the literature and topics that form the bases of an understanding of British planning in general and its particular applications in large conurbations such as London. Some of the material used is, of course, peculiar only to London. But many of the issues raised will apply equally to other metropolitan areas in Britain.

One major intention has been to write the book in language as accessible as possible to students and others with no prior knowledge of planning. Despite this, it has been necessary (for the sake of brevity) to use the many abbreviations and acronyms that form part of the professional jargon of planners. To familiarize students with the meaning of these abbreviations and acronyms, a full list of definitions is provided at the beginning of the book. These definitions are repeated when the abbreviations and acronyms are used for the first time in the text.

The book has four major parts. Chapter 1 deals with the questions of defining what planning and London are, and points to some of the particular problems involved in planning London. Chapters 2–4 analyzes three of the fundamental elements of any city: employment, housing and transport. They emphasize the links between them and the necessity to plan them together, and not in isolation from one another. Chapters 5–7 examine the politics and practice of planning in London. They are focused particularly on the problems and practices that are important to the planning of London. Finally, Chapters 8 and 9 are concerned both with the special characteristics of London as a world city – something which marks it off from other British cities – and the planning achievements of the past and prospects for the future. Although the book is primarily a review of existing material, this part emphasizes the point that planning is essentially a future-orientated activity. It looks to the future of London in the 21st century.

James Simmie
Oxford, January 1994

Acknowledgements

Taking on the task of editing a book such as this is a bold undertaking. Not only is the subject matter so vast that it fills whole library shelves on its own, but also reviewing and simplifying the material is fraught with difficulties in what to include and what to leave out.

What has emerged as *Planning London* is very much the product of the forbearing and helpful collaboration of colleagues. Without their co-operation the numerous restructuring and rewriting exercises would not have been possible. It is appropriate to thank Andy Pratt, Stephen Merrett, David Banister, John Gyford, Mike Collins and Peter Hall for seeing this project through to its conclusion.

Thanks is also due to the many friends and colleagues whose work we have used and quoted as the bases of the various reviews contained in the book. It is hoped that they will feel that citations of their work carry with them the gratitude of the authors of *Planning London*.

Helpful comments were also received on an earlier draft from Mike Bruton and John Glasson. These were most welcome in the suggestions they provided for improving the text. Roger Jones, the publisher, also deserves much thanks for his patience and willingness to persevere to the end of this project.

As usual, despite the best endeavours of all those who have helped with the book, the sins of omission and faults of commission remain solely with the authors.

Permission to use the following copyright material is gratefully acknowledged: The Corporation of London (Greater London Record Office) for Figs 1.1, 6.3, 6.4, 6.5, 6.9; Weidenfeld & Nicolson for Fig. 1.2; Edward Arnold for Figs 1.3, 1.5, 8.1; the Controller of Her Majesty's Stationery Office for Figs 6.1, 6.2, (both © Crown Copyright); the Ordnance Survey for Figs 6.6, 6.12 (both © Crown Copyright); the London Borough of Camden for Fig. 6.8; the Open University for Fig. 7.1; and the Department of the Environment for Fig. 7.2.

James Simmie
Oxford, January 1994

Abbreviations and acronyms

BIF   banking, insurance and finance
CBI   Confederation of British Industry
CDA   Comprehensive Development Area
CG   City Grant
CLPC   Central London Planning Conference
CSO   Central Statistical Office
CURDS   Centre for Urban and Regional Development Studies
DoE   Department of the Environment
DLR   Docklands Light Railway
EC   European Community
EIA   environmental impact assessment
EZ   Enterprise Zone
GDO   General Development Order
GDP   gross domestic product
GLC   Greater London Council
GLDP   Greater London Development Plan
GLEB   Greater London Enterprise Board
GLRPC   Greater London Regional Planning Committee
IDO   Interim Development Order
IDP   Initial Development Plan
ILEA   Inner London Education Authority
ITH   industry, transport and housing
LCC   London County Council
LDDC   London Docklands Development Corporation
LLMA   Local Labour Market Area
LMR   London Metropolitan Region
LPA   local planning authorities
LPAC   London Planning Advisory Committee
LRC   London Research Centre
LRT   London Regional Transport
LTA   London Traffic Area
LUL   London Underground Limited
MGB   Metropolitan Green Belt
MH   Ministry of Health
MHLG   Ministry of Housing and Local Government

MTCP   Ministry of Town and Country Planning
NEDO   National Economic Development Organisation
NIMBY   "not in my backyard"
NSE   Network South East
OMA   Outer Metropolitan Area
PAG   Planning Advisory Group
QUAGO   quasi-autonomous government organization
QUANGO   quasi-autonomous non-government organization
RoSE   Rest of the South East
RTPI   Royal Town Planning Institute
SE   South East of England
SEEDS   South East Economic Development Strategy
SERPLAN   London and South East Regional Planning Conference
SIC   Standard Industrial Classification
TEC   Training and Enterprise Council
TNC   transnational corporation
TTWA   travel-to-work-area
UCO   Use Classes Order
UDC   Urban Development Corporation
UDP   Unitary Development Plans
UP   Urban Programme

CHAPTER ONE

Planning and London

James Simmie

Introduction

Planning London is an introduction to British city planning. It uses London as the case study of land-use problems and the politics and policies involved in searching for solutions to them. While London is not an average or representative British city, being the capital city both in the sense of the seat of government and the major British concentration of economic power, and also in being by far the largest city in Britain, it does contain a full range of planning problems and issues which can be found in varying degrees in most of Britain's other large conurbations. It is for this reason that concentrating on London as a case study serves not only to introduce students to planning in that city alone but also to the range of planning issues that are likely to confront planners in other large cities.

Chapter 1 of the book first of all outlines the basic purposes, principles and administrative structures of the British planning system in general and the parts which have applied in the case of London. Having defined planning in this way, it then goes on to examine the various geographical definitions of London. It concludes by stressing the complex interconnectedness of the planning issues and problems confronting politicians and planners in a city such as London. Despite the importance of considering the interconnections of different land uses, it is also essential to have an individual grasp of the nature and characteristics of some of the key urban functions. For this reason, Chapters 2, 3 and 4 outline three of the most important aspects of any city. These are employment, housing and transport. Developing land-use planning policies to arrange and accommodate these and other city functions is a question of both politics and planning. Chapters 5, 6 and 7 therefore deal with these twin aspects of planning for London. Finally, Chapters 8 and 9 evaluate the past effects and future of planning of in London. These revolve around its special characteristics as not just another large city but as a "world city". The special nature of such cities combines with all the other land-use issues confronting large cities to make planning for London an extremely complex

1

collection of both general and particular problems. The final chapter sums up the experience of tackling these problems in the recent past and looks forward to how they may be tackled in the immediate future.

Before describing and analyzing these issues with specific reference to London, for those completely new to the study of British planning and urban analysis it is necessary to summarize some of the basic elements of the planning system and to define London in geographic terms as the empirical focus of the rest of the book. In what follows, planning is defined in terms of its general purposes and principles, and the administrative structures through which the system is operated are outlined. Alternative geographical definitions of London are described and the significance of different definitions for planning purposes is explained.

What is planning?

Purposes

Turning first to the definition of planning, it may be thought of either as a means to greater ends, along with other public and private policies, or as an end in itself. In the minds of the originators of the British planning system, the broader definition of the purposes of planning was uppermost. Later, as the system became established and bureaucratized, a narrower definition of its basic purpose has been developed.

At first, the coalition government drawn from all parties during the Second World War was receptive to the idea of planning for two main reasons. The first of these was the recent experience of the economic collapse and depression during the late 1920s and early 1930s. This, combined with wartime production needs, gave rise to ideas for and an acceptance of the need for economic planning. The second reason was the need to provide a morale-boosting vision of post-war society. Ideas for economic and land-use planning were developed, along with other aspects of a "Welfare State", as part of this vision.

The ideas for the purposes of the land-use planning part of this vision were developed by elites inside and outside Parliament. According to Hall et al. (1973), these elites followed a unitary model of society in which social stability and harmony were of prime concern. These views failed to recognize the inherent conflicts of interests both between different elites and between them and the rest of the population, which have dogged land-use planning in Britain ever since the Second World War.

These basic conflicts rest on the differences of interest between manufacturing industry and agriculture, often expressed as a difference between town and country, and between these and the mass of the working population. During the war there was some co-operation between manufacturing and agriculture because of their importance to the war effort. There was some acceptance by their elites that better conditions should be promised to the working masses.

The underlying purposes of this initial vision have changed over time. Some

2

indication of these changes is expressed in the planning law that is the statutory basis of land-use planning in Britain. They have been analyzed by McAuslan (1980) in terms of the ideologies of planning law. McAuslan has identified three main ideologies which, at different times, have formed the underlying bases of British planning since the war. They are:
- the protection of private property
- the advancement of the public interest
- the promotion of public participation.

The protection of private property has the longest history and is most dominant. It is fundamental to British society. It defines the acceptable boundaries of public involvement in private property and markets. It also ensures that, in the long run, the coexistence between the public interest and private property will always end up being on terms dictated by the interests of private property.

Looking at the main periods of planning history in Britain, the ideology of private property has been clearly dominant before the Second World War and since 1979. The bearers of this dominant or influential ideology have also been in conflict with attempts to override it during the 1947–68 and 1969–78 periods of British planning history.

The ideology of the public interest in planning developed during the second half of the nineteenth century. It was expressed in terms of regulations over urban conditions, particularly with respect to public health provisions such as clean water supplies and systems of sewers. It was broadened during the war years to include planning and the whole idea of the Welfare State, which was set out in the famous Beveridge Report (1942) Social Insurance and Allied Services. The concept of the public interest received its strongest expression during the immediate post-war period and up to about 1968. The governing elites incorporated elements of both private-property and public-interest ideologies in planning legislation and policies during this time.

In Britain the ideology of participation stands in opposition to the first two ideologies. This is because it forms the basis of claims for all members of the public to be involved in planning decision-making. This runs directly counter to the elitist tradition that decisions are made by major property owners, governing elites and experts.

In British planning, the high point of public participation came during the 1969 to 1979 period. It received its strongest official expression in the Skeffington Report (1969) of the Committee on Public Participation in Planning. Since 1979 it has been intentionally whittled away by an authoritarian central government.

It may be that the public-interest purposes of planning will come to the fore again with the political acceptance of environmental concerns and the currently vague concept of "sustainable development". The driving force behind such a change could be similar to that behind the movement for public health regulations during the nineteenth century. The main difference being that, in the late twentieth century, the capacity to pollute the environment and endanger public health is on a global rather than a local scale.

3

Principles

The operational principles behind the administrative regulations developed to implement the shifting general purposes of planning have themselves changed through time. The first post-war Town and Country Planning Act in 1947 expropriated all the future urban private property rights of owners to change the existing uses of their buildings or to construct new ones at will. The major, and often elite, land users – agriculture, forestry, statutory undertakers, the Crown and the military – were exempt from these provisions. From that time, private property owners wishing to carry out urban development had to obtain planning permission from the relevant local planning authority (LPA). Development was defined broadly as "the carrying out of building, engineering, mining or other operations in, on, over or under land, or the making of any material change in the use of any buildings or other land". A series of subsequent Town and Country Planning and closely related Acts in 1968, 1971, 1980 and 1990 have modified the details but maintained these basic principles of the 1947 Act.

These public regulations have created sharp distinctions between the private property rights of those who can acquire planning permission and those who cannot. The underlying justifications for public distinction between them rest on two quite different principles. On the one hand, the publicly created oligopolistic profits enjoyed by those who can acquire planning permission are justified as legitimate rewards for enterprise. On the other hand, those who cannot acquire the right to develop their property are prevented from doing so on the grounds that such development would cause nuisance to others (Reade 1987: 22).

Local planning decisions that separate these two sets of private property rights are based on two main elements. The first of these elements is the development plan. The second is development control. Both have been subject to change since their statutory arrival in the 1947 Town and Country Planning Act.

Development plans have been through one major change since the Second World War and are currently going through a second. The system introduced after the War made counties and county borough councils responsible for producing "Unitary Development Plans". These showed, on a cartographic base, the precise land uses that could be developed or were planned for particular sites and plots of land. Once approved by the Minister for Housing and Local Government, they became statutory documents. They were very detailed. The processes for modifying them in any significant way were nearly as long and cumbersome as for their initial production and approval. Consequently, it took many years before all counties and county borough councils actually had approved development plans.

This development plan system was changed in the late 1960s when it was expected that the central government would follow the recommendations of the Redcliffe-Maud Commission and reform local government into a single tier of all-purpose local authorities. Accordingly, development plans were separated into general, strategic "structure" and detailed "local" plans. It was wrongly assumed that, with the exception of London, these would be produced and operated within

4

a single local planning authority. In the event, structure plans were made the responsibility of counties, and local plans were given to the districts after the reorganization of local government in England and Wales in 1974.

Initially, structure plans were broad strategic plans which included some economic and social considerations. They had to be approved by the Secretary of State who, by this time, was ensconced in the DoE which had superseded the MHLG. Once approved they became statutory documents. Local plans produced by the districts had to be certified as being in accordance with their relevant county's structure plan.

The history of structure plans is one of the progressive narrowing of their purposes and the reassertion of private property rights as their scope has been whittled away by the Secretary of State. First to go was their economic and social content. This marked a major shift away from planning as a means to greater ends and towards its use as a limited end in its own right. The DoE soon insisted that they confine themselves exclusively to matters of land use. The next nail in their coffin was the Conservative Government's Local Government, Planning and Land Act (1980). This effectively emasculated structure plans by allowing districts to prepare local plans without waiting for an approved structure plan, and placing all control over development, apart from mineral extraction and waste disposal, in the hands of the districts. This was followed in 1985 by the Local Government Act which abolished the Greater London Council and all the other metropolitan counties and placed their strategic planning functions in the hands of the Secretary of State.

Local plans were introduced at the same time as structure plans. They are prepared by the district councils. They can take the form of general plans covering the whole range of local planning issues, "subject plans" concerned with specific matters, and "action area plans" which are related to specific localities. They have always been concerned with the more traditional aspects of land-use planning and especially with questions of layout and design. Even so, the Secretary of State sent out a Circular (22/80) in 1980 requiring them to devote less concern to layout, design, non-conforming uses and public participation. During the 1980s, districts have been under pressure from central government to pay more attention to private property rights and less to their public regulation.

The combination of structure and local plans, which make up the development plan system outside London at the moment, will change for a second time in the near future. It has already been superseded by a new form of Unitary Development Plans (UDPs) in London and the other previous metropolitan counties. The Government White Paper of 1989 proposes to extend a version of this system to the rest of England and Wales. This will also coincide with a further reorganization of local government into all-purpose, single-tier unitary authorities.

Under the proposed UDP system, such strategic planning as will take place will be laid down by the Secretary of State in the form of regional planning guidelines. These will determine the framework within which local plans will have to be produced. It will depend very much on the attitude of central government to private property rights as to how far their interests will be written into regional planning guidelines. The evidence so far suggests that the rights of certain kinds of private property will carry more weight against their regulation than at any time since the Second World War.

The second main element of the British planning system is development control. Development control is the power to decide whether or not a specific development can take place on a specific site, to control the intensity of the development permitted and to control its layout and design. It is at the heart of the British land-use planning system. It is the point at which individual property rights come into direct conflict with public regulation. Development control has traditionally been operated mainly by the lowest tier of government. At first this was the counties and county borough councils. Since 1974 the districts have had the main responsibility for operating the development control system. Decisions are expected to be in accordance with the contents of any relevant public and formal plans. They are also expected to be consistent with the provisions of two central government orders. These are the General Development Order (GDO) and the Use Classes Order (UCO). The GDO specifies which limited types of development can take place without planning permission. The UCO categorizes land uses. Planning permission is not required for changes of use within certain defined categories.

Until the 1980s the development control system regulated strongly urban types of private property rights. Since then its operation has been relaxed and speeded up by central government. The exceptions to these general principles are in what are called "designated areas". These are green belts, conservation areas, national parks and areas of outstanding natural beauty.

In addition to the statutory framework, development plans and development control, planning decisions in Britain are also influenced strongly by circulars from the Secretary of State. These are despatched to LPAs at regular intervals. One of the more important of these was 22/80. The numbers show that this was the 22nd such circular to be despatched in 1980. It recommended to LPAs various ways in which the operation of the planning system should be speeded up and made more responsive to the private property rights of large-scale developers.

Circulars have no statutory force. However, LPAs are advised to follow their requirements because, if they refuse planning permission and that decision is taken to appeal, the Secretary of State is the ultimate judge and jury, through the ministerial inspectorate, of that appeal. He can therefore reverse any decision taken at the local level to accord with his wishes as expressed in circulars.

Administrative structures

Public planning is administered through the relevant departments of central and local government. Parliament determines both the structure of government and the allocation of different planning functions to different parts of that structure. Both have been subject to periodic major changes since the Second World War. Throughout the entire post-war period, however, the relevant central government department has supervised both local government and the planning system. Until

1970 this was called the Ministry of Housing and Local Government (MHLG). In 1970 it was amalgamated with the Ministry of Public Buildings and Works, and the Ministry of Transport, and its name was changed to the Department of the Environment (DoE).

Both the old MHLG and the more recent DoE have the function of supervising local government and planning according to the legislation on these two subjects laid down by parliament. The DoE supervises the planning system, interprets and makes routine government planning policy, and acts as the administrative court of appeal in disputed planning decisions. It is a powerful central ministry.

The day-to-day administration of the planning system was delegated to the largest local authorities after the Second World War. These were the 58 counties, administering mainly rural areas, and the 83 county borough councils in urban areas.

This system was first changed in London in 1965. At that time a two-tier structure of local government was established with the Greater London Council (GLC) as the upper tier, and revised and enlarged London boroughs as the lower tier. Later that decade a Royal Commission on Local Government in England was set up under the chairmanship of Lord Redcliffe-Maud and it reported in 1969. It recommended the establishment of single-tier local government and not the system that had been established in London.

The Conservative government that took office in 1970 rejected the Redcliffe-Maud proposals and instead continued with a two-tier system of local government. In 1974 metropolitan counties like the GLC were established in the other large conurbations. Local government in the rest of England and Wales was divided into two tiers, with counties as the upper tier and districts as the lower tier. A different system was established in Scotland. There the upper tier is regions, and the lower tier is again made up of districts.

Local land-use planning functions were split between these two tiers of government. Strategic planning, in the form of structure plans, was allocated to the counties and regions. Local planning, in the form of local plans, was allocated to the districts. This was a recipe for continual conflict between the two tiers of local government over planning matters. Many of these conflicts did not involve the general public directly. They were more often between property-owning county elites, seeking to protect their property values and amenities, and urban-based developers seeking to build housing, industrial and commercial property in the counties.

The general public had least influence over the most important strategic structure plans. The Secretary of State had a much greater degree of control over them. They had to be approved by him and also to include any modifications which he demanded. Local plans then had to be certified as being in accordance with the relevant structure plan. Even then, the Secretary of State could "call in" any politically controversial proposals or decisions made by the second-tier district councils, and decide the matter for himself.

Paradoxically, it was the rise of popular, participatory planning, in the conurbations during the 1970s, that led the government to propose changes to both the

7

upper tier of local government and structure plans. Conflicts between a Labour-controlled GLC and central government over the non-private property orientated aspects of the Greater London Development Plan (GLDP), the structure plan for London, contributed to the central government abolition of all the metropolitan counties in 1986. Their strategic planning is now conducted within the DoE. Its dictates are then handed down to the boroughs in the case of London. They are bound to follow this "advice" in drawing up the new Unitary Development Plans. It is currently proposed to extend a version of this system of both local government and planning to the rest of the country. This could mean that, at some time during the 1990s, land-use planning in Britain will be conducted by a single tier of local government producing UDPs or their local plan equivalent. Their strategic elements will be handed down by the DoE.

A major new development in this structure of government is the growing importance of European Community (EC) institutions. At the moment two elements of these are of particular relevance for planning in Britain. The first is the Directorate General XVI which deals with regional planning. This has the second largest budget of all the EC directorates after agriculture. Already it has forced the current government to spend funds on declining coalfields before receiving additional EC funds.

The second EC measure which is of significance for British planning is the 1986 directive on environmental impact assessment (EIA). This says that member states are required to assess the effects of both public and private projects that are likely to have significant impacts on the environment as a consequence of their nature, size or location. Despite some recalcitrance on the part of the British government to comply with the spirit of this directive, most notably by avoiding its use on the Channel Tunnel project, they have had to comply with the letter of the directive since 1988. The full implementation of this directive should make it much easier to monitor the effects of major planning decisions in the future, if only because of the information that EIAs will make public.

Having outlined and defined the British land-use planning system in general, it is now necessary to consider how London should be defined. It will be shown that this is a more complex problem than it appears at first sight. It will also be shown that this complexity has led to a long discussion of what the real geographic area of London is. This debate has run concurrently with another on what parts of the existing planning system apply to its various constituent parts and whether or not some unique planning measures and structures are required for planning London.

Definitions of London

There are basically three different ways in which London has been defined. They all give rise to different geographical definitions of the land area covered by London. As the land area changes, not only does the simple physical definition of London change but also the political units and economic functions which it embraces.

These changes make very significant differences to the statistics that are thrown up by analyses based on the different definitions. They also make substantial differences to what needs to be considered in the planning of London.

The three commonly used alternative bases for the definition of London rest on:
- political/administrative boundaries
- its physical boundaries
- the extent of local economic linkages/functions.

In what follows, the marked differences that these different bases lead to in definitions of London will be examined separately.

Political/administrative boundaries

The simplest definition of London can be made in terms of the political/administrative boundaries that carry the label London on maps. The current basis of this definition is the Greater London Act of 1963 which provided the statutory basis for the formation of the Greater London Council (GLC), which was set up in 1965 and later abolished in 1986. This provided a political definition of the boundary of Greater London. This extended approximately to the inner boundary of the Metropolitan Green Belt (MGB) which had been established around the area of London that had been physically developed by 1938. It included the 32 London boroughs and the city of London. The old GLC boundary together with those of the London boroughs are shown in Figure 1.1.

This geographical definition of London is effectively based on the arbitrary point which its contiguous urban development had reached in 1938. It takes no account of the changes that have taken place since then, either in where London has continued to develop or in the patterns of work and life among its residents. In purely objective and analytical terms, it is not a satisfactory definition of the "real" land area of London. It is therefore highly unlikely to be an appropriate basis for land-use planning.

Physical boundaries

The containment of London at its 1938 physical limits by the Metropolitan Green Belt (MGB) has not stopped it expanding and growing in different ways. Powerful restrictions within the MGB have resulted in London growing physically beyond the MGB in the rest of the Outer Metropolitan Area (OMA). In this ring around the MGB "existing towns have swelled; and new towns have grown out of villages, or on virgin fields, into major centres . . . So, in an important sense, towns 20 to 30 miles out, like Guildford, Reading, Chelmsford and Maidstone have become parts of London too" (Hall 1977: 24).

The observable, physical extent of London can be seen in Figure 1.2. It includes not only the old GLC area but also the MGB and towns both within and beyond it. The areal boundary of London defined in this way extends from Letchworth in the north to beyond Crawley in the south. It stretches to Reading in the west and to

Figure 1.1   London's boroughs and the City.

Southend in the east. Despite the green- or brownfield gaps between these urban areas, which have been preserved by the planning system, they all form part of a closely interlocked urban system based primarily on the pre-1938 contiguous urban core of London.

From the point of view of technically coherent land-use planning, there is a need to have some overall strategy for the development of this larger area. This was recognized in the classic Abercrombie plan for Greater London, produced in 1944 and published in 1945. The area covered by this plan is shown in Figure 1.3.

Figure 1.3 shows that, for planning purposes, Abercrombie divided Greater London into four rings. At the centre is Inner London covering approximately the area of the old London County Council (LCC). Surrounding that is the outer urban ring extending up to the boundary of the 1938 built-up area. Beyond that is the MGB. A fourth, outer country, ring includes most of the rest of the OMA. All these rings constituted Greater London and were planned together.

Local economic linkages/functions

These physical definitions of Greater London can now be substantiated statistically by examining the patterns of local economic linkages and functions which can be found in the results of the decennial census. These are indicated strongly by the patterns of regular journeys to work. The geographic extent and strength of these patterns can be aggregated into what are called "travel-to-work-areas"

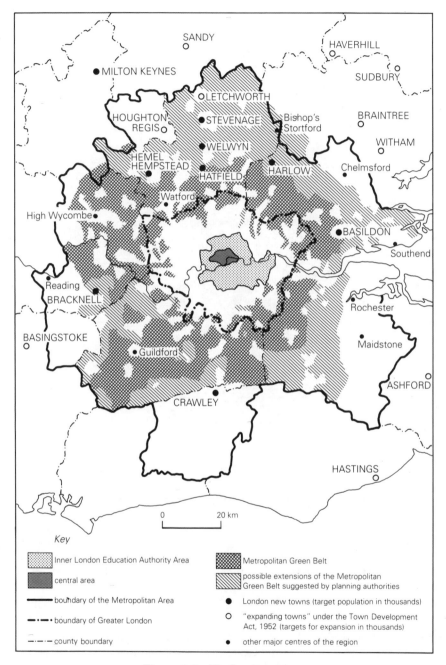

Figure 1.2 The London region.

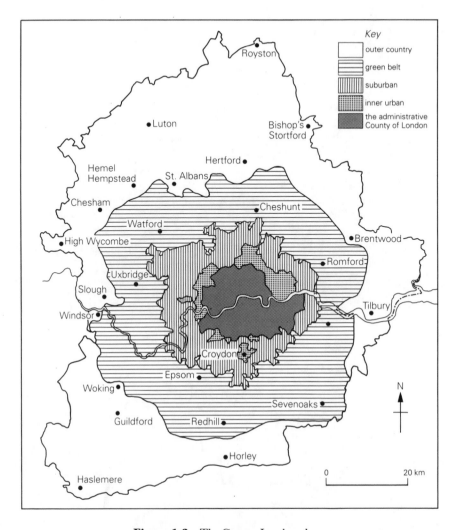

Figure 1.3 The Greater London plan.

(TTWAs). These are areas within which at least 15% of commuters travel to a dominant employment core containing a minimum of 20,000 jobs. The boundaries of these areas in the South East are shown in Figure 1.4.

The use of statistics such as these to define the functional areas of cities has been developed and extended by Hall (1977), Drewett et al. (1976), Hall & Hay (1980) and Berg et al. (1982). The procedures for doing this are described in *Changing places* written by members of the Centre for Urban and Regional Development Studies (CURDS) at Newcastle University (Champion et al. 1987). They are able to define the local labour market areas (LLMAs) which define the geographical extent of different British cities. These are shown in Figure 1.5.

Once these LLMAs have been defined, it is possible to examine the relationships between them. Those that send more than 7.5% of their employed residents to work in one other particular LLMA can be grouped together to define metropolitan regions. Twenty such regions are defined in Britain in Figure 1.5. This confirms that the London Metropolitan Region, defined in economic and social terms, includes at least the whole of the area within the OMA and the administratively defined LMR. This confirms the importance of considering carefully the most significant definition of London from a land-use planning point of view.

The importance of an accurate definition of London is not just a matter of semantics but is also crucial in determining the results of analyses conducted for planning purposes. Analyses based on statistics collected from different geographical areas produce significantly different pictures of London. Two examples will be used to show this: population and employment. Conventional analyses using the GLC definition of London present a picture of population and employment decline. A quite different picture emerges using local economic linkages/functions definitions such that of the LMR produced by researchers at CURDS.

Turning first to population, Table 1.1 shows the old GLC definition of London as experiencing population decline, followed by stabilization at about 7 million.

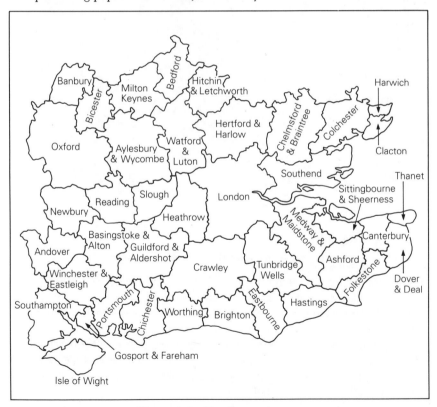

Figure 1.4 Travel-to-work areas.

13

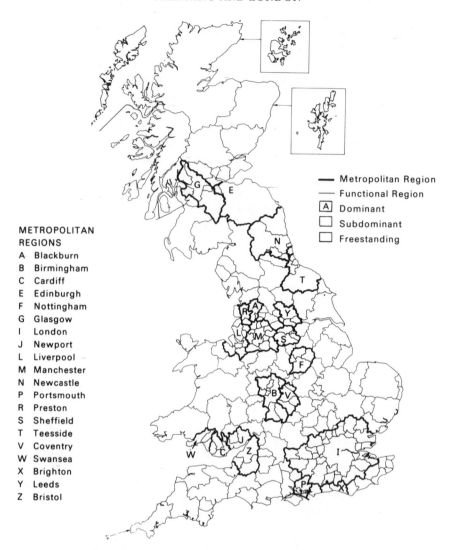

METROPOLITAN
REGIONS
A Blackburn
B Birmingham
C Cardiff
E Edinburgh
F Nottingham
G Glasgow
I London
J Newport
L Liverpool
M Manchester
N Newcastle
P Portsmouth
R Preston
S Sheffield
T Teesside
V Coventry
W Swansea
X Brighton
Y Leeds
Z Bristol

— Metropolitan Region
— Functional Region
A Dominant
   Subdominant
   Freestanding

Figure 1.5 Functional and metropolitan regions.

The addition of the OMA in the definition of London tells a different story. Figures for the LMR show sustained population growth from 12.9 up to 15.2 million. It also shows a decentralization of population in which the OMA comes to accommodate a greater population than the London core.

Similar differences also emerge with respect to employment. Table 1.2 shows a decline in employment in the London core of −975,000 between 1966 and 1989. In contrast, a rise in employment in the OMA of 401,000 leads to a smaller net loss of −574,000 in the LMR as a whole.

Clearly, basic questions such as whether population and employment are

Table 1.1   London's population: actual and forecast, 1966–2000.

	Population (millions)			
	1966	1981	1991	2000
Greater London	7.8	7.3	7.0	7.0
Outer metropolitan area	5.1	6.4	7.4	8.2
London metropolitan region	12.9	13.7	14.4	15.2

Source: Hall (1977), p. 48.

Table 1.2   London's employment: 1966–1989.

	Employment (000s)		
	1966	1989	Change
Greater London	4,450	3,475	−975
Outer metropolitan area	2,060	2,461	401
London metropolitan region	6,510	5,936	−574

Source: Hall (1977), p. 48; Central Statistical Office (1991), p. 36.

increasing or decreasing and by how much are critical to discussions about land-use planning policies. This section of Chapter 1 has shown how crucial clear and statistically based geographical definitions of London are in determining accurate appraisals of the nature and scope of the planning issues and problems confronting London.

Planning London

The different definitions of London show not only the significance of a reasoned selection of the geographical area to be planned, but also the complex interrelationships between the different functions within those areas. Travel-to-work-areas illustrate these important considerations particularly well. They are defined on the basis of the regular relationships between home, transport and work.

The importance of these interrelationships is emphasized and explored in Chapters 2–4. There the authors argue that changes in any of the components – industry, transport or housing – will cause the TTWA to change in size and extent. Among other things, this means that a city is a dynamic thing – the ever-changing outcome of a set of relationships between the three components.

They also argue that the differential investment in each of the three components causes changes in both the operation of the whole as well as any individual's personal experience of a city. For example, a huge investment in transport infrastructure might minimize any transfer problems for goods or people. It would be so easy to get about that location would be relatively unimportant. On the other hand, falling investment or falling standards of management or regulation of transport would make it more difficult to get about and hence make relative location all important. The point they make is that different patterns of investment in each of the components can change both our individual access to, as well as the overall efficiency of, London.

The relationships between geographical definitions of London and the economic and social functions within them also have important implications for the scale of planning required to change or regulate them. In Chapters 2–4 the authors also argue that in addition to the need to take both a longer-term perspective, and to appreciate the interconnectedness of industry, transport and housing, the issue of scale must be considered.

Different processes operate at different spatial scales and this implies that they need to be planned for, or managed at, different scales too. The analysis in Chapters 2–4 notes that industry, transport and housing are themselves segmented. For example, there are separate labour markets for manufacturing and for banking and finance, and these also operate at different spatial scales. These differences are apparent within each function and also between them. Housing markets do not overlap perfectly with labour markets. This conclusion provides another argument for an organization that co-ordinates policy on a spatial scale that is able to link together and effectively manage each separate function. It follows from this analysis that if London is to maintain its rôle as a capital city and a world city into the next century, a longer-term view of a London-wide regional strategy is essential, together with substantial and continuing levels of investment in capital formation and in human resources from both the private and the public sectors, so that the necessary conditions for sustainable economic growth can be generated.

Chapters 5–7, however, show how London's political and administrative units do not coincide with any of the rational definitions of London or the scale of operation of local labour or housing markets and the necessary transport between them. They show that during some periods since the Second World War there have been plans but no institutions which have more or less coincided with coherent definitions of London and the functional elements that needed planning together.

Among the plans have been the classic Abercrombie plan for Greater London (1945), the economic Strategy for the South East (1967) and the land-use Strategic Plan for the South East (1970). Most other plans for the London area have been fragmented between the various core London planning authorities, such as the now defunct London County Council and Greater London Council plans, and those of the London Boroughs within these areas and the "Home Counties" and their boroughs or districts.

In Chapters 5–7 it is also shown that, unlike cities such as Paris, there has never been an elected planning authority for the whole of the "real" London area. The nearest there has been to such an authority for London was the London County Council, followed by the Greater London Council. Neither of these ever administered plans for anything beyond the area contained within the MGB. As has been argued above, this is an arbitrary definition of London which only includes the major urban core of what is, in reality, a much larger city.

Chapters 5–7 show that London planning is now administered by a byzantine collection of institutions. These include:

- central and local government institutions such as the DoE, the London Boroughs, the home counties and their districts
- quasi-autonomous government organizations (QUAGOs) such as the London and South East Regional Planning Conference (SERPLAN) and the London Planning Advisory Committee (LPAC)
- quasi-autonomous non-government organizations (QUANGOs) such as London Pride and London First.

The political problems involved in devising and administering planning for London among this varied collection of institutions are enormous.

Conclusions

The objectives of this introduction have been to outline for the uninitiated reader four major points. These are:

- the structure and contents of the book and the reasons for laying it out in this way
- the general purposes, principles and administrative vehicles of British land-use planning
- the problems involved in defining London and, consequently, which parts of the planning system are relevant to an exposition of the issues and problems confronting the planners of London
- the essential complexity and interconnections of the main urban functions of London from the point of view of its permanent residents, and the byzantine institutional arrangements that currently exist to plan London.

Subsequent parts of the book will return to these issues in more detail. For the moment it is important to remember that, although certain issues will be described and analyzed individually, their separation from the rest is necessitated purely for the purposes of exposition. In reality, and also in the final part of the book, they are all interconnected and should be understood and planned for with that important point constantly in mind.

References and further reading

Allen, J. & C. Hamnett (eds) 1991. *Housing and labour markets: building the connections*. London: Unwin Hyman.

Berg, L. van den, R. Drewett, L. H. Klassen, A. Rossi, C. H. T. Vijverberg 1982. *Urban Europe: a study of growth and decline*. Oxford: Pergamon.

Central Statistical Office 1991. *Regional trends*, vol. 26. London: HMSO.

Champion, A. 1987. Recent changes in the pace of population deconcentration in Britain.

GeoForum **18**(4), 379.

Champion, A. G., A. E. Green, D. W. Owen, D. J. Ellin, M. G. Coombes 1987. *Changing places*. London: Edward Arnold.

Drewett, R., J. Goddard, N. Spence 1976. *British cities: urban population and employment trends 1951–1971*. London: Department of the Environment.

Hall, P. 1977. *The world cities*, 2nd edn. London: Weidenfeld & Nicolson.

Hall, P. & D. Hay 1980. *Growth centres in the European urban system*. London: Heinemann.

Hall, P. , H. Gracey, R. Drewett, R. Thomas 1973. *The containment of urban England* [2 volumes]. London: George Allen & Unwin.

Weightman, G. & S. Humphries 1984. *The making of modern London: 1914–39*. London: Sidgwick & Jackson.

Worpole, K. 1992. *Towns for people*. Buckingham: Open University Press.

CHAPTER TWO

Industry and employment in London

Andy C. Pratt

Introduction

As befits its status as a world city, London[1] accounts for a substantial proportion of all of the jobs in Great Britain: in 1991 nearly four million people worked in Greater London, nearly one in five of all those employed in Great Britain. Impressive though this is, it is useful to take a longer-term perspective in order to place these figures in context. In the mid-1950s one person in five employed in Britain was employed in Greater London; contrary to most people's expectations, Greater London is becoming less dominant in terms of the numbers employed nationally. In fact, total employment in Greater London declined by nearly 5% in the first half of the 1970s and by just over 6% in the second half (LPAC 1987). The rate of decline slowed a little in the 1980s; nevertheless, the fall in employment was just under 8% for the decade. This decline represented the loss of over a quarter of a million jobs. The decline would have been greater but for a temporary increase in the period 1987–9. By comparison the South East (SE) region as a whole performed much better: employment levels were more or less stable over the period 1981–91. An important component of employment change in both Greater London and the SE concerns the increasing numerical importance of females in the workforce.

In Greater London the basic picture is that the number of males in employment is falling while the number of females is rising. Statistics collected by the Department of Employment (1992a) show that in 1981 females accounted for just over 40% of the workforce in both Greater London and the SE; this had risen to over 47% by 1991. Whereas there has been only a modest increase in female part-time employment in absolute terms (i.e. actual numbers of people) decreases in male employment have made it relatively more significant (i.e. proportionately). Most

---

1. When we use the term "London" in this chapter, it refers to the administrative unit of Greater London. The prefixes Inner or Outer refer to the statistical subdivision of Greater London.

of the growth in female employment has been in full-time jobs. While male employment decreased twofold, the overall rate for Greater London female employment increased, albeit by just 3%. In the SE, where employment was more or less stable throughout the 1980s, the *decline* in male employment was 10%, contrasting with an *increase* of 11% in female employment. Thus, what appears to be a relatively stable (albeit declining in Greater London) "headline" figure conceals dramatic changes in the composition of employment. The nature of this change can be related to the decline of employment sectors where males have been historically more numerous (broadly manufacturing), whereas sectors where females have historically be more numerous (broadly services) have expanded.

The information base

Before progressing further, a point must be made about the availability of data on industry and employment matters, as this limits what can be said about this subject. There are three issues that limit data availability: time, categorization and spatial base. First, time. There are three sources of data: the ten-yearly census of population, the occasional (currently tri-annual) census of employment, and the estimates provided by the Department of Employment published on a quarterly basis in *Employment Gazette*. Each source has a different timescale as regards the availability of data. The census of population, collected in the first year of each decade, takes approximately three years to publish detailed data. The census of employment takes anything up to two years to process, but even when published it is largely confidential, being accessible only to planners and official researchers. The estimates of the Department of Employment are published more or less immediately. The paradox is that the most irregular sources are the most accurate. Researchers are left with a difficult choice: to be accurate, or to be up to date. In an effort to be up to date we have relied primarily upon *Employment Gazette*. The degree of inaccuracy in this source increases with the length of time since its updating (it is updated from the results of the census of employment). Fortunately, the last updating was in 1991 (using the 1987 census as a basis for the forecasts).

Secondly, categorization. Our main concern here is how one divides up "industry". The standard way of doing this is to use what is called the Standard Industrial Classification (SIC). Industry is divided into ten broad (one-digit) categories numbered 0–9, as shown in Table 2.1. Each category contains industries that are similar. For more detailed analysis these categories can themselves be broken down into further subdivisions called two-digit and three-digit classifications. For the most part we have used the one-digit classification.

Thirdly, spatial base. All data is collected for specific spatial units. Although information is available for the borough or county, it is invariably subject to restrictions of confidentiality at this scale. The standard units used in this chapter are Greater London, and the South East, and the Rest of the South East (referred to as RoSE, it represents the South East minus Greater London).

Table 2.1 Comparison of employment structure, 1991: GB, RoSE and Greater London. *Source:* DoE (1992a).

Sector		% GB	% RoSE	% Greater London
0	Agriculture, forestry, fisheries	1	2	0
1	Energy, water	2	1	1
2	Metal manufacturing, chemicals	3	3	1
3	Metal goods engineering	10	10	5
4	Other manufacture	9	7	7
5	Construction	4	4	3
61–3, 66–7	Wholesale distribution, hotels	11	11	10
64–5	Retail distribution	10	11	9
7	Transport & communications	6	6	9
8	Banking, insurance, finance	12	13	22
91–2	Public administration, and defence	9	8	11
93–9	Education, health, other	22	24	22

The changing structure of industry and employment

If we really want to get an insight into change in London, we must look beyond the "headline" figures of employment change and consider the performance of separate industrial categories (referred to as sectors). The popular image of London dominated by the City and its financial institutions is reflected in the current industrial structure, dominated as it is by banking, insurance and finance (BIF) activities, closely followed by distribution, public administration, defence and education, and health and other services. Of course, we should not consider London in isolation. If one compares the industrial structure of London with that of Britain as a whole, then the discrepancies and peculiarities become clear: under-representation in manufacturing activities (metal goods and other manufacture) is counterbalanced by over-representation in BIF (Table 2.2). In fact nearly 30% of those working in BIF activities in Britain are employed in London. Although it is not a dominant sector overall in London, over 20% of British transport and communications workers are employed in London (Table 2.2). Table 2.2 also shows how Greater London dominates the SE, accounting for 45% of all employees.

It will come as no surprise to note that agriculture does not play a significant rôle in London's economy, but it is surprising that manufacturing is – relatively – so insignificant. Even as late as the 1960s, commentators on the London economy still referred to it as a manufacturing city (Martin 1966: 60). The manufacturing sector declined in London, as it did in many parts of Britain, throughout the 1970s. However, the decline was particularly severe in London. Between 1971 and 1981 manufacturing employment declined by 25% in Britain as a whole; however, it shrank by 36% in Greater London as a whole and by 41% in Inner London (GLC 1985). From the early 1980s onwards, the BIF sector rapidly expanded both numerically and proportionately in London; although the BIF sector has been steadily increasing in importance in employment terms since the 1950s, it grew by over 30% between 1981 and 1991 (Fig. 2.1).

21

Table 2.2 Significance of Greater London contribution to GB and SE total employment, 1991.

Sector		Greater London as	
		% of GB	% of SE
0	Agriculture, forestry, fisheries	0	2
1	Energy, water	10	43
2	Metal manufacturing, chemicals	6	28
3	Metal goods engineering	7	27
4	Other manufacture	11	46
5	Construction	12	40
61–3, 66–7	Wholesale distribution, hotels	14	43
64–5	Retail distribution	14	40
7	Transport & communications	21	53
8	Banking, insurance, finance	29	59
91–2	Public administration, and defence	18	52
93–9	Education, health, other	15	43

Source: DoE (1992a).

Between 1981 and 1991 the manufacturing sector continued to decline by around 40%, as did both the construction and transport and communications sectors. The only other sector, aside from BIF, that has experienced consistent growth has been the public administration, health and education sector. We can see from Figure 2.1 how the decline in manufacturing and construction sectors is echoed, but to a far lesser degree, in RoSE and Great Britain. The dramatic decline in both construction and in transport and communications in Greater London would seem to be clear evidence of the consequences of the decline in infrastructure

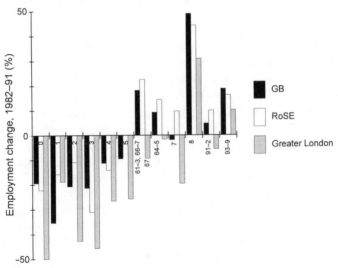

Figure 2.1 Percentage change in employees in employment in GB, RoSE and Greater London, by sector, 1982–91. *Source:* DoE (1984, 1992a).

22

investment and activity that took place in the 1980s under Conservative administrations. Although the percentage growth in BIF in London is small, it does represent many persons, given the large initial base figure. What is perhaps quite surprising, given recent expressions of hope for a recovery led by the retail and tourist sector, is the decline in employment in these sectors in Greater London. The picture is quite different in both RoSE and the SE, where there is evidence of employment growth in these sectors. In summary, we can note that the economy of Greater London is different from that of RoSE. Furthermore, while employment in RoSE is stable or growing, in Greater London it is declining.

Looking back to the figures for total employment change, we can now note that the apparently "stable" period of the 1980s has in fact been one of frenetic structural change. We have already noted the changing gender composition of employment; now we can see that there are similarly dramatic changes in the sectoral composition leading to an increased dominance of BIF employment and a decline of manufacturing employment. While it is only fair to point out that a similar growth rate of BIF employment was evident in the rest of Britain, the significance for London is a tendency towards overdependence. The implications for the future are uncertain. If the banking and financial "boom" falters, then so will the economy of London. In a worrying trend, decline set in with regard to employment in BIF in the 1987–91 period. It is unclear as yet whether this decline represents a contraction in the BIF sector or whether it is simply attributable to a process of new technology replacing workers; in either case, if this trend were to continue then unemployment in London could rise dramatically.

Although the pattern of manufacturing decline (called de-industrialization) was a common feature of the British economy in this period, the compensatory degree of expansion of the service sector, in particular the BIF sector, experienced in London was unusual. The causes are related to two factors. First, to British government policy, and secondly, to changes in the global economy. The first set of factors were manifest as a lack of investment in the manufacturing sector and increased openness of the British economy to foreign investment. The second set of not-unrelated factors concern the globalization of production activities; competition between such global producers has led to cost-cutting strategies. A key strategy has been to relocate manufacturing away from core economies (such as Britain) to the periphery (less developed economies). Even within the core, factors such as the completion of the Single European Market are likely to reinforce manufacturing decline.

The relocation of industry

Within this general process of growth and decline there was also some locational adjustment. For manufacturing activities, production costs could in some cases be reduced by moving to cheaper premises, which could be found on the periphery of Greater London and in RoSE beyond the Green Belt. This notion of migration has been challenged by the work of Fothergill & Gudgin (1982), who found that it was *in situ* rates of growth and decline that were the most significant trend, not the actual movement of firms. Fothergill & Gudgin's argument was that physical restrictions on site led to reduced productivity for firms that remained in inner urban areas. Firms already located in "greenfield" sites did not suffer from such constraints and hence were able to make productivity gains.

The implication is that planning policies may have to be modified so that they are sensitive to the problems of maintaining manufacturing in the urban core. At the other end of the locational spectrum, problems also arise with respect to both the adequacy and the sense of planning restraint in the Green Belt. It might be argued, particularly in the aftermath of the building of the major infrastructure such as the M25 orbital road, that manufacturing employment growth is dependent upon new development land becoming available in and around the Green Belt (Towse 1988). Against this position, apart from conservationists, are the interests of those people currently employed in manufacturing in Inner London. If jobs are relocated to the outer parts of Greater London and the SE, either they will have to move, or more commuting will take place, or new jobs found in Inner London.

It will be clear from the above that the problem of manufacturing decline has causes at both the macroeconomic level and the global scale, as well as at the microeconomic level and local scale; only some of these factors are within the power of town planners to control. Furthermore, that the solution of one set of problems – in this case employment-related – has implications for others, namely transport and housing.

Although globalization processes and deregulation policies hit manufacturing industry with particular severity, they have for the most part served the financial sector well. The deregulation of financial dealing – culminating in the "Big Bang" of 1986 – helped to sustain London as a key world actor in this field. The removal of the limitations on foreign investment by British funds in 1979 opened up a new investment market for British investors and so benefited the City. This last move had the adverse effect of reducing the home funds available to British manufacturing companies, thereby worsening their plight. In the early 1980s the application of a rigorous conservationist planning regime as regards office development in the City of London, caused property speculators to explore other possible locations, with an eye on the potential demand generated by deregulation: Docklands was the prime example. However, a dramatic change in policy in favour of a very liberal planning regime in the City in 1986 (as represented in the City of London Local Plan) opened the floodgates to the redevelopment of the City. By 1988 over a third of the total City office floor-space was in the process of redevelopment. Clearly, there are employment implications here. The later phase of restructuring in the BIF sector, the subsequent downturn in the economy, and the massive scale of development at Canary Wharf in Docklands, have led to the current situation (1994) of hectares of vacant office space in London.

The distribution of employment

So far we have considered the Greater London economy both as a whole and in its context with regard to the RoSE, and to the national and global economies. As indicated, although there are interrelationships between London and RoSE, there are ways in which London seems to perform differently. When the distribution of industry and employment is examined, the picture that emerges is of a London made up of a patchwork of smaller, sometimes overlapping, economies. This unusual, complex pattern is the result of a combination of factors: the particular spatial distribution of industrial sectors, the rates of change experienced within particular sectors, and variations of the rates and duration of unemployment.

The overall changes in employment numbers have not been distributed evenly throughout London. Detailed data on these changes are harder to analyze, as disaggregated figures are available only for the years 1981, 1984 and 1987. Nevertheless, we can note that, while overall employment decline in Greater London was just 1.5% for this period, Barking & Dagenham (−20%), Redbridge (−18%), and Lambeth (−14%) lost a substantial proportion of jobs in their respective boroughs. By contrast, others boroughs gained substantial numbers of new jobs, such as Kensington & Chelsea (+12%), Sutton (+15%) and Tower Hamlets (+14%).

Detailed analysis of the 1981, 1984 and 1987 census of employment carried out by Kowarzik & Landau (1991) relates these patterns of employment change to the relative fortunes of particular industrial sectors which are concentrated in particular boroughs. Barking & Dagenham, for example, is heavily dependent upon manufacturing activity, mainly the car industry. Manufacturing represented 42% of all employment in the borough in 1987; it had experienced a loss of 17% of all manufacturing jobs in the 1981–7 period. Females make up just 33% of the labour force. By contrast Kensington & Chelsea is dependent upon retailing and distribution, this sector representing 35% of all jobs; growth in this sector was 13% over the 1981–7 period. Females make up 51% of the labour force.

At a more general scale, a long-running division within the London economy has existed between the Inner and Outer boroughs. Figure 2.2 illustrates the relative changes in the employment structure in the Inner and Outer London boroughs between 1981 and 1987. The main tendency is towards both greater numbers of employees and a growing dominance of service sector activities in Inner London. Looking to the pattern of sectoral change 1981–7, disaggregated by Inner and Outer London, slightly greater job gains overall in Outer London are composed on the whole of modest sectoral losses and gains. This can be contrasted with loss of manufacturing in the Inner London boroughs, compensated by a huge banking and finance sector growth. Although the sectoral divisions and timescales used in Figure 2.2 are slightly different from Figure 2.1, it is still possible to get a sense of the contrasts between Inner and Outer London, and of both with RoSE. The consequence of this spatial and sectoral employment change has been that the places and sectors showing employment gains are not the places and sectors where they have been lost. The net result is localized unemployment.

25

The structure and pattern of unemployment

Without a doubt unemployment is a major problem in Greater London. It is difficult to comprehend the size of the problem: it is a staggering fact that there are more than one-and-a-half times more people unemployed in London than there are unemployed in Wales and Scotland put together. Unemployment peaked in 1986 at 404,913 in Greater London. After falling off to its lowest level for a decade in 1990 – 199,276 – as we write (March 1994) unemployment has once again outstripped the 1986 figure (Fig. 2.3). Although London seems to have been shadowing the national average, it has consistently performed worse than the SE. Latterly there are signs that this discrepancy is widening.[2] Unemployment is skewed towards Inner and East London and the east of RoSE. What is particularly disturbing is the low level of job vacancies in Greater London (Fig. 2.4). The unemployed:vacancy ratio in 1991 was a massive 10.5 jobs per notified vacancy in Greater London, compared to 5.2 jobs per notified vacancy in the SE. Looking at Greater London in detail shows a further disturbing dimension: 90% of all of those unemployed in October 1991 had been so for more than a month, and 70% for more than three months. Figures 2.5 and 2.6 show this picture broken down by

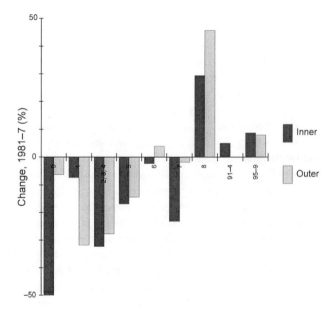

Figure 2.2   Percentage change in employment in Inner and Outer London, by sector, 1981–7. *Source:* Kowarzik & Landau (1991).

---

2. This worsening economic performance was recognized in the dramatic announcement in autumn 1993 of the results of a review of areas eligible for regional assistance. For the first time in the 60-year history of regional policy, parts of the South East and, notably, parts of Greater London, were designated as eligible for assistance.

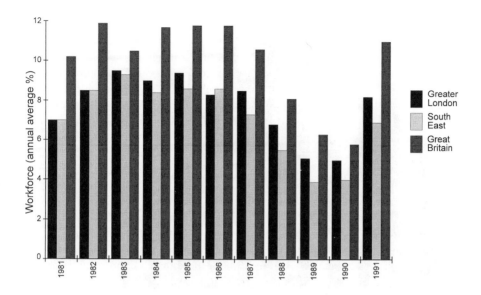

Figure 2.3 Unemployed in GB, SE and Greater London (%).
Source: DoE (1985, 1989, 1992b).

gender; this clearly shows the differing character of unemployment, males experiencing more long-term unemployment. Another line of cleavage – an implicitly discriminatory one – is along lines of ethnic origin. Black and Asian workers generally experience higher unemployment rates than their White counterparts across all occupations; this disparity is especially severe with respect to young adults, namely the 16–24 age group (see Sassen 1991: 302 et seq.). By any measure, unemployment represents a shameful waste of both resources and people's lives.

Let us consider the general issues of labour supply to begin with, as these are far from straightforward. The problem is that "the goal posts keep moving" in London with respect to the overall size of the population and the proportion of the population seeking work. First, we will consider population. Population trends in the 1980s cannot be looked at in isolation. The population of London has been in decline since the 1940s; this can be mainly attributed to outmigration being greater than inmigration. Decline accelerated in the 1960s and 1970s and, surprisingly, reversed altogether for a period in the mid-1980s. Analysts seem unclear as to whether this population upturn is a "blip" or will be sustained (Champion 1987). However, the significance of population increase is that extra pressure will be placed on employment creation in London: even after discounting wider economic trends, more jobs must be created just to maintain the level of unemployment, let alone to reduce it.

The second factor, the proportion of those who want to work (called the economic activity rate), is also interesting. Two additional issues need to be considered here. First, the changing age structure swelling the ranks of those of working age.

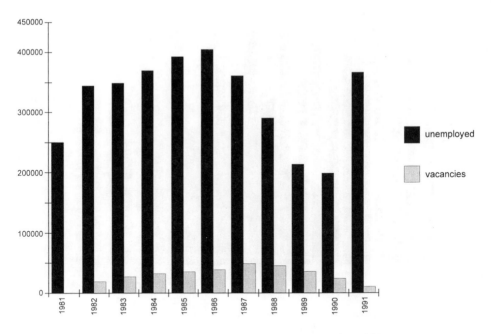

Figure 2.4 Number of unemployed and vacancies, 1981–91, Greater London. *Source:* DoE (1992b), LRC (1991).

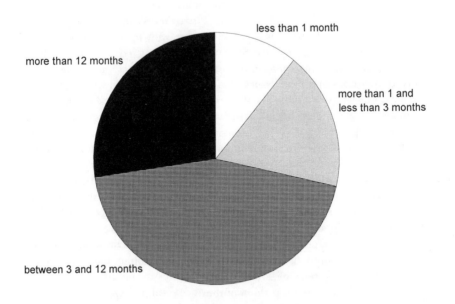

Figure 2.5 Male unemployment by duration, Greater London, 1991. *Source:* DoE (1992a).

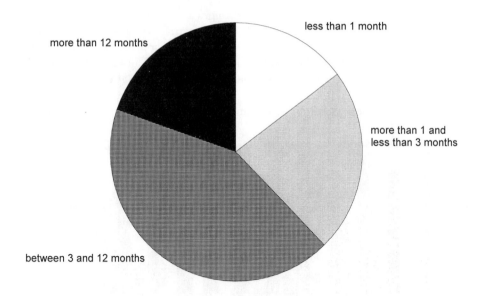

Figure 2.6 Female unemployment by duration, Greater London, 1991. *Source:* DoE (1992a).

Secondly, social changes, primarily where more women are wanting to work; projections suggest that female economic activity rates will continue to rise, and male rates continue to fall (Figs 2.7, 2.8). The net result if these two trends continue is likely to be a growing population and a growing proportion of women looking for work. Greater London is storing up problems, as its economic activity rates are rather similar to RoSE: both are stable or growing compared to the UK as a whole, where they are falling. Female economic activity rates are growing faster in Greater London than even the SE. The net result is more people looking for work in Greater London. Overall, this will put even more pressure on the need to create employment opportunities.

The ratio of notified vacancies to unemployed is currently running at approximately 1:30 (Fig. 2.4). At first sight it would seem as though a major expansion of the economy (job creation) would solve this problem. However, labour markets are not quite so simple. Instead of there being just one London labour market, there are in fact many hundreds, depending upon skill, qualification and location. So, for some occupational groups the ratio of vacancies to unemployed may be lower than average, in other groups it may be much higher. This mismatch of skills to jobs is exacerbated by the spatial characteristics of labour markets; this brings us back to the significance of housing and transport in the formation of labour markets and the reduction of both unemployment and skill shortages.

The Department of Employment has recently carried out an analysis of the Greater London labour market in order to explore the fact that many companies were apparently having recruitment difficulties at a time when so many people were out of work (Meadows et al. 1988). This report, based on specially commissioned survey work of employees and the unemployed, supports the idea that London's labour market is segmented by skill, experience and location. It was found that even where there was some locational correspondence of absolute job vacancies and unemployed people, there was an occupational mismatch. Furthermore, there was a tendency for firms to discriminate against the long-term unemployed.

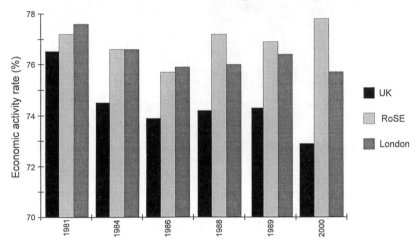

Figure 2.7   Male economic activity rates: UK, RoSE and Greater London, 1981–9, and forecast 2000. *Source:* CSO (1991).

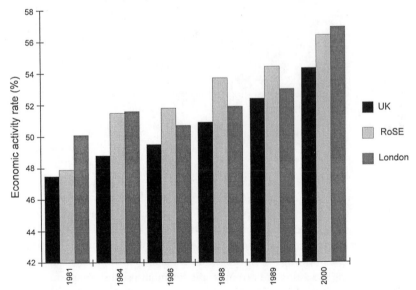

Figure 2.8   Female economic activity rates: UK, RoSE and Greater London, 1981–9, and forecast 2000. *Source:* CSO (1991).

This discrimination operates both in an obvious way and in a more subtle way. For example, many jobs are not notified through job centres but through private agencies or word of mouth. This is particularly the case in the service sector; the net result is that part of the labour market is effectively closed off to those reliant upon job centres as an information source. The report also notes that the most disturbing mismatch existed between the location of the greatest number of unskilled and unemployed people – basically Inner London – and the availability of unskilled jobs – in Outer London. Interestingly the report notes that this mismatch is in no small part related to the lack of availability of cheaper housing, particularly for rent, in Outer London. Looked at another way, the maintenance of numbers of low-skilled manufacturing and services sector employment opportunities would have removed much of the problem in the first place. In either case the operation of planning policy as regards housing and industry (in an integrated fashion) could make a real impact on social and economic wellbeing.

The changing spatial relationship between home and work

The complex nature of labour market formation and its spatial extent is an outcome of the relationship between industry, transport and housing. One indicator of this is the spatial pattern of "travel-to-work-areas" (TTWAs) in London. Not surprisingly, TTWAs do not respect administrative boundaries. In fact London draws in significant numbers of employees from the whole of the South East and beyond. This emphasizes another point; London is not an island. This is another good reason for considering the case for a London, and maybe a SE-wide, regional planning body that could look at all the competing needs over London's sphere of influence.

There are indications that, in the 1980s, employment growth in London was being sustained by employees who were not living in London (18% of those working in London were not resident there in 1981; Hall 1990: 30); that is, the phenomenon of long-distance commuting, particularly from those working in the BIF sector. Detailed confirmation of these trends will come only with the future release of 1991 census data. The reasons for this increase in long-distance commuting are manyfold. Obviously the relationship between high London house prices and improved transport links is important. The high wages paid in the BIF sector gave workers the potential to buy substantial housing in Outer London and country locations (Thrift & Leyshon 1992). Thus, Greater London's economic change, in particular changes in BIF, has impacted upon a whole set of planning and settlement patterns in the wider South East of England.

Industrial and employment policies

It is very difficult to assess the actual investment that private companies make in the London metropolitan region. Nevertheless, the decline in employment – albeit a surrogate measure – does indicate some problems. Despite the rhetoric and bluster of four Conservative administrations, the State still plays a significant rôle in the allocation of direct investment in various aspects of economic development in London. What has changed in the 1980s has been, first, the increasing rôle the private sector has played in partnership with government, and secondly, the centralization of responsibility for economic development and investment and the consequential loss of local democratic control. It is perhaps easiest to consider the period as having two phases. The first, 1979–86, corresponds to the period of the GLC and can be characterized as a two-track policy in London. There was considerable antagonism between central and local government initiatives. The second phase corresponds to the post-1986 period and the fragmentation and redefinition of the rôles of local authorities in economic development.

In the early 1980s, central government activities were characterized by monetarist economic management which in practice involved two elements. First, the reduction and repayment of government borrowing: the immediate impact was a reduction in spending and investment plans. Secondly, the focus on macroeconomic concerns of lowering inflation, even if it led to an increase in unemployment. This economic management policy marked a distinct break from the post-war consensus, called Keynesian policy, characterized by government borrowing in recession to boost the economy, and a commitment, enshrined in the 1944 Employment Act, to create full employment. An additional ingredient in this new form of government was the redefinition of the responsibilities of the State. It was argued, again in distinction from the post-war consensus, that the State should become an "enabler" rather than a "manager" or an operator in the market.

The consequence of such a policy agenda was antipathy for redistributive economic policies and, in the absence of policy, an implicit support for the concentration of development in "favourable" locations. The so-called "overheating" of the SE and London economy, which effectively allowed development to occur at the expense of other parts of the UK and caused considerable problems in London, such as labour market imbalance. The government believed in the now discredited "trickle down" effect, where it was thought that the benefits of such growth would be dispersed to the sectors of society that were in need. One of the few interventions that the Government was prepared to make was to create Enterprise Zones (EZs). EZs were an attempt to remove as many restrictive measures of the State to give the private sector "free rein" to regenerate particularly depressed localities. Perhaps the most famous such EZ was established on the Isle of Dogs. Another attempt to free industry from what were seen as the shackles of the State were Urban Development Corporations (UDCs). The first UDC, established in 1979, was London Docklands Development Corporation (LDDC). The powers of UDCs included those of buying and disposing of land and giving planning permission. Effectively they usurped the Local Authorities where they were located. Unlike local authorities which are accountable to their electorate, UDCs are non-elected bodies responsible to central government.

At the same time the GLC was pursuing an economic policy agenda which had as its aim the restructuring of the economy in the interests of working people rather

32

than large corporations. It stressed the need for local control. The policy was a response to the wanton neglect of the capital's manufacturing sector and both the labour market consequences of the loss of such employment (the Inner–Outer London mismatches discussed above) and the opening up of London to a greater degree of external control. This set of policies focused on the emergent local economic development potential of local government and planners, by way of contrast to the traditional physical plan and land-use concern represented by the Greater London Development Plan.

The key element of the GLC industrial strategy was its focus on *sectors* of industry (GLC 1985). The term "sector" in this context does not mean the same as sectors used for industrial classification (based on the similarity of activities: vehicle manufacturers, general engineering and chemical manufacture all lumped together). Rather, it refers to interrelated activities: the vehicle sector would include steel suppliers, instrument makers, car makers and dealers. The argument was that any intervention had to be carefully targeted. The distribution of employment problems was associated with particular sectors of industry. Industrial sectors usually comprised a majority of smaller firms under local control; however, they needed to be fully integrated in order to compete in new market conditions. Sector strategies[3] were developed to strengthen weak links in sectors and to encourage sector planning. The Greater London Enterprise Board (GLEB) was a key agency in this process, investing in companies in order to assist and influence such restructuring.

The Conservative central government's solution to the GLC's alternative agenda was abolition. In the post-1986 period many further changes have taken place in terms of investment and the local economy. Although GLEB survived the abolition, it was further undermined by the 1989 Local Government and Housing Act. This Act had two key points in respect to the local economy and its economic planning. First, it codified (but restricted) the range of economic development activities that might legitimately be carried out by local authorities. The second, related, issue was the restriction of company shareholding by local authorities. This effectively ruled the activities of GLEB out of court.

In a separate development, the London Planning Advisory Committee (LPAC) was established, post-abolition, to develop a co-ordinating rôle between the fragmented planning bodies (the boroughs) of Greater London. The aim was to act as an advisory body for the Minister to assist in the development of strategic planning guidance. Another significant innovation of this period was the establishment of Training and Enterprise Councils (TECs) from 1988 onwards. Nine of these were established in London, each covering approximately half a million persons. TECs are employer-led partnerships that aim to improve local skills and training (on both a personal and a company basis), to promote enterprise and fulfil local industry needs. As they are so new, it is still unclear how TECs and the economic development functions of local authorities will relate to one another; the danger of duplication of rôles is always possible.

---

3. For further discussion of "sector strategies", see Geddes & Benington (1992).

A whole plethora of inner-city support agencies and policies have been set up by Conservative administrations in the post-1979 period, two recent ones being City Action Teams and Task Forces. However, the mainstay – the Urban Programme (UP), which has its roots back in 1978 – was first established by the Labour administration as a partnership between central and local government to provide grant aid to specific projects for urban regeneration. UP designation is important because it makes authorities eligible for competition for other grants such as City Grant (CG): a private industry led programme introduced in 1988. In real terms UP funding has been falling as CG has been rising[4].

The South East Regional Planning Conference (SERPLAN), a consultative body representing district and county planning authorities, has pressed for strategic planning in the SE in the 1980s (SERPLAN 1985). Overall, its aim was to provide an agreed spatial framework to guide public spending through restraint in the west, co-ordinated infrastructure, land supply and environmental improvements in the east, and more intense support for Inner London, Thameside, and the older industrial towns of RoSE (see Wood 1987: 90). At a regional scale, the South East Economic Development Strategy (SEEDS) was established in the wake of the abolition of the GLC to develop a SE-wide regional strategy based upon sectoral policies. SEEDS (1987) highlighted the fact that there were significant problems within the SE economy – which they termed the South/South divide: echoing the national North/South divide – which required redirection of resources within the region and co-ordination of policy responses of all local authorities rather than the competition that currently exists. Greater London is, of course, the prime example of such chaos. In the absence of Government producing regional or strategic economic planning, SEEDS, SERPLAN and LPAC attempt to fill the vacuum.[5]

To sum up, we can highlight a set of interrelated issues facing industry and employment in London, and by extension the country as a whole. Most of these have been exacerbated by the market-led planning that has been practised in the 1980s. The key point is the loss of a whole sector of industry – manufacturing – in London. Although it is true that, in aggregate terms, most of these jobs have been replaced by gains in other sectors (particularly the BIF sector), the local impact has been devastating. The legacy is a growing rump of long-term unemployed men. In organizational terms the economy of London, like that of Britain as a whole, has become more dependent upon foreign direct investment and external control in the remains of the manufacturing sector, and has developed an increasingly narrow economic base focused upon BIF. Although this configuration has delivered growth in the 1980s, it appears to be a precarious foundation for the 1990s.

---

4. Yet another new initiative was announced in November 1993 regarding the establishment of "London Pride" as part of a programme to devolve central administration "to the regions" and to make links between the Departments of Industry, employment, Environment and Transport. It is likely that many of the existing programmes (such as City Challenge) will be modified as a result of such changes.

5. Of course, the Department of the Environment has produced Regional Guidance Notes for the South East. However, these do not constitute regional strategy or strategic planning.

Structural divisions, spatial divisions

Looked at most broadly, there are some significant spatial divides in London – East and West, Inner and Outer. However, these spatial disparities are the result of a complex interplay of industry, transport and housing relationships. What is at stake is the gap between where people live and where the jobs are to be found. For example, the lack of affordable housing in the Outer London boroughs is a key barrier to the continued economic vitality of London and the RoSE. At present transport networks that favour traditional long-distance commuting patterns are, in tandem with current housing policies, creating a neglected island of unemployed people in Inner London. Transport improvements could help; the need, as regards the economy, is to link deprived boroughs, such as some of those in the East and North, to the rest of London. The third option is to consider an industrial strategy for London. This may have two components. First, to invest in the existing sectors that affect the areas of key employment need. The GLC strategy, and latterly SEEDS's strategy too, seem to offer a good example here. Secondly, to use land-use planning controls to redirect or make provision of industrial development in areas of need. Neither policy will work in isolation. Both require an overarching industrial strategy.

This leads to a key point, the need for strategic planning. It is self-evident that labour markets and industrial sectors do not fit neatly into local authorities areas. At the same time national policy (or the lack of it) does have local effects. There would seem to be a need for an agency between the national and local scales to deal with strategic co-ordination of industrial and employment activity. Such a strategic agency would necessarily incorporate housing and transport concerns as they are integral to the effectiveness of an industrial and employment strategy.

Integrating industry with transport and housing

Industry is always a good issue to begin with as it is the cause of so much movement, as well as being the generator of income, wealth and the products upon which our consumer society depends. Successful and efficient economies and cities depend upon the effective and efficient operation of labour markets. Likewise the successful operation of labour markets depends as much upon the appropriate provision of housing and transport facilities as on education and training.

Its always easy to start from new. In a New Town one might locate facilities in an ideal manner; the objective being, for example, to minimize travel to work and to maintain a functional separation of residential and employment activities. When one is dealing with an already constructed town or city, both physical and organizational constraints have to be taken into account. Any change in the arrangement of activities will impact, for good or ill, upon other activities. In this sense the industry, transport and housing relationship can almost be considered to be like an organism: some changes can be accommodated without too severe

35

effects on health; others can be fatal. All of these points must cause us to look closely at the nature of change. As the structure of employment, not just the total numbers in each sector, but also their distribution. This must be related to corresponding housing and movement. This is perhaps best illustrated with an example.

An example: the impact of a plant closure

Consider the case of a manufacturing plant in Inner London. Typically it might have been established 50 years ago in a good location (then) to serve a growing consumer goods market. A combination of lack of investment and new product development may have left it open to foreign competition. The same goods might well be made more cheaply elsewhere by utilizing new, machine intensive, production techniques. On the other hand the restricted site that the company was operating from may have made the adoption of new production techniques difficult without a move. A move might not have been considered to be practical due to added expense and a loss of a reliable, and trained, labour force. In the end the company may have closed, or been taken over by a competitor. If it was taken over, it might have been closed in a subsequent rationalization programme. Perhaps it might not escape the investigations of the company accountants that the site that the factory occupied was of considerable value in a booming land market. The factory closure and the profit realized from the site is a clear example of short-term decision-making.

What are the consequences of closure? For the multinational company that takes over the plant and sells the land, greater assets are acquired. At the local scale the costs can be wide-ranging. In the period that the firm operated, a whole network of contacts would have been established with local suppliers. Few firms are totally autonomous and self-contained. The loss of the large firm in question might also lead to the closure of some of these suppliers too. It may even have a further knock-on (or multiplier) effect for other larger firms that also relied upon these same supplier networks.

Workers who had lost their jobs may be able to find employment in similar occupations with firms not tied into these supplier networks, if they exist. For some the only choice is to travel some distance to the nearest similar employment source. The problem is that other firms are also operating like this one and they are most likely to have relocated to Outer London. Travelling time for workers is increased, as is congestion on the roads. Public transport is unlikely to be an option as commuting around or to Outer London is more difficult by public transport. Commuting is costly, a daily cost that is met by the employee not the employer.

After some time, those workers commuting long distances may start looking for new housing in the areas where work is to be found. The first problem is that house prices may have been depressed in the area of the closure. Furthermore, generally house prices are much greater in Outer than they are in Inner London, and more expensive in the West than the East, furthermore there are even fewer rented houses in both Outer and West London. People may also consider the social cost too great. For example, moving may be particularly disruptive as regards the schooling of children or the networks of friends and relations invariably involved in both childcare and general social support. This problem may be particularly severe for members of ethnic minority groups. Notably, members of such groups have organized themselves in an attempt to counter discrimination, the result of which is the above average concentration of both unemployment and employment in poorly paid jobs and those occupation, with poor or unsocial work conditions (see GLC 1986: Ch. 3; Cross 1992). One response of ethnic groups is to organize informal, local, savings and loan facilities. Moving away from a locality may thus be difficult in both social and economic terms.

Some former workers may even use their skills and set up small firms. However, the lost wages of those not able to find work will impact on their ability to pay for housing, and to buy goods in the local shops. This is called a negative multiplier. Whereas negative multipliers are normally expressed in terms of money alone, we can also consider them in terms of social factors too. So, for those groups who have lost jobs and have not been able to move, the social fabric of shops and services itself deteriorates further, creating a vicious circle of poverty.

Meanwhile, the industrial site is vacant. Considerable investment may be needed to reclaim the site. A potential industrial user might find it far cheaper to go to a new "greenfield" site and build afresh. In terms of transport costs, a site close to a motorway, such as the M25, may be preferred. Furthermore, if the planning designation of the Inner London site can be changed to retail or offices, then the site value may also be inflated. This provides further incentive for a firm to relocate: in effect, to take the money and run.

Much may be made of the potential new employment opportunities on this former manufacturing site. What are they? If it is a retail superstore, the total employment will perhaps be a tenth of that formerly found in the factory. The work is mainly for unskilled operatives. Much of the work is low paid and part-time. This is not a fact that is likely to boost total household incomes and thus make housing any easier to acquire. In fact most of the posts are likely to be taken by women who did not previously have a job; they may not have even been registered unemployed, and hence have not shown up as unemployed. (If a person is married and their spouse is working, then they will not be eligible for unemployment benefit.) So paradoxically, new jobs may be created but unemployment may be little reduced. Furthermore, an important resource for training in the area may have been lost to the Inner London area.

If the site is redeveloped as an office instead, then the total employment may well be similar to that of the manufacturing unit. Depending upon the type of office, it might be similar low wage and casual operatives as in the retail superstore, particularly if mainly "back office" (routine) functions are being carried out there. There will also be some skilled jobs. But it is most likely the workers taking these jobs will be those who are already living in Outer London. They will commute into work in Inner London. This journey is likely to be easier than that of those having to commute to Outer London. Nevertheless, journeys such as these are time-consuming for employees and wasteful of energy. Once again, the net result is an increase in the number of workers, but little change in the numbers unemployed.

The inefficient labour market

This thumbnail sketch of a manufacturing plant closure could apply to many instances all over London. Clearly, not every case will follow the lines that we have sketched out; in this sense it is a composite or amalgam of various situations. However, this should not detract from the likely impact of a plant closure that extends far beyond a vacant building into the heart of a locality. Hopefully, what it begins to highlight is the complex nature of the interactions between industry, transport and housing (ITH). Each component may act as barrier or enabler of the efficient operation of labour markets. It may be claimed that the expanding size of travel to work areas (TTWAs) is evidence of the "freeing up" of labour markets. People are moving more easily from and to employment opportunities. An alternative view, that which is supported here, is that growing TTWAs may be an indicator of the increasing *inefficiency* of the relationship between industry, transport and housing.

These inefficiencies are manifest in a variety of ways. A good example is traffic congestion. When we see a traffic jam we may say that there are too many vehicles for the road space; the solution is to build more roads. However, this is a rather peremptory reply; we should consider why these vehicles need to be on this stretch of road in the first place. One answer is that other modes of transport might be possible. More significantly we might consider that this is not just a matter of cost and ease of movement. Generally, in their work journeys, people travel because they have to. If home and work were better integrated, there would be a decreased demand for travel. Less energy would be wasted. Fewer resources would be locked up in infrastructure provision, and much time would be saved.

The key point here is that the ITH relationship is constantly under stress and change. But because location decisions are costed on a narrow, short-term, firm-by-firm, basis they do not take into consideration either the extra travelling costs imposed on workers or the housing problems and social disruption that follows. One way of bringing these costs into the decision frame is to take a strategic view. Of course a planning system would have to take full account of the structure of housing opportunities, the type and location of employment, the possibilities for retraining, and the need for transport. These should be material considerations in allowing movement of firms. Clearly, in some cases a better, and in the long term more efficient, solution might be to re-invest in existing industrial sites.

The general point is that investment and co-ordination is required in the efficient integration of ITH. Patently, the market is not very efficient at translating the diverse signals of the elements of ITH into practice. It is questionable anyway whether the market is an appropriate forum for making such decisions, as they are issues that the whole community deserves a say in: both rich and poor. The classic paradox of the market is that, if one is poor, one has a great need, but, in the terms of the market, little "demand".

The fragmented city

Although we have been attempting to understand the general form of changes in the relationship between ITH elements and the problems that they may give rise to in a general sense, it is also useful to make some closing comments on the impact on particular localities of new forms of ITH. The exact nature of the ITH relationship can be considered to be relatively specific to particular occupational groups. People in similar occupations may have similar ITH relations. Furthermore they may actually work in a few locations. When we add in all occupational groups then we have a complex pattern of movement. This can perhaps best be imagined as a composite of a series of pieces of tracing paper placed on top of one another, each with their occupational ITH patterns drawn on. Because people are generally limited by income to certain types of housing, there are real barriers to movement and relocation. Hence, as we have already seen, when a manufacturing plant closes down, all of the former workers do not move house to be near another factory.

In conditions of rigidity in housing markets and limited transport investment the result is often an increase in movement and a polarization of social life. Where, as in the example discussed above, particular occupations are over-represented by particular ethnic groups, we might see evidence of what is termed "institutional discrimination" (see Cross 1988). Real housing ghettos may be created. What is quite strange is that such housing may be in exactly the same place as the employment boom. However, the occupants of the houses may not have access to the educational credentials and training to gain work in the new offices on their doorsteps. This emphasizes a point that is true for all cities and is particularly stark in world cities (Sassen 1991: 265 et seq.). For example, we can easily envisage three broad groups. First, there are people engaged in activities that are tied into the local economy or the local social system, as there have always been. Secondly, there are those who by their employment are tied into national social and economic systems. Finally, there are those tied into the dynamics of the global economy.

The external determinants of these peoples' lives are so different, yet they may all live within a hundred metres of one another and use the same video rental shop on the street corner. In most other ways they are thousands of kilometres apart. This is the real problem; it is difficult to see how such issues could be resolved at anything below the national level. The social fragmentation and creation of an underclass of people who are locked into a (local) social and economic system that offers few options. Others are relatively insulated from these concerns. A momentary blip occurred on "Black Monday" (1987) when overnight the global economy went into temporary free-fall. For once it was the financial dealers who were the temporary clients of the pawn shops. The local economy was relatively unaffected. Such occurrences are most certainly the exception rather than the rule.

Conclusion

By way of conclusion we can point out the complex nature of the ITH relationship. The relationship is not new, it is evolving through time. The changing nature of work, of transport technology and mode, of housing expectations and of the social structure are all important contextual factors that need to be considered here. An accessible account of the changing social context in London and the South East in the 1960s can be found in Young & Wilmot's (1973) classic book *The symmetrical family*. Inefficiencies in the ITH relationship may be manifest in various ways, from local skill shortages to traffic congestion to social fragmentation and ethnic polarization. What is important is an appreciation of the various scales that are involved in the ITH relationship, these are linked to the different scales of economic activity. Achieving co-ordination across scales and between ITH elements would seem to be a key rôle for a strategic planning body. This body would have to be able to take on responsibilities beyond simple land-use decisions. Management and co-ordination across sectors are clearly required. This is not likely to be achieved by market mechanisms. There are good arguments as to why the market is not an appropriate tool for such decision-making in a mature democracy.

References and further reading

Champion, A. 1987. Recent changes in the pace of population deconcentration in Britain. *GeoForum* **18**(4), 379–401.

Cross, M. 1988. Ethnic minority youth in a collapsing labour market: the UK experience. In *Entering the working world*, C. Wulpert (ed.). Aldershot: Gower.

Cross, M. 1992. Race and ethnicity. In *The crisis of London*, A. Thornley (ed.), 103–118. London: Routledge.

CSO 1991. *Regional trends*, vol. 26, Table 10.5. London: Central Statistical Office .

Department of Employment 1984. *Employment Gazette*, Table 1.4. London: Department of Employment.

—1985. *Employment Gazette*, Tables 2.2, 2.3.

—1989. *Employment Gazette*, Tables 2.2., 2.3.

—1992a. *Employment Gazette*, Tables. 1.5, 2.2, 2.6, 2.9, 3.3.

—1992b. *Employment Gazette: historical supplement no. 3*.

Fothergill, S. & G. Gudgin 1982. *Unequal growth*. London: Heinemann.

Geddes, M. & J. Benington 1992. *Regenerating local economies*. Harlow: Longman.

GLC 1985. *The London industrial strategy*. London: Greater London Council.

—1986. *The London Labour Plan*. London: GLC.

Hall, J. 1990. *Metropolis now: London and its region*. Cambridge: Cambridge University Press.

Kowarzick, U. & N. Landau 1991. *London at work: an analysis of the Census of Employment 1981–7*. London: London Research Centre.

Leonard, S., A. Maginn, U. Kowarzik 1991. *Where have all the jobs gone?* London: London Research Centre / Association of London Authorities.

LPAC 1987. *Employment: report by the topic working party*. London: London Planning Advisory Committee.

LRC 1991. *Annual abstract of Greater London statistics*, vol. 22, 1989–90, table 32. London: London Research Centre.

Martin, J. 1966. *Greater London and industrial geography*. London: Bell.

Meadows, P., H. Cooper, R. Bartholomew 1988. *The London labour market.* London: Department of Employment.

Sassen, S. 1991. *The global city: New York, London, Tokyo.* Princeton, NJ: Princeton University Press.

SEEDS 1987. *South–South divide.* Stevenage: SEEDS.

SERPLAN 1985. *Developing* SE *regional strategic guidance: consultative regional statement,* RPC 340. London.

Thrift, N. & A. Leyshon 1992. In the wake of the money: the city of London and the accumulation of value. In *Global finance and city living,* L. Budd & S. Whimster (eds), 282–312. London: Routledge.

Towse, R. 1988. Industrial location and site provision in an area of planning restraint: part of southwest London's Green Belt. *Area* **20**(4), 323–32.

Wood, P. 1987. The South East. In *Regional problems, problem regions and public policy in the* UK, P. Damesick & P. Wood (eds), 64–94. Oxford: Oxford University Press.

Young, M. & P. Wilmot 1973. *The symmetrical family.* Harmondsworth: Penguin.

CHAPTER THREE

Housing

Stephen Merrett

Housing is for people, so we begin with some basic facts on London's demography. With Moscow and Paris, London is one of the three largest population centres in Europe. If sheer size is a necessary condition for the title of "world city", then with more than 6.7 million people in 1991, London fits the bill, as Table 3.1 shows. The area of the metropolis within the Greater London Council's former boundaries is 1,578 square kilometres, so in 1991 the city's residential density was 4,169 persons per square kilometre. (Much of the information in this section is derived from the London Research Centre's excellent *London housing statistics*).

Table 3.1   London's population in 1981 and 1991 (thousands).

	1981	1991	10-year growth (%)
1 Total number of persons	6,806	6,759	−0.7
2 Total number of households	2,643	2,845	7.6
3 Average household size (1/2)	2.58	2.38	−7.8

Source: LRC *London housing statistics 1990*, tables 1.1 and 1.5.

In terms of individual persons, the city's size changed very little in the decade 1981–91. But with respect to the number of separate households, there was an increase of 7.6% in those same years, as average household size contracted with the growth of more people living by themselves. Within the field of housing studies, the number of households is more significant than the number of persons, because people occupy houses and flats as households, traditionally in the form of the nuclear family.

However, Table 3.2 shows that in 1991 married couples, with or without children, made up slightly less than one-half of all households. Lone parents, younger one-person households, pensioner one-person households and "others" each contributed more than 10% of the total household population.

If the "world cities" should be cosmopolitan as well as large, once again London scores, as Table 3.3 indicates. People whose ancestral origin is in the Caribbean or African Commonwealth composed 6% of all persons. Those whose ancestral origin is in India, Pakistan, Bangladesh or the East African Commonwealth also account for 6%. The "other New Commonwealth" includes persons from Cyprus and Sri Lanka in its 3%. And the 85% catch-most category of the "Rest" in Table 3.3 is mainly White and British, but includes large numbers with Irish, Continental European, Middle Eastern, Chinese, Japanese, Australasian and Latin American origins.

Table 3.2   London's population in 1991, by household type.

Type of household	%
Married couple	46
Lone parent	12
One-person (not pensioner)	16
One-person (pensioner)	14
Others	12
TOTAL	100

Source: LRC *London housing statistics 1990*, tables 1.9 and 1.13.

Table 3.3   London's population in 1991, by ethnic origin.

Ethnic origin of persons	%
West Indian or African	6
South Asian	6
Other New Commonwealth	3
Rest	85
TOTAL	100

Source: LRC *London housing statistics 1990*, table 1.2.

We turn next to consider some basic information on London's dwelling stock. Table 3.4 shows that the total number of houses and flats exceeded 2.9 million units in 1990. This is well in excess of the total number of households given in Table 3.1. However, this does not mean that every household seeking a separate home has access to one. Large numbers of dwellings are empty, for reasons good or bad, and some units are second homes.

Moreover, the household total of Table 3.1 is an underestimate: it does not include "concealed households", those people who wish to live separately but who cannot afford to do so. In 1991 the LRC estimated there were about 37,000 concealed family units (married couples and lone parents) in Greater London sharing their housing against their wishes. The figure excludes many single people who would also prefer their own accommodation but who feel they have no option but to live in someone else's household.

43

Table 3.4 shows that the private sector has the lion's share of the total stock figure. Its 69% breaks down into roughly 57% in home ownership and 12% in the private rental sectors. No-one knows the true figures. But London also has a very large public sector stock, divided between council housing and the housing association sector in the ratio 5:1. Such an important rôle in rental accommodation for government and voluntary bodies is not unusual in western Europe. Stockholm probably has a larger public sector stock in proportionate terms, and in Amsterdam 54% of the city's housing is in social rental!

Table 3.4 London's dwellings by tenure, in April 1981 and April 1990 (thousands).

	1981		1990	
	Number	%	Number	%
Local authority[a]	851	32	744	26
Housing association	134	5	154	5
Owner-occupation	1,317	49	1,659	57
Private rental	359	14	349	12
TOTAL	2,661	100	2,906	100

Sources: Department of the Environment, *Housing and construction statistics 1979–89, Great Britain*, table 9.4; and LRC *London housing statistics 1990*, table 2.1.

a. A relatively small number of "other public sector" dwellings are included here as well as (in 1981) the stock of the Greater London Council. This was transferred to the boroughs in the 1980s. For 1990 the private rental/owner-occupier split is the author's "guesstimate".

From an international perspective, London's housing stock is remarkably old, uniquely so for a megalopolis. This is because already in the 1880s London was the largest city in human history and, although it expanded mightily before the Second World War, there has been virtually no net growth since then. About 36% of the London dwelling stock was originally built before 1919 and a further 29% was built in 1919–44.

With reference to type of dwelling, again in comparison with the great cities of continental Europe, London has an unusually large number of houses and correspondingly few purpose-built flats. The data are provided in Table 3.5.

Table 3.6 provides guesstimates on the condition of the housing stock in 1990. It uses the definition in the 1989 Local Government and Housing Act of unfit for human habitation. In addition, the table refers to units which, although not unfit, were in need of renovation, requiring an expenditure at 1990 prices of more than £4,500 to put each one into a good state of repair.

The information gives great cause for concern about the state of metropolitan housing. More than one-quarter is either unfit or requiring substantial renovation work. The problem is particularly marked in the private and municipal sectors. In terms of dwelling conditions, this appears to be the most challenging issue for the city between now and the end of the millennium.

Table 3.5　London's dwelling stock in 1986–7, by physical type.

Type of unit	%
Detached house	6
Semi-detached house	29
Terraced house	23
Purpose-built flat	31
Converted flats	9
Other	2
TOTAL	100

Table 3.6　London dwellings unfit or in need of renovation: "guesstimate" for April 1990, by tenure (%).

Tenure	Unfit	Need for renovation	Fit and in good repair	Total
Local authority	6	34	60	100
Housing association	3	10	87	100
Private sector	10	15	75	100
TOTAL[a]	8	19	73	100

a.　Total includes a relatively small number of "other public sector" dwellings.

The descriptive material presented above on London's population and housing stock provides a useful snapshot of the recent past. But it gives little clue to the substantial changes in the metropolitan housing system over the past 10–15 years. The principal theme of the remainder of this section is that, over that time period, there has been a major restructuring of the forms of housing provision in London. These radical changes are set to continue, even to accelerate, in the next ten years.

The way in which housing is provided in Britain can be interpreted through the nation's housing tenure arrangements. These fall into four principal categories.

- In the council housing sector, local authorities own the dwelling stock, they manage the estates, allocate empty units to new tenants, charge rents to their customers, and repair and refurbish their properties as resources allow. Councils add to their housing stock by designing new schemes and contracting out the building work to private construction companies.
- The housing association sector is a cousin to council housing, for it too is non-profit housing for rent. Often the local authority and housing association sectors are jointly referred to as "social housing". The difference is that housing associations are legally independent of municipal councils. Many are charities, run by committees whose members volunteer for the job. They, too, add to their existing stock of dwellings by contracting out building work to the construction industry, and they receive substantial grants from central government to pay for the bulk of the capital cost.
- In the private rental sector new lettings are at market rents and, predominantly, lack any long-term security of tenure. Landlords vary from resident

owners, through individuals letting just a few houses, right through to large companies with thousands of homes up and down the country. However, since the late 1930s few new houses and flats have been constructed in this sector, since commercial returns on such property have been regarded as too low, with the ever-present risk of government intervention in rent setting and tenancy arrangements.

– The home ownership sector is where the occupier of a house or flat is also the legal owner. At any one time about two out of every three home owners will have an outstanding mortgage (that is, a financial debt to a building society or a bank) incurred when the dwelling was first purchased. The security for the debt is the home itself, and the mortgage can be repaid over a period of up to 20–25 years. Access to this sector is based on paying the market price for a vacant property. New houses and flats are added to the stock by speculative house-builders who purchase and "bank" land, construct an estate using largely subcontracted labour, and sell on the market at the best price they can get.

In the general election of May 1979 a new Conservative government led by Margaret Thatcher was returned to power, and Britain continues to this day (autumn 1994) to be ruled by the Tories, now headed by John Major. The 1979 victory brought a clean break with the broad consensus which had existed with respect to housing policy since 1945. The Conservatives wished to reduce the power and resources of local government. They even went so far as to abolish in 1986 London's elected metropolitan government, the Greater London Council. These municipal powers and resources were transferred to a variety of other bodies: to central government itself, to quangos such as the London Docklands Development Corporation, to the voluntary sector such as the housing associations, to the private sector and to individual citizens. This weakening of local government was particularly evident with respect to housing.

Initially the new policy was carried out in two ways. First, it became much more difficult for councils to gain the Department of the Environment's approval to borrow money to construct new houses. As a result the recorded number of dwelling completions in London by local authorities contracted sharply, as did spending on such works. This is shown clearly in Table 3.7. Lambeth Borough Council had the most vigorous new construction programme of any authority in London in the 1980s

But this only meant that *additions* to the municipal stock were cut back. The second and more important measure was through the 1980 Housing Act, which gave to all council tenants who could afford to do so the right to buy the home they lived in. This had the effect of stripping away units in the *existing* stock of council dwellings. Local authorities were forced to sell their houses and flats whether they liked it or not, and tenants had a legal right to very large discounts on the market price.

Between 1980 and 1990 more than 177,000 houses and flats were sold. This was equal to one-fifth of the rental stock in 1980. Three-quarters were sold under the right-to-buy legislation and the rest came mostly from vacant possession sales

Table 3.7 New dwellings completed in Greater London 1980–90, by tenure.

Year	Local authorities	Housing associations	Private sector	Total
1980	16,249	2,287	4,090	22,626
1981	13,406	1,934	3,821	19,161
1982	7,254	1,535	5,474	14,263
1983	5,149	1,565	6,539	13,253
1984	3,504	1,560	5,434	10,498
1985	2,713	1,061	4,931	8,705
1986	2,153	644	6,289	9,086
1987	1,384	1,177	9,505	12,066
1988	1,390	806	10,257	12,453
1989	922	1,467	12,700	15,089
1990	1,904	1,737	13,807	17,448

Source: LRC *London housing statistics 1990,* p.132.

to individual purchasers, as in the case of the City of Westminster's Designated Sales Policy. In the London Borough of Wandsworth, its policy of stock disposal preceded the Conservative general election victory of 1979 and was more extensive and forceful than the right to buy itself. In 1980–90, 40% of Wandsworth's stock was disposed of. In Bromley and Redbridge, the figures were even higher. The policies of Westminster and Wandsworth have been widely regarded as a form of social engineering, aimed at shifting these boroughs' populations to a younger, more affluent composition, by the privatization of the housing stock. In a provisional report published in January 1994 in a blaze of publicity, the district auditor declared Westminster's Conservatives' policies to be "disgraceful", "improper", "unlawful" and "gerrymandering". Council house sales were much higher in the Outer than in the Inner London boroughs. Inner London has a less desirable public sector stock, more flats than houses, higher house prices comparing like with like, and a higher percentage of tenants on social security. Throughout London it was the more desirable, better maintained, better located and better built properties that were sold. Since 1985 more than 100,000 units have been disposed of, but only 8,000 new homes built by the councils.

From the Conservative Party's point of view nationally, these measures had clear advantages. First, the promise and the delivery of the right to buy was a great success with large numbers of tenants, and paid clear political dividends in the pattern of voting at local and general elections. Secondly, the local authorities lost resources, as part of their housing stock was transferred into owner-occupation, underpinning the Conservative drive to limit municipal power. Thirdly, the reduced volume of new council house-building meant that public expenditure was reduced, another government objective for the economy as a whole. Furthermore, the income from the sale of council houses was treated by the Treasury as negative public expenditure, thereby reducing the public sector borrowing requirement even further. The privatization of council housing in this way dwarfed all other forms of privatization in the period 1979–93.

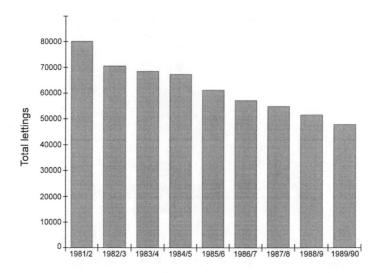

Figure 3.1   Local authority lettings in London, 1981–2 to 1989–90.

Yet, with all its successes, the sale of council housing also had its negative consequences, for both London as a whole and for those households in most pressing need. The annual flow of lettings a local authority (or housing association) can make comes largely from three sources: first, the construction of new homes; secondly, acquiring vacant properties on the open market; and thirdly, the reletting of existing units vacated by former tenants. The reduction by central government of the boroughs' building activity and acquisition programmes severely diminished the first and second supply sources. The reduction in the local authority stock through council house sales, in the course of time, cut back the third supply source. Figure 3.1 shows local authority lettings have fallen by 40% in the eight years since 1981–2.

In the past, council lettings have been the key resource in meeting the needs of those who live in housing poverty. So when the supply dried up, their housing chances deteriorated markedly. The London Research Centre has suggested three factors which made the situation particularly difficult. First, the age group 20–29 is the principal source of newly forming households and in London their number increased by about 150,000 in 1979–90. Secondly, although in real terms the incomes of the low paid and benefit claimants were static in the 1980s, the real cost of mortgage repayments and rents rose. So housing became more difficult to afford, pushing up the demand for homes in the social housing sectors. Thirdly, London attracts a disproportionate number of forced migrants – persons fleeing bloodshed, war and repression in their own countries. Central government, unlike in Sweden, has no plan for distributing these refugees throughout the country, and Greater London's local authorities are legally required to accept them as homeless if they first apply for accommodation in London.

With this surge in need and the decline in lettings, by the early 1990s the situation had become intolerable. In the year 1989–90 more than 33,000 households were accepted as homeless in Greater London, and this excludes all of those people not in "priority need". On any single night in 1990 about 80,000 homeless people were living in temporary accommodation in the city. In April 1990 almost 240,000 households were registered on the boroughs' waiting lists, yet in 1989–90 only 6,000 households from the waiting list could be allocated secure accommodation!

Lettings through the waiting list have been progressively squeezed out by allocations to the priority homeless. Moreover, the ability of council tenants to transfer from one house or flat to another in their borough has been curtailed by the right-to-buy's removal of a disproportionate number of large properties from the council stock.

This loss of council lettings would have had less negative consequences if it had been fully offset by a powerful expansion of the other partner in the social housing sector, the housing associations. Unfortunately the average annual number of dwellings built by the housing associations in Britain in 1980–90 was 17% less than completions under the Labour government of 1974–9.

Table 3.7 shows a static trend in the output of newly constructed housing association properties after the sharp fall in 1980. With respect to the right to buy, this has had much less impact on the associations than on the councils, because no right to buy exists for the tenants of the charitable housing associations. In fact the stock of voluntary sector properties rose by 50,000 dwellings in 1981–9, about four-fifths through acquisitions and the rest from new building. The total number of lettings by housing associations in London in 1989 was 14,500.

Meanwhile, there was no prospect of any long-term revival in the private rental sector. As a rule, investors still regarded the return in this sector as inadequate and the political risks too high. No data exist for the annual number of private lettings in London, so we cannot say precisely by how much they fell. For Britain as a whole, the Inquiry into British Housing chaired by the Duke of Edinburgh (1991) estimated an average loss from the stock of 80,000 units per year in the 1980s!

A minutely detailed, year-long study of one area in Islington (Smith & Merrett 1988) showed that the main reason houses in the private sector were empty was because private landlords were clearing their property to sell it on to homeowners, usually after conversion into flats. This is an example of gentrification, the displacement in residential areas of low-income households by middle- and high-income households. It has been clearly in evidence in London since the mid-1950s (Humphries & Taylor 1986).

The main beneficiary of all these changes was the owner-occupier sector itself. For each thousand council homes sold to their tenants, the local authority stock fell by 1,000 units and the owner-occupier stock rose by 1,000 units, without a single house actually being built. As we have seen above, gentrification was also bringing this switch between housing tenures in the case of the private rental sector. New housing construction for home ownership was also continuing and Table

3.7 shows output in London increased powerfully in the 1980s. Yet, in aggregate and across all tenures, the average annual number of new houses and flats completed in London in the 1980s was less than half the figure for the 1970s.

Because of severe site shortages within the metropolis as well as the tight Green Belt policy of the planners on London's periphery, small new estates were increasingly placed on derelict locations previously used for the transport system, hospitals, factories and warehouses. Docklands is the outstanding example here.

Since the end of the First World War, the rate of house-building for home ownership has always reflected the overall state of the economy. From late 1988 through to 1993, the owner-occupier sector experienced its worst crisis of the century. A series of interest rate cuts through to mid-1988 had brought a strong upward movement in the level of house prices. This was exacerbated by the Chancellor of the Exchequer announcing the forthcoming removal of double mortgage tax relief in the autumn of that year. Couples piled onto the bandwagon to gain access to the subsidy before it was withdrawn, and house prices and sales accelerated even further. But after the summer of that year, a combination of increased interest rates, the cut in subsidy and the onset of the longest recession in the South East for 50 years all dealt heavy body blows to the London market.

The outcome was a dramatic weakening of the effective demand for owner-occupier housing, with a striking similarity to events in Holland a decade before. We saw monthly sales halve in 1989 and 1990 and a rise in the scale of empty property. The rate at which construction of new dwellings was started fell by 50% in 1990 in comparison with 1988. There was also an acceleration in house repossessions. Home buyers found that the lethal combination of a job lost, a high mortgage rate of interest, and debt overhang meant that they were unable to keep up their mortgage payments. Many were evicted by their building society or bank. Others walked away from their dream home in despair.

In a strange twist, the difficulty of selling at a reasonable price led many owners, who had inherited empty property from their parents, to rent out this accommodation to private tenants or to lease it to the local authorities. So private lettings probably increased after 1988. Unfortunately it still appears that this is just a temporary market response, not a long-term shift in investment patterns.

Let me try to sum up. The period from 1979 to 1993 witnessed dramatic changes in what we can call the social relations of housing provision in London. As Table 3.4 shows, the size of the public rental stock diminished and the size of the owner-occupier stock increased. Access to housing through rental lettings contracted while access by house purchase expanded. The housing opportunities of the poorly housed suffered, while those with capital and regular, well paid employment rose. To cap it all, home ownership seemed less secure at the start of the 1990s then had ever seemed possible. New policy initiatives became urgent for the remainder of the decade.

But all the evidence shows that the new government which came to power in April 1992 continues its attack on the local authorities and does nothing to bring about a renaissance of private rental accommodation. The most significant shift in housing provision in the next decade will be the transfer of individual boroughs' own rented housing stocks *en bloc* into the ownership of special housing associations set up for that purpose, as has already happened in 1992 in the London Borough of Bromley. Increasingly in housing, the local authorities seem set to become powerless onlookers.

The preceding pages have set out some of the links between London's housing and general policy trends. In this last part of the chapter, the interconnectedness of housing and industry is highlighted. We have already seen that nearly four million people work in Greater London, of which the services sectors account for some 80%. Between 1980 and 1991 total employment in the capital fell by 9.1%. While public administration, health and education services grew, manufacturing contracted. This was associated with a fall in the number of workers who are men and a rise in those who are women.

But it was banking, investment, insurance and finance (BIF) Sector 8 of the Standard Industrial Classification which experienced the greatest successes. More than one-quarter of all BIF employees in the whole country are located within the former boundaries of the Greater London Council, and BIF is the largest single employment sector in the metropolis, alongside education and health.

The globalization of the world economy tends to strengthen the relative importance of the corporate producer services sectors in the world cities. Moreover, under Mrs Thatcher the Conservative government substantially deregulated British financial institutions. This began in 1979 with the dropping of limitations on foreign investment by British funds and continued, for example, with the Big Bang's de-control of financial dealing in 1986. London – which already in AD 100 had become the financial centre of Britain within the Roman Empire – saw its rôle as a key world actor enhanced (Hamnett 1992).

As a result BIF employment grew by almost one-third in 1981–91, reinforcing its position as the dominant sector of the economy of Greater London. In particular, Chapter 2 indicated the predominance of BIF in 1981–7 employment change in both Inner and Outer London.

As Hamnett (1992) observes, these aggregate employment changes brought with them a regressive redistribution of employment incomes, with a stronger market position for a well paid "service class" and a weaker position for the poorly paid "servicing class". The number of employees in professional, managerial and technical categories grew, as did their individual salaries. This occurred in a decade when the size of Greater London's population in terms of persons was little changed, but when the number of households had increased by 7.6%.

These developments had a powerful knock-on effect for the principal market sector of the London housing system, the home ownership tenure. This is because whenever access to housing is determined by the market – the price system – household income is the key variable from the side of effective demand. Of course, income only rarely provides the cash to buy a house, but it does constitute the flow of money necessary to meet the monthly repayment on the mortgage loan which

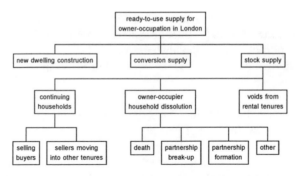

Figure 3.2 The ready-to-use supply for owner-occupation in London.

is used to purchase. So from the demand side all this helps explain the increase in the proportion of owner-occupied dwellings in the Greater London housing stock from 49% in 1981 to 57% in 1990.

But to understand how markets work, we also need a good grasp of supply. Merrett & Sharp (1991) produced a detailed account of the wide variety of supply sources of housing for owner-occupation in London. This is illustrated in Figure 3.2 and Table 3.8.

Table 3.8 Estimated ready-to-use supply for owner-occupation in Greater London, 1987.

Supply source	Dwellings supplied	%
New dwelling construction	9,647	6
Conversions	9,460	6
Void supply from other tenures:		
private rented	13,054	8
local authority	2,716	2
Dissolution of households by:		
death	11,212	7
divorce	5,454	4
marriage	106,464	7
Continuing households moving into the rented sectors	7,287	5
Selling buyers	85,744	55
TOTAL READY-TO-USE SUPPLY	155,220	100
TOTAL OWNER-OCCUPIED STOCK, 1987	1,620,000	

Figure 3.2 shows that supply took nine different forms. Six of these merely recycled during the course of the year the stock of owner-occupied dwellings which had existed at the year's beginning. These were the stock supply from continuing households and from the dissolution of owner-occupier households. But the other three supply forms brought a substantial net investment in the London housing stock which was associated with striking architectural changes in the built environment as well as manifest social changes in the character of individual neighbourhoods.

The supply of newly constructed homes for sale made up 6% of the total ready-to-use supply, as Table 3.8 shows. Between 1980 and 1990, as we have already seen, average annual output equalled about 7,500 units. The majority of this building was on "brown land', that taken out of pre-existing urban uses. The planning system played a key rôle here, for the London Docklands Development Corporation was the single most important source of land for new house-building for home ownership in the 1980s. Moreover, elsewhere it was local planning departments that permitted change to residential use on the other innumerable brown-field sites

The supply of converted homes also made up about 6% of total supply in 1987. These are dwellings created new out of the shell of an existing building, which may formerly have been either residential or non-residential. Once again this is, by definition, brown land and once again the planning system, which was denying access to the Green Belt by speculative house-builders was permitting the change of use or change of structure which conversion entails. The most striking developments are to be found, once again, in London's Docklands.

The stock supply of voids formerly rented made up as much as 10% of total supply in 1987, with a ratio of 4:1 between voids formerly in private rental and those formerly in public rental. The social processes that lie behind this flow have already been described in this chapter.

All of these forms of supply, outside the scope of the recycling of owner-occupied dwellings, contributed to the gentrification juggernaut of the 1980s, as does the later sale on the open market of council and housing association homes first bought at discount under the right to buy. It is likely that gentrification through conversion or through the stock supply of former private rental units has been more important in areas dominated by dwellings built before the First World War, which corresponds very loosely with Inner London.

In a nutshell, the interconnectedness argument here is as follows. The absolute size and the rate of growth of the services industries in Greater London in the 1980s, particularly the scale and rate of growth of the banking, insurance and finance sector, brought with it a very large and growing body of professional and managerial personnel. In the UK the incomes of these groups are high by any standard. Many of these individuals sought owner-occupied housing in the Greater London area, where new building is severely constrained by Green Belt policies. Thus, much of this effective demand for housing was focused on brown-field sites where accommodation was supplied by new construction, conversions and the sale of empty units formerly in public or private rental. In all of these supply processes, the planning organizations of the public sector played a key rôle.

Of course, it is clear that the effective demand for housing by professionals and managers working in Greater London can be expressed not merely within the 32 London boroughs and the City, but also in the Outer Metropolitan Area and even beyond. In these cases the employee travels into Greater London by private car or by public transport. We shall see in Chapter 4 that increased affluence and the buoyant service-sector economy have led to substantial growth in the demand for all forms of travel, particularly in long-distance commuting along the main radial routes into Central London. Because of the underprovision of public transport infrastructure through to 1987, these changes have led to a decline in road speeds and an increase in all forms of congestion.

References and further reading

Allen, J. & C. Hamnett (eds) 1991a. *Housing and labour markets: building the connections.* London: Unwin Hyman.

Allen, J. & C. Hamnett (eds) 1991b. Introduction. *Housing and labour markets: building the connections.* London: Unwin Hyman.

Department of the Environment 1991. *Housing and construction statistics 1979–1989, Great Britain.* London: HMSO.

The Duke of Edinburgh (Chairman) 1991. *Inquiry into British housing.* York: Joseph Rowntree Foundation.

Hamnett, C. 1992. Labour markets, housing markets and social restructuring in a global city: the case of London. In *Housing and labour markets: building the connections*, J. Allen & C. Hamnett (eds). London: Routledge.

Humphries, S. & J. Taylor 1986. *The making of modern London: 1945–85.* London: Sidgwick & Jackson.

London Research Centre 1991. *London housing statistics 1990.* London: London Research Centre.

Merrett, S. & C. Sharp 1991. The denarius hypothesis: house price inflation in owner-occupied London. In *Changing housing finance systems*, M. Satsangi (ed.), 271–312. Glasgow: Centre for Housing Research.

Smith, R. & S. Merrett 1988. Empty dwellings and tenure switching: a British case study. *Housing Studies* **3**(2), 105–111.

CHAPTER FOUR

Transport

David Banister

Introduction

The economy of London boomed in the 1980s, with the service sector accounting for over 80% of all employment. Population remained stable, but the number of cars increased by 22%, with over 62% of households owning at least one car. The increased levels of affluence, together with a buoyant economy in the capital, led to significant growth in the demand for travel, not just by car but by all forms of public transport (Table 4.1). It is difficult to unravel the complexity of the changing situation, but traffic congestion on all forms of transport has increased, at least until 1989 when the effects of the latest recession started to be felt. At the height of the "boom" period (1988), there were 960,000 people coming into Central London (inside the Circle Line) by rail and bus between 0700–1000 hours each weekday morning, and a further 160,000 by car. Even the downturn in the economy since that time has resulted in only a relatively small reduction of 5% in these figures (1988–90), and a further 5% in 1991 (Department of Transport 1992). The numbers of Central London commuters using a bicycle or motor cycle has fallen

Table 4.1 Passenger journeys in London (1981–91).

	British Rail (000s per day)	London Transport (millions p.a.)		Average speed on London roads (mph)	
	To Central London	Underground	Bus	Peak	Off-peak
1981	572	541	1079	17.8	20.6
1985	572	732	1146	17.2	20.9
1991	685	775	1180	16.2	18.9
1981–91	+20%	+43%	+9%	−9%	−8%
1992	641	751	1149		

Source: Department of Transport (1992).

55

by 29% over the past decade, although there are still some 17,000 cycling commuters to Central London and a total of 450,000 cycle trips made daily in London as a whole. There are also over seven million walk trips every weekday, surpassed only by eight million car and taxi trips (Department of Transport 1991a).The types of trips are changing with an increase in the numbers of cross-city trips and a reduction of trips to the centre of London. This trend partly reflects the size of London, which has no single centre but several competing centres for offices, for shopping and for recreation. It also reflects the more varied nature of activities in the 1980s, with longer circumferential movements becoming dominant and the growth in long-distance commuting along the main radial rail routes into Central London. Public transport is ideally suited for radial movements along corridors of high demand. Most of these new patterns of activity are suited for the car and they often take place on residential and local roads which were never designed for such heavy flows of traffic.

Traffic levels on London's roads have increased by over 3% per annum in the suburbs and by about 1% per annum in the central areas. For cars the growth (1980–90) is 38% in the suburbs and 10% in the central area. Outside the central area the car has been the dominant mode of motorized travel for the past twenty years. The numbers of heavy lorries in the centre has actually declined during the decade, which may in part be attributable to the opening of the M25 orbital motorway around London. The net result has been a decline in traffic speeds at all times of the day on all roads (except main routes; see Table 4.1). These figures mask the much lower average speeds in the central areas, which are now only 10.3 miles per hour, irrespective of time of day. There is no peak period in Central London, as traffic is operating under highly congested conditions all the time. Any slight disruption may result in the whole road system within the central area coming to a complete halt: gridlock (Banister 1990a).

Radical changes have also affected public transport with the introduction of zonal fares and travel cards (1981), and the tendering of nearly 40% of London Transport's bus network (since 1985). London Buses have been reorganized prior to full privatization, and all public transport in London now has clear quality of service objectives which should be achieved. Despite these changes, there is still considerable uncertainty about the future, even though patronage levels on London bus services have increased slightly (+4% from 1985–90), while those in the other cities in Britain have fallen by over 26% in the five years since deregulation (Banister & Pickup 1990). However, since 1990, patronage levels have fallen by about 4%, mainly as a result of the recession. The benefits of competitive regulation as practised in London, where all the competition takes place off the road through the tendering process, has allowed co-ordination between services to be maintained, and travel cards are valid on all services. Information to travellers and stability in services have proved crucial to maintaining and increasing levels of demand. Since partial deregulation in London, fares in real terms have increased by 17% for buses, 13% for Network South East rail services, and by 20% for the Underground (Department of Transport 1992). Patronage levels have been maintained and improved, at least until the current recession, despite significant real increases in fares.

The bus is still the most frequently used form of public transport, accounting for 57% of all public transport trips (Table 4.1), but only 7% of the total numbers of commuters entering Central London at the peak use the bus (0700–1000 hours; London Regional Transport 1989). This anomaly represents a considerable under-use of this public transport resource. The principal problem is that buses are caught up in delays caused by cars, and this reduces their effectiveness by lengthening journey times and reducing reliability (Department of Transport 1991b). Congestion and slow traffic have assisted in the long-term decline in commuting by bus, which fell by 18% between 1983 and 1987 (Department of Transport 1989). British Rail and the London Underground on the other hand are "critically congested" (where all seats are occupied and over 60% of crush capacity used; Department of Transport et al. 1989). Selective reallocation of priorities would allow a much greater efficiency of operation and a greater capacity for use of the buses in Central London. There are only 40 miles of bus lanes in the whole of London (Paris has 125 miles).

This chapter reviews transport policy in London over the past ten years, focusing on the issues of investment in transport, congestion and the powerful arguments for strategic transport planning. Two of the most crucial problems are then addressed – the lack of investment in infrastructure and the spreading of the city. Major changes are taking place in the ways in which cities are organized and how they work, yet transport, which has in the past been one of the main facilitators of change, may now act as a constraint on London's continued rôle as the commercial, financial, educational and tourist capital of Europe.

Investment in transport

The heightened levels of congestion on the roads, and a public transport system running at capacity, require important decisions to be made on capital investment. The M25 orbital motorway around London was completed in October 1986, and it is operating to capacity for much of the day. Some sections of the M25 to the West of the city carry over 150,000 vehicles per day and this motorway now carries 12% of all the traffic on Britain's motorways. One lesson which has been learnt is that new road capacity is soon filled with traffic diverted from parallel congested routes and from the expected growth in traffic. The question is when the new road will be operating at capacity, not whether that capacity will be reached. Consequently, new road construction in London is undesirable on transport and environmental criteria. Future road investment is likely to be much more clearly focused on upgrading existing roads (e.g. the North Circular Road), on the construction of new bridges across the Thames (e.g. the M25 Dartford Bridge and the East London River Crossing), and in assisting urban development projects by opening up new areas (e.g. the Limehouse Link).

This change in thinking was crystallized in the four London Assessment Studies which examined a range of Road improvements in congested corridors around Central London. The £250 million package was rejected by the government in March 1990, after a five-year study. Of particular importance in this decision was the opposition of residents to the costs of construction, the demolition of housing, and the traffic-generation effects of the proposed roads. During the lengthy debates on the Assessment Studies, some 6,000 homes had been blighted as they were along the routes of some of the roads being considered. There will be little investment in new roads, but efforts will again be switched to making better use of existing roads through:

- "Red Routes" (where no parking is allowed and enforcement is rigorous)
- reductions in parking spaces and increased enforcement (including wheel clamping and towing away)
- the possibility of road pricing
- limitations on traffic by traffic calming and pedestrianization, and
- the introduction of the new information technology.

Possibilities here include route guidance systems for drivers, smart cards to charge for car parking, and real-time control systems for area-wide traffic control. Passenger transport information systems, again based on real-time information, will be available at bus stations and at individual bus stops to help travellers with accurate information on when the next bus will actually arrive. It should be noted that, although traffic speeds in London have decreased and are now constant across the whole day in the central area, it is when an incident occurs that gridlock takes place. Gridlock occurs when part of the transport network comes to a complete standstill with no moving traffic. Incidents can be unpredictable and may include accidents and road closures, or they can be predictable such as demonstrations and processions. Disruptions caused by both unpredictable and predictable incidents can be minimized by the effective use of road transport informatics systems, as instantaneous incident detection allows emergency services to be mobilized very quickly and traffic to be diverted away from the source of the disruption.

Where London has lagged behind other major cities is in investment in public transport (Table 4.2). All major world cities require substantial and continuing investment in public transport, but for London this investment has taken place only since 1987, and then only in the renewal of existing infrastructure. Total investment in rail infrastructure by London Transport and Network South East (1990/91) is nearly double the level of 1987 at £780 million, with a further £272 million now being invested in rolling stock. It will still be many years before the tube and rail networks are comparable with the quality of networks found elsewhere in European cities. Other investments in public transport have been made, including the electrification of services from Bedford and Peterborough, the Thameslink across-London line (1988), the London City Airport in Docklands (1987), the new air terminals at Stansted (1991), Gatwick (1988) and Heathrow (1986).

Underlying all these investment decisions has been the means by which major infrastructure projects have been financed. One of the great debates over the past

Table 4.2   Investment in road and rail in London and the South East (£ millions, 1991/ 92 prices).

	Roads infrastructure		Rail infrastructure				Rail rolling stock			
	South East	Of which London	NSE	LUL	DLR	Total	NSE	LUL	DLR	Total
85/6	947	244	–	177	40	–	–	13	6	–
86/7	958	278	149	208	19	376	25	26	3	53
87/8	927	317	198	246	76	520	92	24	4	120
88/9	1038	345	229	236	60	525	159	30	4	192
89/90	1253	439	291	269	99	658	130	84	8	222
90/91	1468	491	261	395	125	780	165	86	21	272
91/2	1458	1470	253	273	135	661	147	96	27	270

Notes:
– The 1992 figures are provisional.
– Figures include both private and public investment. Road figures cover expenditure on new construction and improvement, and capital maintenance by government and local authorities, including New Towns and the LDDC.
– South East covers an area comparable to that of Network South East: all counties in the South East standard region, plus Dorset and Cambridgeshire.
– Network South East figures include some expenditure by InterCity and Freight.
– NSE: Network South East; LUL: London Underground Limited; DLR: Docklands Light Railway.
Source: Department of Transport (1992).

decade has been the rôle of government in providing resources for public expenditure. Both British Rail and London Transport have been set strict limits on the levels of capital expenditure which in turn relate to their financial performance. If targets are not reached, the investment may be delayed, so long-term decisions become influenced by short-term changes in the economic cycle. The government has also tried to raise capital from developers, but this has proved of limited value in terms of the amounts obtained and the period over which payment takes place. The private sector prefers to make its own decisions (e.g. to build a new airport terminal) or argues that it will not be the only beneficiary from a major transport investment. The free-rider problem characterizes the reluctance of the private sector to invest in the infrastructure which it claims is a common good available to all its competitors. Many of the beneficiaries from the investment will not pay directly for the service – they are the free-riders – and the private sector cannot recoup their costs from these beneficiaries. The dedicated link from Paddington to Heathrow would cut journey times to 15 minutes and cater for nearly 20 million passengers a year, given the expected growth in demand, yet the relatively modest cost (£400 million at 1993 prices) has only recently been found by the British Airports Authority in partnership with others. Similarly, the negotiations over the proposed contribution of £400 million from Olympia and York, agreed with the government as a part contribution to the extension of the Jubilee Line from Charing Cross and Waterloo into Docklands, has delayed construction for nearly five years. Investment in transport must not be postponed and it must continue throughout the downturns in the construction and economic cycles which occur on a shorter-term cycle than the transport investment cycle. In both these examples, the government has insisted that the projects are funded at least in part by the private sector. This in turn has meant delay, continuing congestion and reductions in levels of confidence.

An audit of the problems

The basic question is whether, in terms of capacity, the transport problems and quality are really as bad as stated, and whether the threat of gridlock reduces the attractiveness of London as a capital city. In 1991, congestion and traffic jams were perceived as the most pressing problem for those living in London (50% of respondents mentioned this factor) and rated higher than house prices (43%), burglaries and assault (34%), poor public services (30% litter and rubbish), homelessness (28%), cost of living (27%), vandalism and graffiti (21%), unemployment (20%) and poor public transport (16%). But improvements to public transport, reduced fares and improved roads were all seen as more important policy actions than the possibility of road pricing (NEDO 1991).

A clear strategic policy must be agreed for transport, and resources must be allocated to investment in all forms of transport, both public and private. Apart from the direct effects of inefficient and poor-quality transport, it has a major impact on the environment, it affects decisions of people to live and work in the capital, it influences business efficiency, it reduces tourism in the city, and it influences peoples' perceptions of London as a world city.

The present situation is not unexpected. Over the past five years (1989–93) there have been some twenty major reports from academics, professional organizations, government bodies and pressure groups covering transport in London. Indeed, there is a remarkable degree of agreement between the documents about the causes and nature of the problems. There is also a fair degree of consensus as to the range of transport options available to ease the problems of congestion, safety and pollution, and to improve the quality of the city environment, and at the same time increasing economic efficiency and promoting accessibility.

Proposals include the Jubilee Line extension, the CrossRail between Paddington and Liverpool Street, the Chelsea to Hackney Underground line, the new high-speed rail link east from St Pancras / Kings Cross and Stratford to the Channel Tunnel, a new terminal at Heathrow airport, a 1,000 mile network of cycle routes, and "Red Routes" on all 300 miles of major roads. All of these projects have been costed and approved, but none of them has been started (November 1993). Similarly, none of these projects has been assessed in terms of its strategic importance or its impact on accessibility, its environmental benefits and its contribution to the economic efficiency of London.

Whatever the ideological differences between central and local government, London is still one of the few major world cities without a metropolitan transport authority. Such an organization is essential to provide the stability and continuity in transport decision-making across the city and to provide the financial resources for new investments. There would be close links with the boroughs and the sponsors of new development to ensure that land uses were compatible with the transport infrastructure. This would mean that the transport investment would take place at the same time as the development, so that the one was not at odds with the other. If investment capital were not available from central government, other means of raising funds would have to be established. These could include government-guaranteed loans and joint ventures with the private sector, which might include the possibility of the private sector running services on publicly financed infrastructure. Other means to raise capital include the more effective use of planning gain, the possibility of an employment tax in London (as in Paris), transport bonds to raise capital over the short term, and positive encouragement to the private sector through tax incentives by making their contributions 100% tax deductible. The present system is only concerned with meeting short-term financial targets set by the Treasury and the Department of Transport. For real progress to be made, transport investment in the capital must be placed on a longer-term financial basis with a continuous commitment, irrespective of economic conditions.

In the longer term, other proposals are also being considered. The road pricing option is at present being assessed by the Department of Transport. The possibilities of parkway stations and another London orbital motorway are being advocated by the road lobby, while dedicated bus routes and strict parking enforcement, together with market pricing of all parking spaces, are being promoted as the only short-term solution.

Decisions are required now and investment must follow. Car ownership in London is already close to the national average, and it is further expected to increase to about 70% of households by the year 2000. New office developments in Central London (e.g. in Docklands, Hammersmith and the City) will generate more traffic, whereas out-of-town regional shopping, retail and leisure centres located around the M25 and other accessible parts of the road network will all create more car traffic. With the opening of the Channel Tunnel in 1994, tourist and other traffic across the channel will double, and much of that traffic will require accommodation in London (British Tourist Authority 1989). In addition to these particular London factors, other changes taking place in society are also likely to generate more trips; included here are increases in leisure time, earlier retirement and an ageing population, more dispersed patterns of employment and increases in levels of affluence. Major investment is required now to anticipate this new demand. The alternative is a continuation of a transport system that is inappropriate to the needs of a capital city in the year 2000.

Infrastructure

The success of cities and regions has always been based on the quality of their infrastructure. This in turn requires a commitment over a long period of time to continued new investment and replacement of the existing stock. Infrastructure is the durable capital of the city and its location is fixed – it includes roads, railways, water, sewerage, electricity, gas and telecommunications. Often the services obtained from the infrastructure have a spatial dimension (e.g. the distribution of water), with the benefit from that service declining as distance from the supply point increases (e.g. reservoirs). Their key characteristics are that many people and industries benefit from a single infrastructure, that they can be used over and over again, that the infrastructure remains when people move in and out of an area, and that it provides the means for the integration and co-ordination of activities over time and space. The infrastructure forms the arteries of the city, and the health of the city is dependent upon these networks.

In London, capital expenditure on the infrastructure has failed to keep pace with changes in the demand patterns. Following the constraints imposed by the International Monetary Fund (1976–7), public expenditure was severely cut back to allow more resources to be channelled into producing exports and investment in private industry. Markets (not the government) were seen as the most efficient means to provide services and distribute resources. Government policy was to reduce public expenditure, and this objective was much easier to achieve in the capital programme. The cuts were made even more severe by the upward pressure on current expenditure, particularly for social security payments. The magnitude of the under-investment is illustrated in Table 4.3 where *net* investment (i.e. allowing for depreciation) over the decade is shown as a percentage of measured capital stock in manufacturing and in the other main industry groups. Thus, total net

Table 4.3   UK net fixed-capital formation (1979–89) as a percentage of the 1979 capital stock.

Transport	−5.9%
Manufacturing	+5.1%
Distribution and banking	+111.6%
Oil and gas	+43.8%
Other (excluding housing)	+31.1%

Source: K. Coutts et al. 1990. *Britain's economic problems and policies in the 1990s.* Institute of Public Policy Research Economic Studies 6, chart 1.10.

investment in manufacturing over the period (1979–89) was only 5% of the opening net capital stock, and there was a decline in the transport sector. It is only in the sectors such as distribution and banking and oil & gas that the private sector has invested heavily, with the resulting net increases in the capital formation. However, the private sector has invested neither in the transport infrastructure nor in the public utilities such as water and electricity. The private sector's case is clear.

Investment will take place only if there are clear returns on capital to the investor through profits and dividends to shareholders. Investment in roads gives no clear competitive advantage to the private investor and it may help their competitors. This is the "free-rider" dilemma for government: why should a private company invest in a project when it is known that someone else will pay for it?

The only situation where the private sector has shown interest in investment in transport infrastructure is when they charge for the use of that road *and* they can exert effective monopoly control over the route. For example, the Queen Elizabeth bridge (opened in 1991) across the Thames, which duplicates the existing M25 tunnels, has been financed and run by a private sector consortium (Table 4.4).

Table 4.4   The Queen Elizabeth road bridge on the M25.

This road bridge was opened in 1991 and it marks the first time this century that a major road has been privately funded in the United Kingdom

Construction	By Dartford River Crossing Ltd	
	Trafalgar House plc	49%
	Kleinwort Benson plc	17%
	Bank of America	17%
	Prudential Assurance	17%
	Cost £170 million	
Operation	The company has taken over the outstanding debt on the existing Dartford Tunnels from Essex and Kent County Councils, and operates both the tunnel and the new bridge as toll facilities.	
	The bridge provides four lanes for southbound traffic and the existing tunnels provide four northbound lanes.	
	The company has a maximum of 20 years to recoup their costs and make a profit.	
	Tolls will not increase in real terms above the levels prevailing at 1 January 1986.	

Source: Banister (1990b).

In the non-transport sectors, the government has decided to privatize many of the industries involved in infrastructure provision (e.g. British Telecom, the water companies, the electricity companies, and British Gas). Private monopolies have been established with agencies being set up to protect consumers against the abuse of that monopoly control. Part of that control is designed to raise the levels of investment in the infrastructure, thus reducing the necessity for public investment. The costs of the private investment are recouped directly from the consumer.

However, it is with respect to transport infrastructure in London that most debate has taken place, particularly in the context of proposals for the new cross-London rail links. Originally, it was the government's intention to look for contributions to the capital investment costs of the two new full-size rail tunnels extending from west to east (Paddington to Liverpool Street) and from north to south (Euston / Kings Cross to Victoria), together with the new Underground line from Chelsea to Hackney, from the private sector. Their argument was that the schemes would enhance land values and generate significant benefits to businesses and landowners, and that the beneficiaries would negotiate with railway operators over the choice of routes, alignments and location of stations "in return for a significant financial contribution to reflect the benefits they would derive" (Department of Transport et al. 1989). Only in situations where expected revenues from fares and the contributions from developers are not sufficient to pay for the scheme would the government consider making a grant, but even then only if there are sufficient non-user benefits (e.g. in the relief of road congestion). The result has been a stalemate, as there are no clear direct advantages to the developers, the scale of the proposed investment is vast (of a scale similar to the Channel Tunnel), and the risks are high, including forecasts of demand, design standards, the inquiry process and the acquisition of land.

The main conclusion must be reached that the public sector still has the principal responsibility for investment in the capital infrastructure in all situations where the capital formation is not controlled directly by the private sector. A clear partnership is required between the government, the statutory agency running the service and the London Boroughs within which the service operates. Planning is a crucial element in the preparation of sites for development. The required infrastructure must be available at the time the development is ready for occupation. This means that an assessment of the infrastructure requirements for any new development should be a material consideration in the planning decision for the individual project. It also means that each individual project should be assessed in terms of an overall plan or programme for the area. Projects in themselves may not generate and attract much traffic, nor will they place undue demands on the telecommunications networks, the utilities or the quality of the urban environment, but taken in conjunction with all other developments their effects may be substantial. The key new rôles for planning in relation to infrastructure provision are in the assembly of land for development, in the extension of development control powers, and in the assessment of how individual developments fit into other developments in the locality and the vision of the city as a whole. The private sector can then construct and operate the infrastructure as a private project or in conjunction with the public sector as a joint venture, with the risks and rewards being shared.

Docklands provides a classic example of the problems created by the absence of appropriate infrastructure provision before development takes place. The London Docklands Development Corporation (LDDC) was set up in 1981 to buy land and control development in the old London docks. The government also exempted developers in part of the area from property taxes for ten years. Only limited road investment took place and the low-capacity Docklands Light Railway (DLR) didn't even link the docks area with the commercial centre of London. The Bank extension (costing £150 million) was opened in July 1991, four years after the original line, and it is only now that capacity is being increased with longer trains and more frequent services. Even then, the scale of investment is not commensurate with the amount of office space in the docks. The Canary Wharf development will provide 10 million square feet of office space, and over 25 million square feet is being provided in the Isle of Dogs.

It was only in 1989 that the government approved the extension of the Jubilee Underground line into Docklands, but only on the condition that developers owning land along the route contributed to its estimated £1.9 billion cost (1993 prices). These payments, and hence the future of the line, have been in doubt ever since, with plans never getting beyond the design stage. The Minister has now given his approval, and construction on the 16km route between Central London, Docklands and Stratford will begin before the end of 1993. It will take four and a half years to build and it will create some 20,000 jobs. An initial £98 million has been provided by the European Investment Bank, and a further £300 million will be paid by the Canary Wharf company over the next 29 years. The total private sector investment will be less than 10% of the total discounted costs, yet this contribution has been the major cause of the five-year delay in starting the project.

Major road investment has taken place with the Limehouse Link, improvements in the main roads (e.g. the A13), and the upgrading of the roads within the Docklands area itself. Nevertheless, the accessibility of the area is still very poor, with no links to the south of the river and congested routes to the City. The government needs to have the means to recover the costs of infrastructure from the chief beneficiaries. This mechanism is analogous to the private sector's ability to charge directly for the infrastructure used. The irony of the situation is that the benefits of infrastructure are capitalized in property prices, but those values cannot be realized until the infrastructure investment takes place. This is the impasse.

The government has been reluctant to use tax revenues to invest in transport infrastructure, even though the position of London as an international and national centre would suggest that a special case could be made. Good transport infrastructure in London, particularly for public transport, is an asset from which the whole nation benefits. Revenue could also be raised from domestic council taxes to help investment, but this is more likely to support concessionary fares and other forms of subsidy, which specifically benefit London residents. The argument here is that many of the people who benefit from London's transport system are not residents. These include tourists, long-distance commuters and freight companies. Is it fair that Londoners should subsidize their travel in the Capital? One means to raise money from commercial property owners would be through a supplement to the Unified Business Rate. Alternatively, a business (or employers') levy could be raised from those benefiting from improved transport infrastructure. If the money raised were invested in the transport system, companies would benefit from reduced congestion and the better quality of public transport service. The users of the transport system should also pay a fair price which would cover the operating costs and make some contribution to the maintenance of the system, but it is unrealistic to expect major capital investment to be funded out of fares revenues.

More speculative proposals for London include road pricing and supplementary licensing. With road pricing, the motorist is charged according to the time spent on the road system, whereas supplementary licensing is a fixed charge to enter the central area. The justifications in both cases are based on the premise that the motorist pays only the private costs of road use, and that road pricing and supplementary licensing allow the full social and environmental costs to be charged. However, it is unlikely that the revenues raised from pricing road space will be used to finance capital expenditure. At best, the revenues may be used to support improved public transport services and at worst they will "disappear" as another form of exchequer revenue. Unless a clear commitment is given to using the revenues for transport investment, public resentment is likely to be substantial. The impact of road pricing on the city centre is unclear. It may accelerate the decentralization of the city as firms seek to locate in areas with lower rent levels outside the priced area. It may increase boundary pressures on locations immediately outside the pricing area, and there are substantial equity issues raised. Although the overall impact may be progressive on all households, as car-owning households are rich and those who drive most are the richest, the impact on car-owning households is regressive, as low-income households would be priced off the road (Banister 1993).

In summary, an agenda for infrastructure investment in London can be drawn up:
- Infrastructure investment must be increased and maintained at a significant level to protect London's position as a major world city.
- The public sector is the main agency in providing the level of investment required. The private sector will only be prepared to invest where it has a monopoly over the provision of that infrastructure (e.g. water supply), where there is no competition (e.g. the new M25 bridge), or where it might be the principal beneficiary (e.g. Canary Wharf).
- Capital can be raised from the taxpayer, the traveller (including the motorist), and from a variety of property and employment taxes.
- Planning has an important rôle in linking development with the appropriate infrastructure investment, and in ensuring that the system as a whole is operating efficiently. This means that distances for travel and distribution should be minimized. There should also be a balance between development and infrastructure provision. Assessment should cover both the direct impacts that any new project has and the wider indirect effects on the efficiency and quality of life in the city as a whole.

Decentralization

Over the past fifty years London has been spreading as the urban area has grown and the labour-market areas have expanded. People no longer live close to their workplaces, but commute long distances, often travelling two to three hours a day. This separation between homes and workplaces has taken place as people are pre-pared to sacrifice time spent in commuting for more space and a better environ-ment. Such a change has been made possible through increases in income, the availability of high-quality road and rail links, and the fact that most activities are now no longer work based. The growth in travel has taken place in social, shop-ping and recreational activities, many of which take place in the countryside and in purpose-built car-accessible locations (e.g. regional shopping centres and sports facilities). Greater accessibility can be achieved through the use of the car in the countryside than the use of public transport and the car in London.

Simple patterns are being replaced with more complex patterns as travel demand no longer takes place along well defined radial corridors (suited to public transport), but along more elaborate circumferential and peripheral movements (suited to the car). With the decentralization of employment from Central London and the pressures for development on greenfield sites, average journey lengths have increased substantially. Locally based facilities and jobs, suitable for access by "soft" modes of transport (i.e. walk, bicycle and bus) are no longer attractive to car users, who prefer to use the car and to travel farther to larger facilities.

All these factors have led to certain anomalies. Homes had traditionally been located near to workplaces, but, with the advent of trams, buses and the Under-ground in London, homes were soon being constructed in the suburbs. Workers commuted to office jobs in Central London and to the main manufacturing cen-tres in other parts of London by public transport. With regional decentralization, there is now a mismatch between jobs and homes, and this has resulted in long journeys to work. Both workplaces and homes have become almost randomly dis-tributed across the South East. The traditional logic of home and work proximity is further distorted by the more complex patterns of employment within the fam-ily. In the past, only one person in each household worked, but now there are often two or more workers within a household, and the household itself is a much looser unit. There are many single-parent families, households with young returning adults in them, and couples cohabiting. The "typical" family unit (two adults and two children) is now the exception and not the rule (Banister & Bayliss 1991). Pat-terns of part-time working, flexible hours, working from home, and travelling to different employment destinations – all add further variability to the picture.

The patterns of activities that have emerged are high in consumption of resources (human and natural), with considerable environmental disbenefits. Lower densities of development lead to increases in energy consumption and a greater dependence on the car. It might be expected that London is efficient in terms of energy consumption in transport, as it has a relatively high density of pop-ulation and a high proportion of total travel by public transport. However,

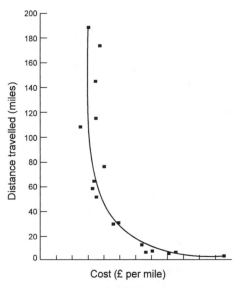

Figure 4.1 Costs of commuting to Central London by rail, by distance travelled (1991). *Source:* Roberts (1992).

because of the larger number of trips made by Londoners and the higher than average journey lengths, total energy consumption in transport in London is higher than that in other cities in Britain (Banister 1992).

The third anomaly may help explain some of these distortions. There is a distance inversion in the costs of commuting to Central London by rail (Fig. 4.1). As distance increases, the costs per mile of travel decreases. This does not mean that it is cheaper to travel by rail if one lives a long way from London, but it does mean that it is cheaper per mile travelled (Roberts 1992). In addition, it is often quicker to travel to Central London from a longer distance on the InterCity network than it is for a shorter distance on Network South East. For example, travel times by rail from Oxford (100 km) and Reading (50 km) from the West on the InterCity network are similar to those from East Grinstead (50 km) and Oxted (30 km) on Network South East to the South of London. The differences in travel times between British Rail and London Underground for comparable distances are even greater. The combination of this cost and time inversion make the prospect of long-distance commuting more attractive.

These patterns and anomalies are not unique to London, but within Britain they are nowhere more evident than in the capital. Decentralization has led to a high level of consumption of resources which is not sustainable, certainly in environmental terms, and parts of the capital are being left empty as dereliction can be found next to new development. Population and development densities, particularly in the central parts of London, are being reduced as new construction is delayed and as land prices remain significantly higher than those elsewhere in the South East. With the recent oversupply of office space and other commercial developments in Central London, and the loss of confidence in the construction industry, rental levels are falling, but it may take several years for this process of market readjustment to take place. In the meantime, development pressures will continue to be greatest on greenfield sites in the South East.

Conclusions

The arguments presented in this chapter are not a statement of support for a return to the 1960s or 1970s style of planning, but a much more active form of intervention at the strategic and local levels. At the strategic level, clear objectives and targets must be set to re-establish London as the capital of Europe, with vibrant national and local economies, cultural and educational excellence, and a high quality of life for its residents and visitors. Achievement of these objectives involves both the public and private sectors operating in the same direction in partnership. There must be a continuous process of investment in infrastructure and in priorities being established to balance the needs of the motorist against those of others, including pedestrians, cyclists, public transport users, residents and businesses. Planning in a new form has a key rôle in establishing those objectives and targets at the macro level, and in the implementation of them at the local level. Planners should be seen as agents of change operating in concert with politicians, businesses and local communities. They should also ensure fairness and justice in their actions and that the needs of all groups in society are met. The market can operate in some situations, but there are also situations where controls and regulations are needed to moderate the adverse impact of the market. Equally, there are other situations where the market fails and direct intervention is needed. It is the balance between these different priorities that needs to be addressed. In the transport sector this balance has never been achieved – in the 1970s there was too much intervention, in the 1980s there was too little. The challenge for the 1990s is to achieve the optimum.

References and further reading

Banister, D. (ed.) 1990a. *The final gridlock. Built Environment* **15**(3/4; special issue).
—1990b. Privatisation in transport: from the company state to the contract state. In *The state in action: public policy and politics*, J. Simmie & R. King (eds), 95–116. London: Pinter.
—1992. Energy use, transport and urban form. In *Sustainable development and urban form*, M. Breheny (ed.), 160–81. London: Pion.
—1993. Equity and acceptability questions. Paper presented at the OECD/ECMT seminar on Internalising the Social Costs of Transport, Paris, September/October.
—& D. Bayliss 1991. *Structural changes in population and the impact on passenger transport demand.* European Conference of Ministers of Transport, Round Table 88, Paris.
—& L. Pickup 1990. Bus transport in the Metropolitan Areas and London. In *Deregulation and transport: market forces in the modern world*, P. Bell & P. Cloke (eds), 67–83. London: Fulton.

British Tourist Authority 1989. *Strategy for growth 1989–1993*. London: British Tourist Authority.

Coutts, K., W. Godley, B. Rowthorn, G. Zezza 1990. *Britain's economic problems and policies in the 1990s*. Institute of Public Policy Research, Economic Studies 6.

Department of Transport 1989. *Statement on transport policy in London*. London: HMSO.

—1991a. *Transport statistics for London 1980–1990*. Transport Statistics Report, Government Statistical Service, October.

—1991b. *A bus strategy for London*. Consultation Paper, London, March.

—1992. *Transport statistics for London 1992*. Transport Statistics Report, Government Statistical Service, October.

—and London Transport and British Rail 1989. *Central London rail study*. London: HMSO.

London Regional Transport 1989. "Long-term strategy and medium-term objectives." Chairman's Planning Statement, London, LRT.

NEDO 1991(November). *A road user charge? Londoners' views*. A report prepared by the Harris Research Centre for National Economic Development Office, the London Planning Advisory Committee and the Automobile Association.

Roberts, J. 1992. Do transport policies meet needs? In *Transport, the environment and sustainable development*, D. Banister & K. Button (eds), 248–56. London: Chapman & Hall.

CHAPTER FIVE

Politics and planning in London

John Gyford

The planning of any city is more than a purely technical exercise in which only professional planners are involved. The design and implementation of planning policies is an activity which has significant implications for the city's inhabitants as they go about their daily lives in their economic, domestic, recreational and other rôles. Decisions on the future development of particular sites or localities can directly affect the value of property, the prospects for employment, access to housing, the ease of travel, the facilities for enjoyment, or the very appearance and aesthetics of the local environment. Major strategies for urban growth or containment can replicate such impacts at a larger scale, affecting not only the people who live within the city itself but also those who live in the surrounding region.

Because it may affect people's interests so directly, and sometimes so drastically, planning can generate considerable controversy, provoking not only public debate but also political action, as those affected attempt to defend their interests. They may seek to promote a particular development, or to defend a threatened neighbourhood; they may operate in a variety of ways, campaigning and lobbying, both in public and in private. In any particular city the nature of the debates about planning and the ways in which they are resolved will reflect the specific history, institutions and culture of that city. In this chapter we begin by identifying two major themes in the continuing debate about London and its future and then explore the ways in which the planning of London has been shaped by the evolving political institutions and political culture of the city and its region.

Debates about London

During the past hundred years London's rôle has undergone a transition from that of imperial capital to world city. In the 1890s London ranked with Berlin, Vienna, Paris and St Petersburg as one of the capitals of the great empires of the day: in terms of her population and of the scale of the empire that was ruled from her hub,

71

she was the greatest of the imperial capitals of her time. In the 1990s London is matched with New York and Tokyo as a world city from which are directed the operations of a global economy.

The failures of Berlin, Vienna and St Petersburg and perhaps, as yet, Paris to make the transition from imperial capitals to world cities reveal the extent to which the fates of cities have been influenced by the major political events of the twentieth century, most notably perhaps two world wars, the rise and fall of fascism and communism, and the dismantling of empires. The fact that London alone of these cities escaped the traumas of invasion, occupation, revolution and totalitarianism may help to account for its relatively secure transition from one leading status to another. So too perhaps may the fact of its imperial rôle being already bound up with a seaborne trading empire rather than one organized on a continental basis, thereby bequeathing it a set of financial institutions and practices capable of operating in both an imperial and a post-imperial global context.

Not surprisingly, London's continuing eminence first as an imperial capital and then as a world city has occasionally provoked lively debate on whether the two rôles have benefited London as a place and Londoners as its people. There is not the space here to recapitulate the whole body of the debate on what might be called the "Rights and wrongs of London" (Fisher 1992: 17). However, two concerns within that body of debate are worth at least a brief mention, not least because they have been given utterance over a space of a hundred years or more, maintaining their resonance despite the city's changing international rôle during that period. One is the concern over the size, form and fabric of the city; the other is that of concern for a socially divided London.

The physical growth of London as it developed into a major metropolis provoked unease and downright hostility in some quarters. Most notoriously of all perhaps, the radical journalist William Cobbett (1826) berated "the infernal Wen" from which "the smoke . . . ascendeth for ever more" and, as an MP, warned the House of Commons that

Of all the mistakes ever fallen into by the Government, none was greater than that of expending large sums of money on this particular spot. As it was, however, something was taken away from every part of the country in order to enlarge London. (*Hansard*, 7 May 1833)

Other critics combined a distaste for the size of London with an aversion to its visual aspect as an industrial and commercial centre. Thus the designer and poet William Morris (1868: 3) contrasted the growing city of his day with his preferred image of a small pre-industrial London:

Forget six counties overhung with smoke,
Forget the snorting steam and piston stroke,
Forget the spreading of the hideous town;
Think rather of the pack-horse on the down,
And dream of London, small and white and clean,
The clear Thames bordered by its gardens green;

72

It would be wrong to imagine that London has lacked defenders as a great city. To the Danish architect Steen Eiler Rasmussen (1960: 242) London was "a wonderful city", a "modern, sprawling city" sometimes "hateful" yet "constantly attractive". Its attractions lay particularly in the modest scale and simplicity of its domestic architecture, in its squares and its parks, all of them features contributing simultaneously to London's aesthetic merits and to its geographical dispersal. These very same features have however also been amongst those most liable to damage during periods of commercial boom and development pressure. It is against the background of just such a period of energetic redevelopment in and after the 1980s that we find a contemporary observer, Richard Rogers (1992: xliv) calling for action "to revitalize this great humanist city, to create beautiful buildings, tree-lined avenues and new parks . . . a metropolis of social and ecological harmony". Rogers does not here confine his concern to aesthetics, any more indeed than did William Morris a century earlier with his fusion of romantic radicalism and Marxism. Rogers also identifies a London becoming "increasingly divided into ghettos of poverty and affluence" and thereby reminds us of that second major focus of concern which addresses the question of social division in the city.

We have already encountered, in the previous chapters, the contemporary "coexistence of fabulous wealth with abject poverty particularly in Inner London" and the "growing underclass consisting of the poorly paid, unemployed and/ or ethnic minorities". Such descriptions of social division in today's London echo the "two worlds" of late-Victorian London, "one dark and mysterious, the other dazzling and ostentatious" (Briggs 1968: 317). Accounts of deprivation and dereliction in Inner London in the 1980s and 1990s, such as Paul Harrison's *Inside the inner city* (1983) and Patrick Wright's *A journey through ruins: the last days of London* (1991), have their forerunners in Andrew Mearns' *The bitter cry of outcast London* (1883) and William Booth's *In darkest England and the way out* (1890). Mearns' concern for what he called, in his book's subtitle, "the abject poor" and Booth's fears for, and perhaps of, the "submerged tenth" of "darkest London", again find echoes in the late twentieth-century concern about an urban underclass. There is perhaps a similar historic parallel to be found in the fact that many accounts of social division and distress in late nineteenth-century London focused upon "the vast and unlovely territory beyond the Tower . . . such as Whitechapel, Spitalfields, Bethnal Green, Poplar and the Isle of Dogs" (Lees 1988: 110), precisely those areas some of whose territory was to become an arena of conflict in the 1980s and 1990s as different economic and social groups contested the future development and planning of the London docklands and its environs.

It is thus possible to draw certain parallels between the aesthetic and social critiques that were made of London at the earlier zenith of its imperial rôle and at the more recent emergence of its rôle as a world city. Such parallels do not however imply a critical continuity, for the passion and the alarm which so often characterize the two sets of end-of-century commentary was rather less common during the intervening one hundred years. During that intervening period, of course, social division and distress were to become moderated and muffled by the emergence of the Welfare State, and the problems of London's growth and form began to be addressed through the creation of new structures of London government and through the evolving machinery of town and country planning. In particular, for many decades during the twentieth-century, debates about the condition of London and of Londoners took place within the confines of very stable arrangements of governmental structure, party politics and strategic planning policy. These arrangements effectively persisted until around 1970 when they began to unravel, thereby giving scope to a more fragmented and more contentious debate heralding the rise of our contemporary end-of-century critiques.

Government and politics

From 1889 to 1965 the major institution of local government in London was the London County Council (LCC), whose boundaries even at its birth were already failing to match the spreading built-up area of the city, but which in the course of its life secured international recognition as the government of London. In 1965 the LCC was replaced by the Greater London Council (GLC), whose boundaries embraced the great bulk of the built-up area inside the Green Belt but were regarded by some as yet again too narrowly drawn. The GLC however had a far shorter, and perhaps more troubled, life than its predecessor. After twenty-one years it was abolished in 1986, leaving London with no single organ of democratic local government able to speak on behalf of the city. The act of abolition itself provoked considerable protest and a renewed debate about how London should be governed.

The question of how London should be governed has indeed been a matter of recurring political controversy. The issues debated have included the "correct" geographical boundaries for metropolitan government, the desirability or otherwise of a two-tier system of local government and, perhaps most crucially, the proper rôle for any top-tier authority (e.g. the LCC and GLC). The latter issue has tended to focus around whether or not there are appropriate functions to be performed (a) of a *strategic* nature (e.g. planning, transport and infrastructure provision) and (b) of a *redistributive* nature (i.e. between richer and poorer areas). However, the debate on such functional questions may often have concealed from the lay observer, if not from some of the participants, a partisan political ambition – a concern not only over how London should be governed but over who should govern it.

As the most populous conurbation and as the capital, London has long had a symbolic value as "a political prize of great consequence, with national as well as metropolitan implications" attaching to its control (Young 1986: 90). The value of the prize is often accentuated by the attention it receives from national media based in the city. Control of County Hall just across the river from Westminster has proved to be both a morale-booster for the parliamentary opposition and an irritant for the government, as Herbert Morrison's LCC in the 1930s and Ken Livingstone's GLC in the 1980s each showed in their time on behalf of the Labour party. Indeed in much of the debate about the abolition of the LCC and of the GLC there was a barely hidden agenda derived from a search for those arrangements most favourable to the (Conservative) government of the day.

In the lifetime of the LCC there was little doubt that it was that body which was the first prize in the political contest. Since it embraced the whole of the then county of London within its borders, it was clearly symbolic of the city in terms of administrative geography, even if metropolitan growth made those same borders increasingly anachronistic as time went on. It was moreover a prize that was tenaciously defended, for control of the LCC changed hands only twice during its 76 years of life. From 1889 to 1907 it was run by the (Liberal) Progressives, from 1907 to 1934 by the (Conservative) Moderates and Municipal Reformers and from 1934 to 1965 by the Labour Party. For each party London was thus at some point not only a prize but also a stronghold from within which long-term objectives could be pursued. Its utility in the latter respect was enhanced by the fact that the LCC possessed a greater range of powers and functions than did the 28 metropolitan boroughs created within the county as lower-tier authorities in 1899. The LCC's functions embraced education, social services, health, housing, town planning, highways, drainage & sewerage and the fire service. The functions of the metropolitan boroughs in contrast were confined largely to housing, parks, museums and libraries, refuse disposal, street-lighting and other minor duties. With such a division between the tiers, there could be little doubt as to the dominant powers of the LCC in London's local government. Acceptance of this fact of life came to be facilitated when, during and after the 1930s, Labour increasingly dominated both levels of local government in London. The outcome was that "Labour boroughs and the usually Labour-controlled Metropolitan Boroughs Standing Joint Committee largely accepted the tutelage of the LCC" (Young & Garside 1982: 300).

In 1965 the picture changed with the advent of the GLC and the 32 London boroughs. The GLC, like the LCC before it, did possess the symbolic prize value of geographical identification with the new, greater, London. However, it held no unquestioned dominance as far as powers and functions were concerned. Social services became a function of the boroughs, as did education in Outer London: in Inner London (the old LCC area) education became the responsibility of the Inner London Education Authority (ILEA) on which both the GLC and the Inner London boroughs were represented. Housing and planning functions were initially divided between the two tiers, but over time gravitated towards the boroughs. Moreover the GLC and the boroughs were not a reliable political fiefdom for any party, so there could be no question of any "tutelary" arrangements being established within the parameters of single-party dominance. Indeed in the very earliest years of the new system, when there was temporarily a coincidence of Labour Party control at both levels, a dispute over housing powers saw "the newly formed and Labour-controlled London Boroughs Committee . . . torn between party commitment to a strong GLC and defending the powers of its members" (Young & Kramer 1978: 34).

For 21 years, from 1965 to 1986, local politics in London thus offered two worthwhile prizes, control of the GLC and control of the London boroughs. The GLC continued to have political prize-value by virtue of its claim to represent the metropolis as a whole. However, the boroughs now presented a prize of almost equivalent value because of their active rôle in service provision, and public and political perceptions of this were evidenced by comments such as "London belongs to the Tories by landslide" (*Evening Standard*, 10 May 1968) and "The leadership of London is now ours" (*London Labour Briefing*, June 1982) after the borough elections of 1968 and 1982.

With the abolition of the GLC the focus of local political conflict shifted to the boroughs themselves. However, the first borough elections after GLC abolition, in May 1986, produced no conclusive verdict, with Labour controlling 15 boroughs, the Conservatives 11 and the Liberal/SDP Alliance two, with four being "hung" with no one party in overall control. Four years later, the 1990 elections gave Labour control of 14 boroughs, the Conservatives 13, the Liberal Democrats three: in the remaining two, Labour provided a minority administration in one (Havering), and in the other (Brent) power shifted with the changing political allegiance of one or two councillors.

Thus it is now far less easy than in the past to answer the question "who has political control of London?" other than by pointing perhaps to the government of the day at Westminster. Over the past two or three decades there has been a steady shift away from the stable situation of the LCC era in which latterly one political party (Labour) dominated a single, powerful institution of London metropolitan government, whose primary rôle was accepted by lower-tier institutions (most of them usually controlled by the same political party). The shift has been towards a more complex and perhaps less stable balance of forces, with the emphasis increasingly on the rôle of the submetropolitan London boroughs as the chief, but divided, voices of political London. The emergence of a fragmented system of local government in London has thus been accompanied by a fragmentation of political control. What had once been largely (in the days of the LCC) or partly (in the days of the GLC) political war on a single major front has now become a series of 32 "small wars" for the parties to contest.

In respect of both government and politics, the preceding account can be summarized briefly as one that describes a journey from stability and simplicity to one of instability and complexity, at least in relative terms. For three quarters of a century (1889–1965) the government of London meant in effect the LCC, with 28 small metropolitan boroughs in a very junior rôle. For a further two decades a geographically larger but functionally less powerful GLC contested supremacy with 32 powerful London boroughs. Since 1986, with the abolition of the GLC, the boroughs have emerged as the sole units of democratic local government in London, but sharing their powers with joint bodies set up specifically to deal with certain city-wide issues after the abolition of the GLC, such as the London Fire and Civil

Defence Authority, the London Waste Disposal Authority, the London Boroughs Grants Committee and the London Planning Advisory Committee. The government of London is thus now fragmented; whether that arrangement will prove to be stable remains to be seen: the continuation of debates about yet further alternative arrangements suggests that it may not be (cf. Travers et al. 1991).

If the government of London has now become fragmented, then the pattern of government for the whole metropolitan region of London and the South East has always been so. In the absence of any level of regional government a series of *ad hoc* arrangements have had to be constructed. In the field of planning, for example, a Greater London Regional Planning Committee (GLRPC) was established in 1927 covering local authorities in the county of London and the surrounding counties of Essex, Kent, Surrey, Buckinghamshire, Middlesex and Hertfordshire. This body's contemporary successor, the London and South East Regional Planning Conference (usually known as SERPLAN) now represents no fewer than 12 county councils, 32 London boroughs, plus the City of London and 98 district councils. Its objective is to enable all those local authorities "to secure greater co-ordination of their planning policies . . . and to provide a means by which they can express a collective view" on regional planning issues (SERPLAN 1991: 1).

However, in seeking to achieve these aims SERPLAN is unable to call upon any effective executive powers of its own, but must rely upon the processes of deliberation and negotiation amongst its members. It is these 143 member authorities who constitute the fragmented local government of planning in London and the South East. For many of these authorities, solving the problems of London is not necessarily their chief priority.

This is not a new situation. The early GLRPC for example was split asunder in the mid-1930s by conflicts between the LCC, anxious to use land at Fairlop for out-county housing, and the Ilford Borough Council and Essex County Council who sought its development as an airfield (Mayrick 1992). During the life of the GLC the outer London boroughs showed little enthusiasm for helping Inner London with its housing problem through the release of suburban land (Young & Kramer 1978). In the counties around London, the defence of the Green Belt and of the countryside beyond it has often had just as much importance as assisting the city with its own problems. With no effective level of regional government to balance the respective aims of the city and the surrounding counties and districts, much therefore has often depended on political negotiation and manoeuvre. It is arguable that, for some while at least, London entered into such proceedings with one major asset: a clear and consistent planning strategy that was maintained for several decades.

Planning and political change

The political stability enjoyed by the LCC was a key factor in enabling that body to pursue consistent planning strategies over a long period of time, especially in the years between 1934 and 1965 when uninterrupted Labour control was combined with parliamentary legislation granting the council new powers, particularly in the field of planning. In their discussion of housing policy, Young & Kramer (1978: 218) stress the importance of the LCC being "able to pursue longer-term objectives" since "the life-span of a single project could be anything up to ten years or more. Major changes in the direction of policy . . . would take a decade to carry through". Very similar remarks could be made about planning policy.

Indeed one historian of LCC planning policy (Saint 1989: 215–6) identifies a very long-term consistency in the policy, arguing that "for the whole of its existence the LCC itself, irrespective of the party in power . . . encouraged and promoted the process of 'decentralization' or 'dispersal'" of the city's population. It did so even though the result was "to weaken its own power base" as people and jobs moved beyond its boundaries, for the council was in the grip that "persistence among all British political parties of the puritan distaste for cities and urban life" which we have already seen evoked by William Cobbett and William Morris.

The means by which such a dispersal policy was pursued varied over time. They included the promotion of cheap workmen's fares from the suburbs, the building of so-called "out-county" housing estates, the development of the post-1945 New Towns programme and the planned expansion of existing small towns around London. From the 1940s onwards the policy took increasingly coherent form in the shape of successive plans, initially advisory in nature, but eventually backed by the full force of the town & country planning legislation introduced in and after 1947.

However, the development of this dispersed metropolis was not secured without controversy, for it entailed the emergence of several conflicts. In the specific context of London's westward expansion for example, Hall (1973: 481) made the following observation:

One of the most important of these conflicts, actually and potentially, is simply between existing residents and possible new residents. Especially in the countryside, the existing resident may frequently prefer the status quo. He is not worried by land shortages; indeed they keep up the resale value of his property. Providing local services are adequate, he has no reason to see them expanded for the sake of newcomers, while there is always the risk that newcomers will simply put a greater strain on the existing stock of public and private services, whether these be telephones or schools or shops. Change in general will not be welcome; it will be tolerated insofar as it seems to be minimal in terms of disturbance or distortion of the existing style of life. A few newcomers, especially if they have the same accents and clothes and life styles, may be absorbed and even welcomed; a mass incursion, especially of people regarded as coming from a different class or culture, will be resisted.

As this passage suggests, the planning decisions involved in the growth of a dispersed metropolis could have major consequences in economic, social and cultural terms and could thus generate considerable public and political conflict. However, although there might be certain possible conflicts between existing residents and new residents, the existing residents themselves were by no means always homogeneous. They might well contain particular groups for whom an influx of Londoners could bring some positive advantages.

In the case of Stevenage, in Hertfordshire, in the late 1940s, for example, one observer found a variety of views about the initial proposals to develop a New Town there in accordance with the principles outlined in the *Greater London Plan 1944*. The opponents of the scheme included the following: farmers, wishing to preserve agricultural land; conservationists, concerned for the protection of rural landscapes; property owners, worried about compulsory purchase; ratepayers, fearful about future rate bills; the "respectable" middle-class, alarmed at possible proximity to working-class Londoners; and ideological opponents, for whom the whole process of planning was an infringement of personal freedom. On the other hand, the proposals did have some supporters: local trades unions, who anticipated more jobs and houses; the discontented, for whom "old Stevenage was a place of limited and outdated civic and recreational facilities; and Labour Party supporters, for whom the scheme was part of the wider programme of the postwar Labour government. One group could not be placed securely in the camp of either the opponents or the supporters: local traders, who found it hard to know, for instance, whether they would gain from a growing market or lose out to increasing competition, as newcomers arrived" (Orlans 1952: ch. 5).

In cases such as Stevenage, as part of the New Towns programme, hostile local opinion might not make much headway since the final decisions rested with central government, and implementation was the responsibility of an unelected development corporation. (Four decades later, of course, similar conflicts and frustrations were being worked out in London's docklands, where a determined central government and a development corporation were being accused of overlooking established local interests in favour of newcomers and developers from outside the area.) However, where London's dispersal proceeded in a more incremental fashion, as through the expansion of small towns, there was more scope for political pressure since key planning decisions rested with the elected local authorities who were free to sign – or not – town development agreements with the LCC and the GLC.

At Banbury, for example, where a further expansion from an already agreed 40,000 to 70,000 was much encouraged in the mid-1960s by the government, the GLC and Oxfordshire County Council, "the decisive power lay with the Borough Council . . . and the opinions of the political parties[were] important . . . The local aim of both parties was of course control of the Council. Each had to calculate whether expansion would be likely to bring this about" (Stacey et al. 1975: 74–5). Labour thought that a further influx of industry and manual workers would improve the prospects for a Labour-controlled council and make the local parliamentary constituency marginal or possibly Labour; the Conservatives could make the same estimates, but saw them as less attractive. In the end the council's decision went against further expansion on the casting vote of the Conservative mayor.

As the previous paragraphs indicate, London's decentralist planning strategy

79

had varying implications for the potential receiving communities; with diverse political, economic, social and cultural interests at stake, there was always the possibility of conflict developing. Nonetheless, the LCC held firm to its strategy, which over the years embraced the dispersal of people and industry both to New Towns and to expanding towns in the surrounding region.

The character of the LCC's plans has been described as that of "unitary plans; each portrayed a single desirable physical–spatial pattern towards which future development was to be directed". They assumed that "forces for growth would not be unduly disruptive and that a strong system of planning controls could and would be maintained" (Foley 1963: 172). In addition to being unitary in character, these plans also reflected a certain "long-held, monocentric concept of urban order for the city" based on a dominant centre at the heart of the city, a concept reflecting "a broad-based *political consensus* regarding ultimate objectives" (Hart 1976: 144, 185; italics in original). As the statutory planning authority for its area, the LCC provided through its development plans of 1951 and 1962 the essential machinery for the promotion of a monocentric yet dispersed metropolis.

However, the abolition of the LCC and the metropolitan boroughs, and their replacement by the GLC and the new London boroughs in 1965, changed the rules of the game. Not only did the new GLC area embrace many suburban communities formerly beyond the reach of the old LCC, the new boroughs were larger and were granted far greater planning powers than their predecessors. Suburban boroughs in particular were not prepared to accept the geographical or political subordination implied in the monocentric planning strategy of the "old" London of the LCC, not least because the very processes of dispersal of people and jobs out of the old LCC area had produced some new and thriving suburban centres. Thus the GLC's *Greater London Development Plan* (GLDP) statement of 1969 identified "major strategic centres" at six suburban locations (Ealing, Wood Green, Ilford, Lewisham, Croydon and Kingston) whose growth was to be encouraged. In effect "a new *polycentric* form for London was being proposed", with the former monocentric concept being "quietly but effectively abandoned" (Hart 1976: 144; italics in original).

Agreeable though this move towards polycentrism was for the six London boroughs covering the new strategic centres, it was not enough to satisfy many of their colleagues who argued the case for the inclusion in the plan of many more such centres. Eventually, in the wake of the public inquiry into the GLDP, no fewer than 28 strategic centres were identified. When the GLDP came up for alteration in 1984, certain boroughs were again key influences on policy: some Inner London boroughs, spurred on in some cases by local community groups, had persuaded the GLC to adopt a "community areas" policy around the "central activities zone" to prevent the loss of mainly working-class residential areas to commercial redevelopment pressures (GLC 1982, 1984, 1985).

If the boroughs thus made active incursions into strategic planning issues during the GLC era, they also of course focused very firmly on planning their own territory. As well as promoting the idea of a polycentric Greater London, they proved equally enthusiastic about imparting a monocentric character to their own individual boroughs. This "borough effect" has entailed the "consolidation of a borough's core . . . often accompanied by urban renewal and road improvement projects", along with "a downgrading of secondary centres" in the boroughs and a strong tendency to steer low-status activities such as retail warehousing towards peripheral sites near borough boundaries (Herbert 1991: 201–206). Such a "borough effect" in London's planning hardly seems likely to decline with the departure of the GLC and it suggests an increasingly fragmented approach to planning, compared to the unitary approach that prevailed until the 1960s.

The changing nature of the political institutions of London has thus had considerable significance for the sorts of planning policies pursued, with a clear shift of approach following the abolition of the LCC in 1965. A few years later, commentators were taking note of a further set of changes, this time in the political culture and behaviour of Londoners, which were also to have implications for planning.

An American researcher, Stephen Elkin, investigating the politics of planning in London in the final years of the LCC, was much struck by the fact that London's local politicians at that date seemed to operate in a wholly different political environment from their opposite numbers in the United States. Whereas American politicians saw "a heterogeneous electorate most of whose major social and economic differences are politically relevant" councillors in London "saw an electorate which was relatively homogeneous with only one important political cleavage" (Elkin 1974: 78). That single cleavage was class and it expressed itself through a two-party system of local politics. Other possible cleavages, based on race, ethnicity, neighbourhood issues and organized interest groups, were conspicuously absent. London's politicians were also prone to believe that once elected they could reasonably be left to "get on with the job".

> Councillors in London were not political entrepreneurs. They did not have to engage in a continuous dialogue with their market, the public, to see what would sell and, compared to their American counterparts, had little incentive to invest any significant amount of resources in trying to monitor and mould citizen opinion. (Elkin 1974: 14)

Elkin's account of London politics in the early 1960s could hardly be applied to the politics of London in subsequent decades. Indeed, by the time Elkin came to write up his research in 1973, he was already conscious of changes under way, with "a citizenry growing more knowledgeable of and involved with local government decision-making". He noted "higher levels of conflict both in and outside of government", "a changing political culture, manifested in an increase in citizen organization", and "a citizenry becoming more concerned with issues and more active in local politics" (Elkin 1974: x).

With the benefit of hindsight we can now see that the quiescent form of urban politics which Elkin had encountered in London in the early 1960s was about to be displaced by something rather different. To some degree this displacement reflected certain fundamental changes within British society at large after the mid-1960s. British political culture, with its traditional assumptions of respect for, and trust in, public bodies and of deference towards established authority, was now displaying much more questioning, sceptical and assertive attitudes. The onset of economic decline in particular meant that questions of resource allocation became much more hotly contested now that prizes could no longer be made available for everybody. The growth of secondary, further and higher education provided for a more articulate and self-confident population. The development of the mass media and the use of investigative journalism raised public awareness of how governmental decisions were made and of how they might be challenged. The experience of what government – local or central – actually did also provided public unease on occasion, especially in the case of major disturbances to local environments in the wake of urban redevelopment schemes during the 1960s. In the words of one historian of the period:

> A new activism was afoot among middle-class residents groups which broke through the standard apathy of British political culture. Motorway schemes, urban and rural, the siting of new airports, the invasion of suburban streets by heavy goods vehicles, all of these brought militant, and often highly successful, protest groups of (relatively) ordinary citizens into being, giving some real substance to the word "participation" . . . (Marwick 1982: 176)

The middle class were not alone in taking action to defend their territory. Community groups in working-class areas also organized themselves – "people in deprived areas looking at their own problems and seeking their own solutions" (Baine 1975: 17) – and doing so through varying mixtures of self-help, campaigning and mobilization of the hitherto inactive. There was, then, a quite widespread move towards what Donnison (1973: 384) came to describe as the "micropolitics of the city", an "'unofficial' arena of administration and politics" operating at a scale smaller than that of the formal lower tier of local government, the London boroughs. The emergence of this new form of local activism was recognized not merely by academic observers. A long-serving London MP recalled the change in his own constituency in Fulham:

> There was a stronger tendency towards group action. In 1945 I would receive letters which said, in effect, "Conditions in this street are awful; please do something about it." The 1970 version would be, "We have formed a residents" association to deal with some problems in this neighbourhood; will you please come to the inaugural meeting." There was much greater understanding of the value of education. In the 1940s parents would ask that their child be allowed to leave school before the statutory age in order to take a job. By 1970 such requests were unknown; their place was taken by pleas from parents' associations that repairs to a school should be expedited and by enquiries about grants for further and higher education. There was keener interest in environmental problems. I became President of the newly formed Fulham Society which concerned itself with traffic, planning, conservation, and the use to be made of the Bishop of London's Palace, which had passed into the care of the Borough Council. (Stewart 1980: 256–7)

The "keener interest in environmental problems" in the early 1970s was confirmed by the editor of the London *Evening Standard*, who found that local environmental issues were forming the most frequent topic of letters written to the newspaper (Jenkins 1973). This degree of environmental concern, combined with the "citizenry . . . more active in local politics" noted by Elkin, thus provided for an increasing degree of public involvement in the debating and resolving of planning issues at the turn of the 1960s and 1970s.

Perhaps the first major example of this was the case of the London Motorway Plan, a set of proposals for three ringways and thirteen radial routes contained in the GLDP proposals of 1969. The public response to these proposals was such that:

A kind of insurrection took place in London between 1969 and 1973. Thousands of citizens not normally involved in politics were so incensed with the way their elected governing bodies were attempting to improve their city that they went to unusual lengths to oppose and eventually overcome the will of established authority. (Thomson 1977: 59)

The range of political activity entered into by opponents of the motorway plan was considerable. Some 100 locally based bodies, such as civic societies and residents' associations, lobbied and campaigned locally within their boroughs. The London Amenity and Transport Association brought together a group of professional people to argue the case at the metropolitan level, and the London Motorway Action Group launched a Motorway Fighting Fund. Both organizations gave evidence against the proposals at the GLDP public inquiry. A Homes Before Roads group put up candidates in the GLC elections of 1970 and in the borough elections of 1971, motivated at least in part by a feeling that neither the Conservative nor the Labour party could be persuaded to abandon the proposals which had been conceived under a Labour GLC and brought forth under a Conservative one (Wiggins 1971). Others continued to work within the political parties: in the end, once the GLDP inquiry was over, "the Conservative party . . . began a strategic withdrawal from the road proposals which they had so long defended" (Hart 1976: 173), while on the Labour side pressure for change produced a manifesto commitment for the 1973 GLC elections "to abandon the disastrous plans to build motorways which threaten the environment of Central London" (Greater London Labour Party 1973: 10). The Labour victory at those elections brought about an abandonment of the proposals, though not before some rearguard attempts "to keep major chunks of the London motorway system and call them something else" (Livingstone 1987: 51).

The successful "insurrection" of 1969–73 was perhaps the first major public political challenge to planning policy in London. Since then innumerable challenges have occurred on a more modest scale throughout the city, sometimes with success, sometimes without. Examples include an experimental traffic scheme in Barnsbury, where middle-class residents were instrumental in redirecting traffic into poorer adjoining streets (Ferris 1972); the battle over Covent Garden, eventually saved from large-scale redevelopment but with its character fundamentally changed (Hain 1980, Anson 1981); the struggle over Tolmers Square near Euston, eventually lost to redevelopment (Wates 1976); the fight to reserve the Coin Street site near Waterloo for local housing needs, culminating in "one of the most extraordinary victories ever by a community group" (Cowan 1986; see also Brindley et al. 1989: ch. 5); the defence by the owner-occupiers of Croydon's "deep South" of their residential exclusivity against proposed increases in housing density (Saunders 1979); the eventually abandoned scheme to redevelop part of Peckham High Street for a new Town Hall, vigorously opposed by an action group "comprising Peckham amenity groups and the local residents, shopkeepers and businessmen" (Goss 1988: 92); the "battle for land" in Spitalfields between housing development for local needs, especially those of the Bangladeshi community, and commercial development for City needs, a battle described by one of those involved as a "most uneven fight, between Britain's poorest and most recently settled residents and some of the world's most powerful financial institutions" (Forman 1989: 141); the many conflicts that have arisen in the course of the redevelopment of the London docklands by the London Docklands Development Corporation (Brownill 1990); and the long-drawn-out campaigns that were waged in the areas around London centred on possible sites for the third London airport (Buchanan 1981, Cashinella & Thompson 1971, Cook 1967, Hall 1980, McKie 1973).

In all the cases just cited, organized groups of one sort or another played key parts in representing local bodies of opinion, some of which felt themselves inadequately represented, or overlooked, by the formal procedures of representation through local councils. Amongst such groups were: the middle-class Barnsbury Association and its opponent the Barnsbury Action Group; the Covent Garden Community Association; the Tolmers Village Association; the Waterloo Community Development Group, the Coin Street Action Group and the Association of Waterloo Groups; the Federation of Southern Croydon Residents' Associations; the Peckham Action Group; the Spitalfields Housing and Planning Rights Service and the Spitalfields Community Development Group; a variety of Docklands groups including the Association of Island Communities on the Isle of Dogs, the North Southwark Community Development Group and the Newham Docklands Forum; and such anti-airport groups as the Defenders of Essex, the Wing Airport Resistance Association, the Northwest Essex and East Herts Preservation Society (and its opponent the Stansted Area Progress Association), and the Bedfordshire Airports Resistance Association (and its opponent the Thurleigh Emergency Committee for Democratic Action) – in each case with the "opponent" group counterposing working-class claims for jobs against middle-class concern over the environment.

The forms taken by the conflicts in these and other cases naturally took on particular characteristics reflecting local circumstances. However, one key factor has been identified by some observers, namely the ways in which local groups do or do not manage to establish successful links with the formal institutions of political decision-making. An analysis of the disputes over the motorway proposals, Covent Garden and the future of the London Docklands led to the conclusion that

"London's politics of land use flows through established [political] organizations. Citizen groups may sprout at the grass-roots level, but they are most often transplanted into one or another of these organizations" (Savitch 1988: 229). Winning over a political party and/or a level of local government was seen by Savitch as a key development: for example "In the motorways case separate interest groups and a single-issue party were incorporated into either the Labour Party, the boroughs, or the GLC" (ibid.). A similar point is made by Forman in comparing the eventual success of the campaign to secure housing rather than office development on the South Bank at Coin Street with the much harder struggle in Spitalfields. The Coin Street organizations "had the support of the GLC and the two borough councils throughout . . . the planning policies for the area clearly favoured what the community wanted. In Spitalfields things were different. The council and community were at loggerheads." (Forman 1989: 165).

An alliance between the formal structures of local politics and the *ad hoc* groups of community protest and campaigning may perhaps be a necessary condition of success in land-use conflicts in London, but it may not however always be a sufficient one. Politicians and protesters are not the only actors in a world city also inhabited by market-orientated entrepreneurs and a market-worshipping central government for whom global market pressures may be more important considerations than purely local non-market interests.

Amenity and community groups are naturally likely to be particularly preoccupied with the planning problems of their own locality, rather than with the global economy or indeed the city as a whole. However, in the wake of the abolition of the GLC, several groups were brought together by the Civic Trust to create a forum for the discussion of London-wide issues. The London Forum of Amenity and Civic Societies, founded in 1988, now embraces over 70 groups, organizing conferences, seminars and exhibitions, and pressing for a more effective strategic planning framework, improvements to public transport and traffic restraint, protection and improvement of open spaces, and more powers to protect listed buildings and conservation areas. The forum's members have also begun to address the issues arising from London's rôle as a world city, not least in calling for a new strategic authority – a "Voice for London" – without which they fear "London's present favourable position in the league table of world cities will certainly disappear" (*News Forum,* January 1992).

Whose world city?

The foregoing account has highlighted key features in the political history of London and its planning. These may be summarized as follows:

- London's historic rôle as a major international city has been closely tied up with developments in twentieth-century politics and economics during the transition from the age of empires to the age of the global economy.
- There has been a long history of debate over the "rights and wrongs" of Lon-

don, especially over the questions of social divisions and of the form and fabric of the city.

- During the past century or so, the years from 1889 to 1965 provided a period of governmental and political stability in the city.
- The same period 1889–1965 was also one in which a coherent metropolitan planning strategy evolved, based on a monocentric urban form and a commitment to dispersal.
- However, the implementation of this planning strategy was often contested by public and political opinion in the counties surrounding London.
- Since 1965 London government has become increasingly fragmented and its politics more complicated.
- Also since 1965 planning has shifted in the direction of a more polycentric vision of the metropolis, increasingly expressed in a "borough effect".
- In the years around 1970 changes in London's political culture produced a greater degree of public interest and activism in planning issues.
- One consequence of the latter changes has been the emergence of an active world of civic and amenity societies and community groups, initially concerned with local problems but sometimes addressing broader issues at the level of Greater London, including its rôle as a world city.
- There has thus emerged a politics of planning in London reflecting Harold Lasswell's (1936) interpretation of politics as "Who gets what, when, how". It has encompassed conflicts over such questions as who gets Barnsbury's traffic? Who gets to use and redevelop the land at Tolmers Square or Coin Street or Spitalfields? Who gets the benefits of the jobs or bears the costs of the disturbance associated with the third London airport (or indeed the Channel Tunnel and its rail links)?

Perhaps the ultimate question now facing the politics of planning in London will prove to be that of who enjoys the benefits and who suffers the costs of its status as a world city. The question of "Whose interests will be served: those of the resident population or of transnational corporations?" (Friedmann & Wolff 1982: 309) is one way of formulating the issues. Yet some parts of the resident population may well benefit from London's world city status, just as other parts may not. Friedmann & Wolff recognize this with their reference to the prosperous "citadel" of the transnational elite and the deprived "ghetto" of the underclass. Similarly Gordon & Harloe (1991: 392) speak of a "dualization of London politics" in the 1980s in which radical strategies of Right and Left reflected "the respective concerns of the gainers and losers in the restructuring of opportunities in the city" and displaced the "more and less affluent members of the 'middle mass' from the centre of the political stage in London".

Such political perspectives on London's emergence as a world city cast a more sceptical light than those which seek to exploit and celebrate that status. The latter perspectives tend to be those which talk of "the abstracted forces of technological change, knowledge, creativity, learning, amenities, quality of life, etc."; more political perspectives raise additional questions of "class, politics, struggle, gender, race, inequality, poverty and suffering" (Warf 1991: 1821). Both perspectives clearly relate also to the century-old debates about London's form and fabric and about its social divisions. Indeed an observer of London in the 1990s, witnessing the dazzling office towers and the inner-city dereliction, the City wine bars and the beggars in the streets, might perhaps wonder along with William Morris in the 1890s:

> Was it all to end in a counting-house on the top of a cinder-heap . . . and a Whig committee dealing out champagne to the rich and margarine to the poor . . . ? (Morris 1894: 243)

References and further reading

Anson, B. 1981. *I'll fight you for it: behind the struggle for Covent Garden*. London: Jonathan Cape.

Baine, S. 1975. *Community action and local government*. Occasional Papers on Social Administration 59, London School of Economics.

Booth, W. 1890. *In darkest England and the way out*. London: Salvation Army.

Briggs, A. 1968. *Victorian cities*. London: Penguin.

Brindley, T., Y. Rydin, G. Stoker 1989. *Remaking planning: the politics of urban change in the Thatcher years*. London: Unwin Hyman.

Brownill, S. 1990. *Developing London's Docklands: another great planning disaster*. London: Paul Chapman.

Buchanan, C. 1981. *No way to the airport*. London: Longman.

Cashinella, B. & H. C. Thomson. 1971. *Permission to land*. London: Arlington.

Cobbett, W. 1826. The ruling passion. In *Cobbett: selections*, A. M. D. Hughes (ed.) 1961, 70–71. Oxford: Oxford University Press.

Cook, O. 1967. *The Stansted Affair: a case for the people*. London: Pan.

Cowan, R. 1986. The penny drops at Coin Street. *Roof* (March/April), 6–7.

Elkin, S. 1974. *Politics and land-use planning: the London experience*. Cambridge: Cambridge University Press.

Ferris, J. 1972. *Participation in urban planning; the Barnsbury case*. Occasional Papers on Social Administration 48, London School of Economics.

Fisher, M. 1992. London: a plan for development. In *A new London*, R. Rogers & M. Fisher (eds), 3–225. London: Penguin.

Foley, D. L. 1963. *Controlling London's growth: planning the great wen 1940–1960*. Berkeley/Los Angeles: University of California Press.

Forman, C. 1989. *Spitalfields: a battle for land*. London: Hilary Shipman.

Friedmann, J. & G. Wolff, 1982. World city formation: an agenda for research and action. *International Journal of Urban and Regional Research* **6**, 390–43.

GLC 1982 *A community areas policy*. Report P239 to the GLC Planning Committee, 25 March 1982.

—1984. *The Greater London Development Plan as proposed to be altered by the Greater London Council*. London: Greater London Council.

—1985. *Community Areas Policy: a record of achievement*. London: Greater London Council.

Gordon, I. & M. Harloe 1991. A dual to New York? London in the 1980s. In *Dual city: restructuring New York*, J. H. Mollenkopf & M. Castells (eds), 377–95. New York: Russell Sage Foundation.

Goss, S. 1988. *Local labour and local government*. Edinburgh: Edinburgh University Press.

Greater London Labour Party 1973. *A socialist strategy for London*. London: Greater London Labour Party.

Hain, P. 1980. *Neighbourhood participation*. London: Temple Smith.

Hall, P. 1973. London's western fringes. In *The containment of urban England*, vol. 1: *urban and metropolitan growth processes*, P. Hall, H. Gracey, R. Drewett, R. Thomas, 447–83. London: Allen & Unwin.

—1980. *Great planning disasters*. London: Weidenfeld & Nicolson.

Harrison, P. 1983. *Inside the inner city*. London: Penguin.

Hart, D. A. 1976. *Strategic planning in London: the rise and fall of the primary road network*. Oxford: Pergamon.

Herbert, M. 1991. The borough effect in London's geography. In *London: a new metropolitan geography*, K. Hoggart & D. Green (eds), 191–206. London: Edward Arnold.

Jenkins, S. 1973. The press as politician in local planning. *Political Quarterly* **44**, 47–57.

Lasswell, H. 1936. *Politics: who gets what, when, how*. New York: McGraw-Hill.

Lees, A. 1985. *Cities perceived: urban society in European and American thought, 1820–1940*. Manchester: Manchester University Press.

Livingstone, K. 1987. *If voting changed anything, they'd abolish it*. London: Collins.

Marwick, A. 1982. *British society since 1945*. London: Penguin.

McKie, D. 1973. *A sadly mismanaged affair: a political history of the third London airport*. London: Croom Helm.

Mearns, A. 1883. *The bitter cry of outcast London: an enquiry into the condition of the abject poor*. London: London Congregational Union.

Morris, W. 1868. The Earthly Paradise: a poem. In *Collected works of William Morris*, M. Morris (ed.) vol. III, 1910. London: Longman Green.

—1894 (1979). How I became a socialist. *Justice* (June 16). In *Political writings of William Morris*, A. L. Morton (ed.), 240–45. London: Lawrence & Wishart.

Orlans, H. 1952. *Stevenage: a sociological study of a New Town*. London: Routledge & Kegan Paul.

Rasmussen, S. E. 1960. *London: the unique city*. London: Penguin.

Rogers, R. 1992, London: a call for action. In *A new London*, R. Rogers & M. Fisher (eds), xiii–xliv. London: Penguin.

Saint, A. 1989. Spread the people: the LCC's dispersal policy. In *Politics and the people of London: the London County Council 1889–1965*, A. Saint (ed.), 215–35. London: Hambledon Press.

Saunders, P. 1979. *Urban politics: a sociological analysis*. London: Hutchinson.

Savitch, H. V. 1988. *Post-industrial cities: politics and planning in New York, Paris and London*. Princeton, NJ: Princeton University Press.

SERPLAN 1991. SERPLAN: *functions and organisation*. Paper RPC 110.

Stacey, M., E. Batstone, C. Bell, A. Murcott 1975. *Power, persistence and change: a second study of Banbury*. London: Routledge & Kegan Paul.

Stewart, M. 1980. *Life and Labour: an autobiography*. London: Sidgwick & Jackson.

Thomson, J. M. 1979. The London Motorway Plan. In *Public participation in planning*, W. R. D. Sewell & J. T. Coppock (eds), 59–69.

Travers, T., G. Jones, M. Hebbert, J. Burnham 1991. *The government of London*. York: Joseph Rowntree Foundation.

Warf, B. 1991. Review of *Urban Affairs* annual reviews, volume 35: cities in a global society. *Environment and Planning A* **23**, 1819–21.

Wates, N. 1976. *The battle for Tolmers Square*. London: Routledge.

Wiggins, D. 1971. The revolt in the cities. *The Times*, 3 April 1971.

Wright, P. 1991. *A journey through ruins: the last days of London*. London: Hutchinson.

Young, K. 1986. Party politics in local government: an historical perspective. In *Aspects of local government*, Research Volume IV of the Report of the Committee of Inquiry into the Conduct of Local Authority Business, 81–105. London: HMSO.

—& P. L. Garside. 1982. *Metropolitan London: politics and urban change 1837–1981*. London: Edward Arnold.

—& J. Kramer 1978. *Strategy and conflict in metropolitan housing: suburbia versus the Greater London Council 1965–75*. London: Heinemann.

CHAPTER SIX

Land-use planning since 1947

Michael Collins

Introduction

Since its inception in 1909 the British planning system has, in the main, been a function of local government. As a consequence it has had to reflect the political importance that successive governments have attached to economic, environmental and social considerations. Inevitably the interplay of national and local politics determines the resources that are available to local authorities, which in turn shape their policy stance and operational response to global, regional and local issues. The previous chapters have already examined the relationship between land-use planning and London's political organizations and social systems. It is generally agreed that the planning system has become increasingly politicized and that, in the case of Inner London, " The spectrum of organized political opinion is broader and the active political agenda longer" (Crawley 1991: 103).

The statutory planning system has also had to confront new problems and issues such as inner-city regeneration, oil and natural gas exploration, energy conservation, toxic waste disposal, hazardous industrial activity and processes, nature conservation and, even, crime prevention. In the case of London there is considerable evidence to support the view that the metropolis is beset with problems that call into question its future status as a world city (Porter 1990). This evidence will be evaluated to determine whether London's planning system can tackle these problems, let alone exploit the development potential of the East Thames Corridor and the Channel Tunnel rail link. It is worth recalling, however, the timely warning issued in 1951: "Planning legislation does not solve problems, it only provides the framework within which solutions can be found" (MTCP 1951: 15). The Chief Planner at the Department of the Environment (DoE) developed this theme further and advised that:

> The physical environment cannot *solve* the problems of urban poverty or drug addiction. Improving the environment may, or may not, be less important than solving these other problems. What is undeniable is that whatever

society does about these problems, we will still have urban areas and we still have to tackle physical problems. But in tackling them we clearly need to be aware of, and take into account – perhaps even contribute to the solution of – these other problems. So much for the general background. (Burns 1973: 3)

Regional planning, 1900–93

The origins of regional planning, as of so much else, lay in Ebenezer Howard's cartoon diagrams of 1898, above all his long-lost and long-neglected vision of the Social City: the group of slumless, smokeless cities, multiplying without end as each reached a predetermined limit. It was a brilliant concept for the progressive decentralization of thousands of people from the slums, pollution and congestion of the tightly bounded Victorian city. It rested on the impeccable logic that it made no economic sense to keep poor people on expensive land, and it anticipated the economics of mid-twentieth century industry. Applied in the first garden city at Letchworth, it failed initially to attract much attention or enthusiasm except for the idealists. But then, slowly, the industrialists began to locate there. When it came to the second garden city at Welwyn, nearly twenty years later, the message was already heeded; to this day, Welwyn Garden City is dominated by the Shredded Wheat factory, archetype of all the other new factories that located themselves on greenfield sites around London during the inter-war years.

In 1927 Neville Chamberlain, a politician who had early become interested in planning while Lord Mayor of Birmingham, used his position as Minister of Health to create a Greater London Regional Planning Committee, covering some 1,800 square miles within a 25-mile radius of Central London, and with 45 members from local authorities. Raymond Unwin, earlier the architect of Letchworth and subsequently architect to the Ministry, became its technical adviser. An interim report of 1929 proposed that the entire basis of planning should be reversed: instead of planning authorities reserving land for open space, they should allocate certain areas for building, and assuming that the rest would be left open: towns against a background of open space, as Unwin liked to call it. This would necessitate a Joint Regional Planning Authority with powers over major decisions. Local planning authorities should be able to refuse applications for development, but should pay compensation on the basis of a common value pool.

This proved much too radical, and in 1933 the Committee's work was frozen. But meanwhile, it had produced a powerful vision of a green belt or girdle around London, to be bought outright by the local authorities, and of towns against a background of open countryside outside that. New industrial zones should go into self-contained satellite towns within 12 miles of Central London, and in garden cities between 12 and 25 miles away. But the necessary legislation to ensure it was not forthcoming. Although Unwin emigrated to America, his plans of 1929–33 had provided an essential basis for Abercrombie's 1944 Plan.

In the intervening years, much happened: the establishment of the Barlow

Commission on the Distribution of the Industrial Population in 1937, and its report in 1940; the Uthwatt Committee on Compensation and Betterment (1942), and the Scott Committee on Rural Land Use of the same year; the establishment of a Ministry of Town and Country Planning in 1943; and the decision by the London County Council (LCC) to employ Patrick Abercrombie as consultant, working alongside the county planner J. H. Forshaw and his brilliant assistant Wesley Dougill, on a plan for the County. The resulting plan of 1943 needs to be considered as a whole with the subsequent Greater London Plan, which Abercrombie produced on commission from the central government, for both in effect constitute a seamless web.

The County of London Plan borrowed best practice from regional planning concepts developed by planning's founding fathers, over the previous three decades. From Scotland came Patrick Geddes' method of survey before plan, in order to establish the half-hidden village structure of London. From America there came Clarence Perry's neighbourhood unit principle, allied to with Clarence Stein and Henry Wright's insistence on a hierarchy of roads to separate pedestrians and vehicles. And from nearby Scotland Yard came Alker Tripp's insistence on precinctual planning (Tripp 1942). Together, these created in effect a new spatial order for the metropolis, in which highways simultaneously solved the traffic problem and defined the neighbourhoods, thus producing a structure for a cellular, organic metropolis – a brilliant illustration of how to kill two birds with one planning stone (Forshaw & Abercrombie 1943: 3–10; Hart 1976: 54–87).

In the Greater London Plan, Abercrombie retained exactly the same organic structure. But this time it was subtly turned inside out. From the County of London Plan, Abercrombie borrowed the notion of concentric rings, four in number: Inner (slightly larger than the County, with Central London forming an innermost ring), Outer or suburban, Green Belt, Outer Country. Each represented a band of decreasing density of population and of employment. Each was defined by a major ring road, either bounding it or running through it: the A ring through the inner ring, bounding the central area, the arterial B ring around Inner London, the C ring through the middle of the suburban ring and the arterial D ring at its edge, the parkway E ring through the Green Belt near its boundary with the Outer country ring (Abercrombie 1945: 7–10).

Together, the Abercrombie plans entailed an enormous relocation of population. Reconstruction and redevelopment in Inner London would displace no less than 1,033,000 people; of these, all but 125,000 would move beyond the Green Belt – 644,000 to the Outer Country Ring (383,000 to New Towns, 261,000 to extensions of existing ones), and nearly 164,000 even beyond this ring but within 50 miles of London, 100,000 farther still. The Greater London Plan proposed eight New Towns, each with a maximum population of 60,000 people, between roughly 20 and 35 miles from the centre of London (Abercrombie 1945: 14). It was an extraordinary triumph of regional planning: the most that any city had attempted until then, and greater than almost any has achieved since. Lewis Mumford, writing from the United States to Frederic Osborn, rightly described it as "the mature form of the organism whereof *Garden cities of tomorrow* was the embryo" (Hughes 1971: 141). The question, as Mumford immediately recognized, was whether it could ever be realized politically. Almost miraculously, it was: the new Minister for Town Planning under the 1945 Attlee government, Lewis Silkin, quickly accepted the principle of the New Towns and appointed a predecessor, John Reith, to head a committee to recommend the best administrative means of achieving them. The New Towns Act – based on the Reith Committee's recommendation that the New Towns should be built by development corporations –. was passed in 1946; by 1949 all eight Abercrombie New Towns were designated (sometimes in different places), and were substantially complete by the mid-1960s. Finally, in 1952 came the legislative machinery for the other major element of Abercrombie's grand design, the planned expansions of existing country towns, in the form of the Town Development Act; results were slower to come, but here too major progress was being made by the late 1960s, and eventually some of these places – Andover, Basingstoke, above all Swindon – emerged as impressive as the New Towns themselves.

The Town and Country Planning Act 1947 provided the means whereby the proposals in the Greater London Plan could be safeguarded pending implementation. These proposals were to be incorporated, as appropriate, in the development plans that the county councils and county boroughs were required to prepare. These plans had to observe the policies set out in the Memorandum on London Regional Planning issued by the Ministry of Town and Country Planning in 1947. This Memorandum was the result of a joint study undertaken by the Ministries and local authorities, who were expected to adhere to it in the control of development and the preparation of development plans. It was agreed that the population of the region should not increase materially over 10 million, and that over 1 million people, together with equivalent amounts of employment, should be decentralized from the congested inner areas to planned communities located beyond the Metropolitan Green Belt (MGB) (TPI 1956: 10–12). The population targets adopted by the local authorities in the London Region are set out in Table 6.1. It can be seen that the population of the London Region was expected to increase by just over 426,000 (4%) between 1951 and 1971. Local authorities, with the exception of Hertfordshire County Council, believed that this population increase could be accommodated without any major encroachments on the MGB by virtue of subdivision, infilling and the observance of higher occupancy rates. It is generally agreed that these development plans were ". . . harmonised to a surprising degree by acceptance of the Abercrombie principles" (Self 1971: 91). The main departures from these principles were to reflect several factors, including the findings of more up-to-date surveys, the emergence of new trends such as the natural increase in population, and the need for the plans to focus upon the proposals which could be implemented within a 20-year period.

Table 6.1 Population estimates for local planning authority areas in the London region.

Planning authority	1951 census	Development plan forecasts for 1971
County of London	3,348,336	3,150,000
Middlesex	2,268,776	2,241,550
Hertfordshire	609,735	886,615
Inner Essex	1,162,478	1,351,300
East Ham CB	120,873	111,150
West Ham CB	170,987	165,000
Inner Kent	672,410	752,660
Surrey	1,351,963	1,426,010
Croydon CB	249,592	266,136
Buckinghamshire (part)	173,578	224,520
TOTALS	10,148,728	10,574,941

Source: TPI (1956), p.15.

The 1960s

Great as was the achievement of the 1950s and 1960s, nevertheless important matters went awry. First, the Abercrombie plans were posited on the quite untenable assumption in the Barlow Report (1940): that employment growth and in-migration to London and the South East could simply be halted. Secondly, unexpected by everyone, from 1955 to 1964 birth rates rose. By the mid-1960s the population of Britain was increasing at about 700,000 annually: "a Bristol a year", as the phrase went. And almost half this growth – 1.1 out of 2.4 million between 1951 and 1961, for instance – was occurring in the South East, making a nonsense of the assumptions on which the Abercrombie plans had been based. It formed a solid ring of growth in Abercrombie's Outer Country Ring, 15 to 35 miles from the centre. By the 1960s, the growth had slowed to about one-third of the national total, and it had spread farther into a discontinuous ring some 25–70 miles from the centre. The Outer Metropolitan Area (OMA) gained one million in the 1950s, 800,000 in the 1960s; of this, the New and Expanded Towns took only a small part. Suburban speculative building was again the norm, except that it was occurring not on the edge of London but on the edges of a score of places in the OMA.

The result around 1960 was a crisis in planning policy, resulting in a radical shift. In 1964 the *South East Study* officially admitted that between 1961 and 1981 the South East (including East Anglia) was expected to grow by no less than 3.5 million people. To meet the need, the *Study* proposed new cities at Bletchley, at Newbury and between Southampton and Portsmouth, plus large expansions of Ashford, Ipswich, Stansted, Northampton and Swindon. Soon Newbury was abandoned (or, effectively the same thing, combined with Swindon); Ashford, Ipswich and Stansted were all dropped, and it was decided that South Hampshire could grow without much encouragement. But Bletchley became Milton Keynes, and both Northampton and Peterborough joined it as Mark Two New Towns,

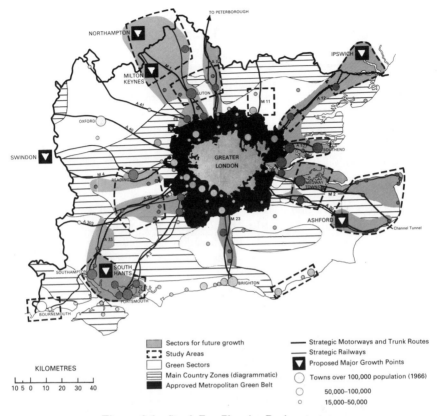

Figure 6.1   South East Planning Region strategy.

designated in 1967–8. Meanwhile, in 1967 the South East Economic Planning Council – a new official advisory body, created in 1965 – suggested joining London to the major growth centres by discontinuous corridors of growth; this caused a minor furore, to which the government responded by instituting yet another study in co-operation with the local planning authorities (see Fig. 6.1).

The result, in 1970, was the *Strategic plan for the South East* (DOE 1970a), hailed as the successor to the Abercrombie plan and certainly the significant planning document for the region to appear between World War II and the present day. It reiterated the message of the 1964 Study: the need to plan for growth. The forecast increase for the entire South East region, between 1966 and 2001, was from 17.0 to 21.6 million; since Greater London itself would continue to lose, that would mean 3.1 million more in the OMA, 2.4 million in the Outer South East. The most effective way to accommodate such huge growth, the Plan argued, would be to develop five very large growth centres, at distances between 40 and 80 miles from London, with eventual populations of between 0.5 and 1.5 million: these would be not single cities but planned urban regions, which could attract factories and offices, and offer a range of jobs, social opportunities and entertainment, thus becoming counter-magnets to London (Fig. 6.2). They would take more than half the projected growth down to the 1990s. Thus, the South East would no longer be dominated by London, but would become a polycentric city region rather like Randstadt in Holland (Hall 1989: 44).

Radical as the *Strategic plan* was, it represented a continuity in regional planning philosophy that could be traced back through Abercrombie to Howard, only the scale grew progressively larger over time. Essentially, the major urban units in the 1970 plan are a reinterpretation of Howard's polycentric Social City of 1898, or the Unwin–Abercrombie prescription for planned dispersion. Unfortunately, this time there was a difference: in a region and a country already profoundly influenced by the spirit of NIMBYism – "not in my back yard" – (an acronym imported from the United States), the proposal brought fierce local opposition, compounded by a sudden and unexpected demographic downturn. A review of the plan in 1976 reduced the 1975–91 regional population growth projection from 2.8 million to a mere 174,000. Besides that, London's population loss was far more serious than earlier supposed: the review forecast that its 1991 population could be not 7.0 million as previously forecast, but a mere 5.7 million. Growth in the Rest of the South East (RoSE) was reduced from 3.4 million to some 2.0 million. So, the review concluded, the five major growth zones of the 1970 Plan would still be needed, although not on the earlier scale. And the government's response of 1978 accepted this broad approach.

LONDON

■ Major growth
● Medium growth
▬ Road framework
▌▌▌ Agricultural area
▓▓▓ Environmental area

Figure 6.2　A strategic plan for the South East.

Table 6.2   The South East Strategic Plan proposals, 1970.

Population, actual and planned

	Population (000s)				
	1966	1981	1991	2001	1966–2001
South East	17,000	18,700	20,100	21,600	+4,600
Greater London	7,800	7,300	7,000	7,000	−800
Outer Metropolitan Area	5,100	6,400	7,400	8,200	+3,100
Outer South East	4,000	4,900	5,700	6,400	+2,400
ROSE	9,100	11,100	13,100	14,600	+5,500

The major growth areas

	Miles from London	Population (000s)		Growth
		1966	2001	1966–2001
Reading–Wokingham–Aldershot–Basingstoke	30–50	500	1,200	+700
South Hampshire	70–90	800	1,400	+600
Milton Keynes–Northampton	60–80	300	800	+500
South Essex	30–50	600	1,000	+400
Crawley–Burgess Hill	30–40	200	500	+300
TOTAL, 5 areas		2,400	4,900	+2,500
TOTAL, South East		17,000	21,600	+4,600

Source: GB South East Joint Plan Team (1970).

The great 1970s U-turn

But, by then, there had been a major change in British government policy; almost certainly, the most significant in the entire post-1945 period. Government had discovered the inner-city problem. The trigger was the publication, in 1977, of three major consultants' reports – on Liverpool, Birmingham and Lambeth (1977a,b,c). The problem was not exactly new; academic observers had been writing about it for several years (Donnison & Eversley 1973). What was new was official recognition: it was now clear that there was a new landscape of change in Britain. No longer was it an issue of prosperous South East versus the declining and deprived North; rather was it a question of the depressed inner cities versus the prosperous shires. But the resulting politics were interesting: Conservative shire councillors, faced with growth pressures that they devoutly wished would go away, were content to make common cause with left-wing Labour councillors from London boroughs, to swing resources away from greenfield development and into inner-city regeneration. This has been a policy constant since that time, under Labour and Conservative administrations alike. Its effect has been to turn attention away from New Town schemes, by whatever means, and to focus it on large-scale urban projects: first London Docklands, and then the East Thames Corridor.

The advent of minimalist planning: 1979–

Meanwhile, shortly after the great policy reversal, in 1979 came the election of a radical right-wing government, committed to a minimalist approach – which meant minimalist planning. Nowhere was the new approach better illustrated than in the new government's first regional review for the South East, in August 1980. In place of one main report and five supplements of 1970 were three type-written pages setting out the new priorities: to promote economic recovery, to restrain public expenditure, to stimulate the private sector, to sweep away obstacles to commercial enterprise, to achieve more home ownership and housing for sale. Interestingly, after the rhetoric, it reaffirmed the 1970 policies: a clear distinction between growth areas and conservation-restraint areas.

True, at a wider national–regional scale, there was a complete reversal of policy: no longer would government seek to steer growth out of the South East, through controls on industrial development. Yet, given the scale of de-industrialization and its impact on all inner-city areas, including London, that reversal was probably inevitable. And the message was sharply underlined by the inner-city riots of 1981: here, in the cores of the cities, as the new locus of decay and deprivation, must be the new focus for intervention. The means of intervention were different: Enterprise Zones, with a ten-year holiday from local property taxes and a minimalist planning regime; and Urban Development Corporations – modelled on the 1945 town apparatus, to recycle urban land and attract private capital.

What was notable was the new focus. Strategic planning, officially described in 1983 as a discredited notion of the 1960s, was formally abandoned; thus the 1970 plan was effectively forgotten. Though it was a Thatcherite government that made this great U-turn, the intriguing question is that any government might have done the same: the economy was in deep recession, the inner cities were apparently being torn apart, formerly prosperous and fastidious areas now welcomed new factories and warehouses. Liberating the spirit of enterprise might thus seem the only feasible option.

Meanwhile, the irony was that, despite the new emphasis on the inner city, the tide of movement was still strongly outwards. Indeed, it was farther and farther out: in the 1950s the belt of maximum growth was 20–35 miles out from London, in the 1960s 35–45 miles out, in the 1970s up to 60–70 miles out; by the 1980s, it had washed even beyond that, to the areas at the very fringe of the South East and beyond it, between 80 and 110 miles from London. There was however another most significant feature: in thus rolling outwards, this belt of growth increasingly broke up and reconcentrated into a relatively few city regions at, or just beyond, the South East boundaries. A final irony was that several of these were precisely the areas proposed for major growth in the more-or-less forgotten 1970 plan: Reading–Wokingham–Aldershot–Basingstoke, Crawley–Gatwick, and Milton Keynes–Northampton. One other, Bournemouth–Poole, had been proposed as a medium-growth area in that plan. And two others, Swindon and Peterborough–Huntingdon, had not been included simply because they were right outside the regional boundaries.

It is significant however that several of the 1980s growth areas – Swindon, Milton Keynes, Northampton and Peterborough – were based on new or expanded town schemes that essentially dated from the 1960s, that is before preparation of the 1970 plan, which simply took them on board. In other words, they represented the legacy of the golden age of strategic planning, finally coming to fruition in an age that had officially rejected it. That legacy was rapidly exhausting itself, as these 1960s schemes came to planned completion in the late 1980s and early 1990s. They have not been followed by anything on an equal scale. Indeed, even the attempt by the major private builders (organized in 1983 into Consortium Developments, with the objective of developing modestly sized new residential communities in the South East) largely failed: proposal after proposal – at Tillingham Hall north of Tilbury, Foxley Wood south of Reading, Stone Bassett east of Oxford, and Wilburton north of Cambridge – was defeated by local opposition and/or doubts on the part of successive Secretaries of State for the Environment.

So it could be argued that during the 1980s, regional planning in the South East arrived at some kind of impasse. The government, in a statement of 1983 which presaged the end of the Greater London Council, declared roundly that strategic planning was an outmoded concept of the 1960s. It even contemplated abolishing County Structure Plans (DoE 1989a), although this was later abandoned. The clear implication was that well organized builders would deal directly with local district councils, which – together with proposals for "Simplified Planning Zones" – should ensure speedier and simpler development. But it did not work out that way, because it foundered on local opposition. The spirit of NIMBYism emerged as a major fact of political life at the Department of the Environment.

The prescription that emerged by the late 1980s was a new form of regional planning. County planning departments co-operate through their own organization – the Standing Conference on South East Regional Planning (SERPLAN) – in producing regional advice to government. Another QUANGO – the London Planning Advisory Committee (LPAC) – does so for Greater London. In return, after due deliberation, the government produces succinct statements of regional guidance, which constitute regional policy in all but name. Subsequently the job of development control passes to the Districts, who – at least in the boom years of the late 1980s – found themselves faced with an increasing volume of applications and, perhaps more significantly, repeated appeals against refusal to grant permission. However, perhaps the most interesting fact was that the largest schemes (like Consortium Developments' new communities) did not succeed on appeal. The system seemed to have settled down to an incremental style of planning, in which development proceeded in small or medium-sized packages. The outcome was concentration at the broad spatial scale into a few fringe growth areas, but dispersion at the more local scale within (and indeed outside) those areas. Big, bold schemes were out, because they attracted too much political opposition and because they were against the political spirit of the times.

The exceptions of course were those within or just beyond London's urban envelope: Docklands in the 1980s, the even bolder East Thames Corridor scheme of the 1990s. These corresponded to the new model of the large urban project, achieved through public infrastructure spending which would leverage massive private investment. The first was politically very contentious, since it involved a development corporation taking the powers of local authorities. The second, interestingly, was almost completely uncontentious: it involved an alliance between conservative central government and development-minded local authorities, mainly Labour. And equally, it implied less pressure on the beleaguered NIMBYite authorities on the other side of London, which were subject to the most intense pressures for development. There was an implicit regional plan, or at least regional project, here: it was to reverse the historic westward drift of London's most dynamic economic sectors and most prestigious residential areas, which had been taking place since the sixteenth century. In 1994, it is too soon to say whether, or how far, it may be successful.

Development plans 1947–65

Introduction

In 1944 the Coalition Government issued a White Paper entitled "The Control of Land Use" (MHLG 1944) which constituted a direct and positive response to the recommendations of the Barlow, Scott and Uthwatt Reports, examined earlier in this Chapter. This White Paper paved the way for the Town and Country Planning Act 1947 which sought to unify the previous legislation, thereby providing a more effective planning system than had existed in the 1930s. It also set out the policies that local planning authorities (LPAs) were required to incorporate in their development plans.

LPAs were about to enter a halcyon period in which development plans would not only remedy the environmental defects of nineteenth-century urban development but also prepare for the changes that were needed to mirror the shifting patterns of national and local life (MHLG 1956: 42). The re-emergence of town planning was greeted with expectancy and a sense of euphoria (Rodwin 1956: 20).

The main aims of the 1947 Planning Act were:

– to provide a framework, or pattern, of land use, against which day-to-day development could be considered, i.e. the development plan
– to bring all development under control by making it, with certain exemptions, subject to the sanction of a local planning authority or, in some cases, the sanction of central government

- to deal with certain specific problems of amenity such as the preservation of trees and woodlands, and of buildings of special architectural and historic interest, together with the control of outdoor advertisements
- to solve the problems of compensation and betterment
- to extend the powers of public authorities to acquire and develop land for planning purposes.

The 1947 Planning Act required each county council and county borough to prepare a development plan which:

- defined the sites of proposed roads, public and other buildings and works, airfields, parks, pleasure grounds, nature reserves and other open spaces, or allocate areas of land for use for agricultural, residential, industrial or other uses specified in the plan
- defined as an area of comprehensive development, any area which the LPA felt should be developed or re-developed as a whole to deal with extensive war damage, poor lay-out, obsolete development, or to facilitate the relocation of population or industry, the replacement of open space or any other purpose specified in the plan
- designated land for compulsory acquisition by any Ministry, local authority or statutory undertaker for the purposes of any of their functions;
- designated land for compulsory acquisition if it was in an area defined by the plan as an area of comprehensive development,
- other land which, in the opinion of the LPA, ought to be acquired compulsorily for the purpose of securing its use in the manner proposed by the plan.

Development plans were expected to be realistic and to include only firm proposals that were likely to be carried out within 20 years. Although local authorities were expected to indicate the phasing of development, it was recognized that the rate of implementation depended upon national policy for industry, housing and agriculture, as well as the opportunities for capital investment. The Minister of Town and Country Planning was empowered to approve any development plan submitted to him either without modification or subject to such modification as was deemed expedient. He was responsible for not only major questions of land use but also detailed matters including outdoor advertisements and proposed alterations to the appearance of a building (Sharp 1969: 18). The Ministry issued advice on the information that was needed (e.g. its availability and whereabouts) and guidance about the content of the Report of Survey. This report was to take the form of maps, accompanied by a written analysis. The maps were to summarize the main conclusions of the survey investigations in respect of land use, road and rail traffic, population density, and so on; while the written analysis would draw attention to the chief problems revealed by the various surveys and show the steps by which the authority had arrived at the conclusions that lead to the specific proposals in the development plan. LPAs were warned not to spend much time on the preparation of elaborate and detailed layouts for planning schemes, but to concentrate on broad decisions regarding the pattern of future development for individual towns and in particular stretches of countryside (MTCP 1951: 25).

The development plans which were prepared under the 1947 to 1962 Planning Acts are now referred to as "old development plans", and they continue to remain in force over much of England and Wales. The 1990 Planning Act, as amended in 1991, provides that, if an "old development plan" is still in force in a district, immediately prior to the commencement of the 1990 Act, then it will form part of the development plan for that district. In due course these "old development plans" will be revoked by the Secretary of State as soon as the country is covered by adopted district-wide local plans.

Progress 1947–65

It was anticipated that the whole of Great Britain would be covered by development plans by 1 July 1951, but this proved to be an unrealistic target because of the immense amount of work entailed and to the shortage of trained staff. Some 126 of the 148 LPAs were granted extensions of time in order to complete their draft plans. By 1960 some 145 plans had been approved, leaving only those for Derbyshire, Glamorgan and Manchester still outstanding (MHLG 1961: 54). It can be seen from Table 6.3 that progress in the South East of England was equally varied, and it was not until the end of 1958 that the whole of the region was covered by development plans which had been approved formally by the Minister.

Table 6.3 Approval of development plans in South East England.

Year	County councils	County boroughs
1951–4	3	2
1955	5	3
1956	1	6
1957	1	1
1958	4	1
TOTAL	14	13

Source: MHLG annual reports, 1951–8.

The absence of a standing regional body for London meant that the Ministry had to assume responsibility for co-ordinating planning activity in London and the Home Counties. This task was simplified by the transfer of planning powers to the county councils and county boroughs, thereby reducing the number of LPAs in the London Region from 136 to 10. In 1947 the Ministry issued a Memorandum on London Regional Planning, which required LPAs to observe the policies set out in the Greater London Plan 1944, subject to such modifications as were contained in the Memorandum. This meant that overall growth of London was to be restrained, the Green Belt was to be strictly enforced, and the Greater London Plan's programmes for planned decentralization and major roads were to be implemented (Foley 1963: 32).

London's problems, needs and priorities had already formed the subject of several reports and advisory plans, including the Bressey Report 1939, the County of London Plan 1943, the City of London plan 1944 and, as noted above, the Greater London Plan 1944. It was generally agreed that the main problems posed by London were (and, as noted earlier this book, still include) traffic congestion, the prevalence of slum housing, the haphazard admixture of industry and housing, and a general lack of open space in the Inner London boroughs (Stirling 1952: 1). Other bodies such as the RIBA and the Royal Academy of Arts were also preparing advisory schemes for London's future redevelopment. There was no shortage of answers to the following question, posed by W. S. Morrison (Minister of Town and Country Planning):

> What sort of place should the centre of a world capital, with an ancient and glorious history and a thriving and growing modern life, be? (*Journal of the Town Planning Institute* 1943–6: 208)

The administrative County of London: 1947–65

The London County Council (LCC) was able to draw upon a range of established policies and proposals when work commenced on the preparation of a development plan for the administrative county of London. There was even general agreement about the social policies that should be pursued, e.g. the quest for the best possible living conditions, the redeployment of population and industry, and the maintenance of full employment (Foley 1963: 32–3).

The main objectives of the development plan prepared by the LCC were as follows (LCC 1951: 1–3):

- to preserve London's character and improve its efficiency as the Commonwealth centre, capital city, commercial and industrial centre, a port and a home for millions
- to restrain the future growth of London's population by the establishment of the principal density zones of 200,136 and 70 persons per acre
- to recognize and develop the existing system of communities
- to house those in urgent need, to resume slum clearance, to secure the provision of out-county accommodation, and to provide sites for related facilities such as shops and churches
- to pursue the decentralization of employment, to reserve the land needed for the relocation and reorganization of existing industries, to segregate housing from industry, and to use zoning and plot-ratio controls to ensure that future developments did not conflict with the decentralization of employment and population
- to improve the existing road system and to collaborate with other authorities and private owners to secure adequate parking provision
- to provide the sites required for the London School Plan and the London Scheme of Further Education
- to acquire the land needed to achieve an interim public open space standard

of 2.5 acres per 1,000 population, as a first step towards a long-term standard of 4 acres per 1,000 population
- to promote the comprehensive reconstruction of war-damaged and obsolete districts
- to review the possibility of providing helicopter landing facilities, and an airway terminal, in Central London.

The logistics of the plan still make impressive reading: for example, some 5,665 acres were set aside for new housing, 910 acres for schools, 1,071 acres for new open space, and some 2,288 acres were designated as areas of comprehensive redevelopment. The road improvements amounted to 11 miles of new trunk road, 7 miles of major road widening, 2 miles of new tunnel, 43 new or improved road intersections, and the rebuilding of two bridges over the Thames. Sites were set aside for hospitals, London University, and such important national projects as the BBC Television Centre and the National Library. It was envisaged that the exercise of development control powers would ensure that the substantial volume of private sector development played its part in creating a new London.

The LCC Development Plan was submitted to the Minister on 31 December 1951, and it was subjected to over three years of public inquiry and Ministerial investigation before it was approved on 7 March 1955 (see Fig. 6.3). Nearly 7,000 objections were lodged when the Plan was placed on exhibition, but almost 30% of these objections were either withdrawn before the Public Inquiry or were not made the subject of debate. In this context it is worth noting that about 20,000 individual objections were lodged against proposals contained in the plans for London and the Home Counties, as compared with a total of about 41,000 objections to all the development plans for the whole of England and Wales. The Minister, when approving the plan in 1955, expressed the view that ". . . the preparation and adoption of this comprehensive design for the world's greatest city is a significant event, which in years to come will be accorded a notable place in the pages of London's history." He considered that this plan provided a sound and wisely conceived framework, within which the life of London could continue to advance and develop in the year ahead (Ling 1955: 126–8). In his letter approving the plan, the Minister referred to the fact that congestion was the root cause of most of London's planning problems. With this in mind he concluded that the plan's additional land allocations for employment uses were not wholly consistent with the stated objective of decentralizing industry and commerce in proportion to the proposed reduction in population. Some 380 acres of land, which had been zoned for industry and commerce, although at present used for residential purposes, were re-zoned for residential use. The Written Statement, as amended, now stated that planning permission would not normally be given to change the use of residential property which still possessed a useful life for that purpose. A further provision was that such land as remained zoned for industrial development should be reserved primarily for the relocation of industries that were badly sited in other parts of the County. This land was no longer available for new industries or for the expansion of existing firms if the nature of their business permitted them to move

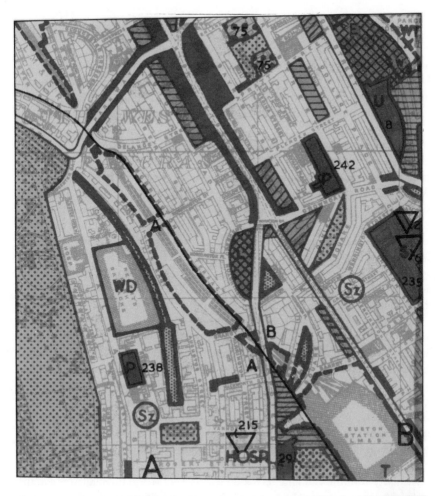

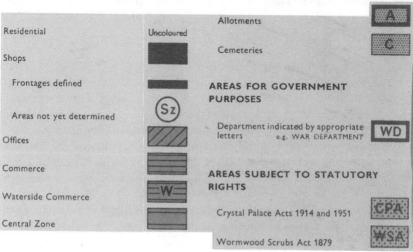

Figure 6.3 Extract from Administrative County of London development plan.

outside the County. The Minister expressed the hope that the Council would make funds available for the purchase of factories vacated by firms moving out of London. He also instructed the LCC and the City Corporation to undertake a fresh survey of existing proposed office floor-space in Central London.

The survey undertaken in 1956 confirmed that nearly 18.25 million square feet of office floor-space had been built in Central London between 1948 and 1955, and that planning permission had been granted for a further 17.5 million square feet. This led the LCC to reduce the permitted plot ratio (i.e. the ratio between the gross floor-space of a building and its site) from 5.5:1 to 3.5:1 in large parts of the West End. An additional plot ratio of 1.5:1 for residential use was also permitted in parts of the West End (see Fig. 6.4). In 1957 the LCC embarked on the First Review of the development plan. The Council undertook a fresh survey of land use and parking provision in the central area, together with an investigation of employment trends. The First Review made further provision for restricting office development, notably by re-zoning some 145 acres of land from offices to other uses and by reducing plot ratios. Further reductions were also made in respect of the amount of land zoned for industrial use (LCC 1960: ch. 15).

Almost 1,400 objections to the First Review's proposals were lodged, and they formed the subject of a public inquiry which lasted for several weeks. The Minister published details of the modifications that he proposed to make, and these formed the subject of a second public inquiry. In his letter approving the First Review of the LCC Development Plan in 1962 the Minister underlined the importance of securing as much residential development in the county as possible, by making more land available for the purpose and by permitting the maximum density appropriate to each particular site. The Minister pointed out that this last matter depended on the ratio of persons per room or dwelling which the council assumed when considering proposals for development. This could alter as time went on, particularly with the changing make-up of households and the tendency towards fewer persons per room. The Minister asked the council to consider this in consultation with the Department.

Development plans in the rest of the London region: 1947–65

It was noted above that the number of LPAs in the London Region had been reduced from 136 to 10 (i.e. including the LCC). The development plans prepared by the 9 LPAs which surrounded the LCC were in effect statements of the proposed pattern of land use in 1971. These plans were required to observe the land-use planning principles and strategy set out in the Greater London Plan 1944. Inevitably these plans also had to reflect the various economic and social changes which took place during the late 1940s and early 1950s (MHLG 1955: 42–3).

The employment policies contained in these development plans attached considerable importance to restricting the further growth of industry within the London Region. In the cases of Essex, Kent, Middlesex and Surrey, industrial

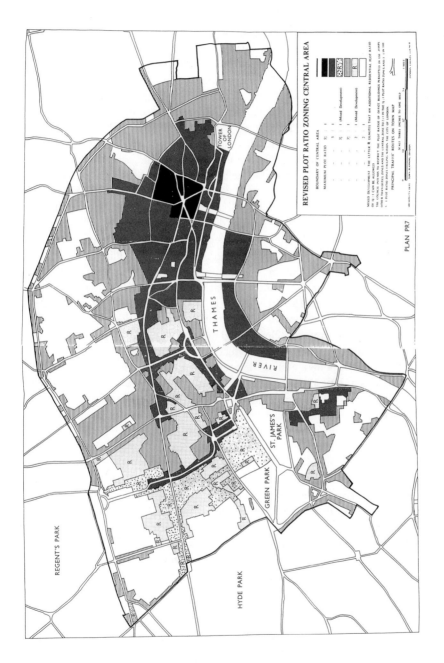

Figure 6.4   London County Council plot ratio map, 1957.

expansion was to be discouraged in the inner urban ring. Provision was made for those firms that wished to relocate from the county of London. Firms were encouraged to move to the small towns located in and beyond the MGB. Industrial development in the Thames Corridor was to be restricted to firms dependent upon water-front access. The inward movement of firms from outside the London region was to be actively discouraged. Buckinghamshire County Council considered that there was no need to introduce additional industry having regard to labour shortages and an unemployment rate of 1% (Buckinghamshire County Council 1951: 25). In the case of Hertfordshire, however, some 15 million square feet of industrial floor-space was constructed between 1946–61. The county council's industrial policies were modified in 1956 in an attempt to maintain a balance between the further growth of employment and population.

It was not until the late 1950s that belated attempts were made to curb the growth of office employment in Central London by "steering" new development to suburban and outlying town centres. Doubts were expressed at the wisdom of this approach because it simply increased the total number of jobs in the region. The rising costs of London's journey-to-work pattern resulted in attempts to stagger working hours. These *ad hoc* policy responses led a Town Planning Institute Working Party to conclude that the ". . . failure to integrate the planning of communications with the planning of land use must be strongly criticised" (Town Planning Institute 1956: 51). In 1963 the Location of Offices Bureau was established to promote the decentralization of office employment. Additional controls over office development, whereby developers had to obtain an office development permit from the Board of Trade, were introduced in 1965.

The transport component of these development plans was perhaps the weakest element notwithstanding the fact that the Greater London Plan had formulated comprehensive proposals for roads and railways. It suffices here to note that the 1947 Memorandum virtually ignored the railway proposals set out in the Greater London Plan, and many of the plan's key road proposals, including the "A" and "B" ring roads, were abandoned in 1950. The LPAs in the London region considered that additional road capacity had to be provided to accommodate the increasing volume of vehicular traffic. For example, Middlesex County Council proposed that the county's road system should be expanded to accommodate an increase of 100% over the 1939 volume of traffic. The road proposals in the development plans consisted of schemes for improvements to, and extensions of, the main radial routes, together with a few major proposals such as the Dartford Tunnel and the South Orbital Road. This *ad hoc* approach was due in part to the prevailing restrictions on capital investment. However, it also reflected concern at the sterilization of development and land values which often resulted when a road scheme was inserted in a development plan. As a consequence the construction of a new road depended upon the willingness of the local authority to raise the necessary money from rates to cover interest and amortization, and the willingness of central government to make available the grant. In 1960 the Royal Commission on Local Government in Greater London concluded that while ". . . improved administrative machinery will not of itself solve London's traffic problems, that problem is insoluble under the present machinery" (Herbert Report 1960: 119).

One important common feature of the "old development plans" was the strong commitment to the preservation of a large area of open countryside around London in order to prevent its outward growth. The Metropolitan Green Belt (MGB) was the only one defined in the original plans already submitted to the Minister. The authorities concerned gave further consideration to the depth of the Green Belt, and by the end of the year proposals for extending it had been received from the County Councils of Essex and Hertfordshire. Berkshire, Buckinghamshire, Surrey and Kent County Councils were also known to be considering the desirability of extending their sectors of the Metropolitan Green Belt (MHLG 1956: 44). By 1963 over 5,200 km^2 of land around London were subject to Green Belt policies (Elson 1986: 19). Throughout the 1950s and 1960s the principle objectives of the MGB were the containment of urban sprawl and the maintenance and encouragement of agricultural and rural uses. Less importance was attached to recreational activity until the late 1960s when the area devoted to agricultural use began to decrease. It was always recognized that the national interest would require that special (i.e. favourable) consideration be given to defence projects, reservoirs, minerals extraction and other forms of development, such as educational and research institutions, which retained the open character of the site in question.

The Greater London Council 1965–86

The Herbert Commission reviewed the case for the reform of local government in London and recommended that the Greater London Council (GLC) should be established to undertake those functions that could only be effectively performed over a wide area. Notwithstanding this recommendation, the Commission envisaged that the newly created London boroughs would be the primary unit of local government (Herbert 1960: 192–3). These recommendations were enacted in the London Government Act 1963, which also included provisions for the reform of London's development plan system. Section 25(3) of the London Government Act required the GLC to prepare a development plan which laid down general policy with respect to the use of land, including guidance as to the future road system. During the interim period, the development plans already prepared by the LCC and the county councils and county borough councils were to constitute the Initial Development Plan (IDP) for Greater London. The IDP was to have statutory effect in respect of development control, compulsory purchase orders and enforcement notices, etc., until superseded by adopted local plans. Provision was made in Section 25(4) of the London Government Act for each London borough to prepare a local development plan which restated the relevant provisions of the IDP and the Greater London Development Plan (GLDP). It was envisaged that these borough plans would bridge the gap between the strategic framework provided by the GLDP and the detailed land-use framework required to prepare local plans. In other words they were expected to fulfil the rôle of urban structure plans.

It is important to recall that the Herbert Commission was thinking of the 1947 development plan system, as was the government when it accepted the Commission's recommendations. The development plan provisions of the London Government Act 1963 pre-dated the Report of the Planning Advisory Group (PAG 1965), and the reformed system of structure and local plans set out in the Town and Country Planning Act 1968. A detailed examination of the problems which arose as a result of this historical sequence is to be found in the Report of the GLDP Panel of Inquiry (Layfield Report 1973: 15–34). It was not until the GLDP Regulations were issued in 1966 (MHLG 1966), and subsequently amended in 1968 (MHLG 1968) that it became apparent that the GLDP would differ considerably from an "old development plan" (Layfield Report 1973: 20). Perhaps of greater significance is the fact that detailed guidance regarding the form and content of structure and local plans was not issued until 1970 (DoE 1970b). The Minister's announcement in late 1970 that the London boroughs would no longer be required to prepare individual development plans reinforced the growing doubts and the relevance of the GLDP (Self 1971: 21).

 ## *The Greater London Development Plan*

When the GLC and the London boroughs came into being in 1965, they inherited the established regional policies and framework set out in the South East Study, together with the detailed policies, proposals and planning standards contained in the IDP. It was not until 1969 that the GLDP was forwarded for Ministerial consideration and approval. The plan consisted of a written statement, a metropolitan structure map and an accompanying report of studies. It was based upon the findings of the London Transportation Study initiated by the LCC in 1962, and subsequent GLC surveys of land use (1965), future travel demands (1966), employment (1966) and housing (1967). The plan-making process was deemed to be "elephantine" (Young & Garside 1982: 326), and the Council's approach to the preparation of the GLDP was deemed to be both ". . . narrow and old-fashioned" (Self 1971: 18). This resulted in a draft plan which was deemed to be ". . . alarming and horrifying" (Thorburn 1970: 64) and which had to be virtually rewritten in the light of changing circumstances (Eversley 1973: 102–107).

The GLDP written statement confirmed that the Council was prepared ". . . to do everything within its power to maintain London's position as the capital of the nation . . . and to foster the commercial and industrial prosperity of London and its cultural status" (GLC 1969: 10). Particular importance was attached to improving housing conditions, the improvement of public transport and the road system, the conservation of London's distinctive character, and the improvement of public and private sector design standards. The Council's main aims were to:

– liberate and develop, so far as planning can, the enterprise and activities of London, promoting efficiency in economic life and vitality in its society and culture

- treasure and develop London's character – capital of the nation, home and workplace of millions, focus of the British tradition
- conserve and develop London's fabric, of buildings, spaces and communications, protecting the best while modernising what is out of date or inferior
- promote a balance between homes, work and movement as principal elements upon whose relationship London's overall prospects depend
- participate in necessary measures of decentralization and help forward the part that London plays in national and regional development
- encourage continual improvement in metropolitan environments and make them congenial and efficient in the service of London's people
- unite the efforts of all who can help to realise these aims and to give new inspiration to the onward development of London's genius. (GLC 1969: 11)

The housing component of the GLDP comprised little more than a brief review of existing problems, together with general statements of good intent. Although the links between population, residential capacity and density, and labour force were identified, this did not result in the adoption of an integrated approach such as that advocated earlier in this book.

The GLC's Transport plan constituted the most ambitious and controversial part of the GLDP. It was based upon a firm commitment to the development of a primary road system, including the Motorway Box, and to the piecemeal improvement of the secondary road system and specified local roads. The public transport component consisted of little more than a restatement of the investment plans of individual public transport operators. One commentator concluded that the transport plan was ". . . for all its deficiencies the most carefully documented . . ." part of the GLDP (Hall 1970: 49). However, this view was not shared by the London Amenity and Transport Association (Thompson 1969), by over 19,000 objectors and by the Layfield Panel. Particular concern was expressed at the Council's failure to adopt a co-ordinated approach to public transport, the road network, traffic restraint and management, environmental improvement, and short- and long-term changes in the nature and location of the land uses that generated and attracted traffic.

The GLDP provided more policy guidance for town centres than was required by the 1966 Regulations. For example, the Council designated 6 major strategic centres and 22 strategic centres where future shopping development was to be concentrated. The main aims were to establish a convenient distribution of town centres, to determine the respective rôles of Central London and the suburban centres, to indicate which uses should be encouraged, and to provide a guide to the distribution of future retail floor-space. Although particular attention was paid to the needs and problems of Central London, the Council failed to identify the activities that needed to be located there. By 1972 the Council had changed its views about the benefits and importance of tourism, and concluded that the continued growth of tourism would adversely affect the environment and attractions of London. The section devoted to urban landscape listed 23 Areas of Special Character, together with a statement of general policy for each area. Policies were also included for high buildings, metropolitan open land, the MGB and trees.

The size, complexity and controversial nature of the draft GLDP led to the appointment of a Panel of Inquiry on 29 May 1970 to consider the objections to the plan. This Inquiry proved to be one of the largest statutory inquiries ever held in the UK. Some 28,392 objections to the plan were duly lodged by 19,997 objectors, and the inquiry lasted for 237 days.

> Although the length of the Inquiry was largely due to the number of Objectors who wished to be heard orally at the Inquiry, much time was taken in discussion of the written objections and, of course, in our own questioning and examination of the Plan. We held eighty-three private meetings as a Panel and there were innumerable smaller meetings among groups of Members. Furthermore, we visited, in some cases several times, all the areas of London which were the subject of specific objections; in particular we inspected the proposed routes and vicinity of all the proposed urban motorways. We also visited Stockholm, Hamburg, Dusseldorf and Frankfurt in order to gain first-hand knowledge of public transport operation, the environmental effects of urban motorways, and the operation of traffic management schemes. (Layfield 1973: 3)

The GLDP was formally approved by the Secretary of State on 9 July 1976 (see Fig. 6.5). Recourse to the approved Written Statement confirms that the draft GLDP had been subjected to major modifications. One of the main aims of these modifications was to ". . . set out the basic requirements of residents and others using London in the context of its wider functions, especially in relation to national and regional policies" (GLC 1976: 1). The Secretary of State agreed with the Panel's view that local planning decisions could only have a limited influence on the size, distribution and composition of London's population. The question of residential density was deemed to be too important to be determined on an individual borough basis. It was decided that densities of over 140 habitable rooms per acre (hra) would be acceptable only in special circumstances. New developments for family housing were normally to be restricted to the lower part of the 70–100 hra range.

The Secretary of State modified the Plan's transport policies to place more emphasis on public transport in order to create a better environment. Greater importance was to be attached to value for money when considering major transport projects. The most significant modification was the deletion of the Motorway Box, and the southern part of Ringways 2 and 3, notwithstanding the proven need to facilitate the orbital movement of road traffic in and around London. Although he agreed with the Panel's view that environmental and other considerations should be taken into account when planning new roads, he did not accept their recommendations about mitigating the effect of major roads on the environment.

The urban landscape policies survived almost unscathed and thereby confirmed that the planning issues posed by high buildings, London squares, trees and street furniture, were suitable subjects for inclusion in the general policy guidelines for the future development of the metropolis. The Secretary of State removed the

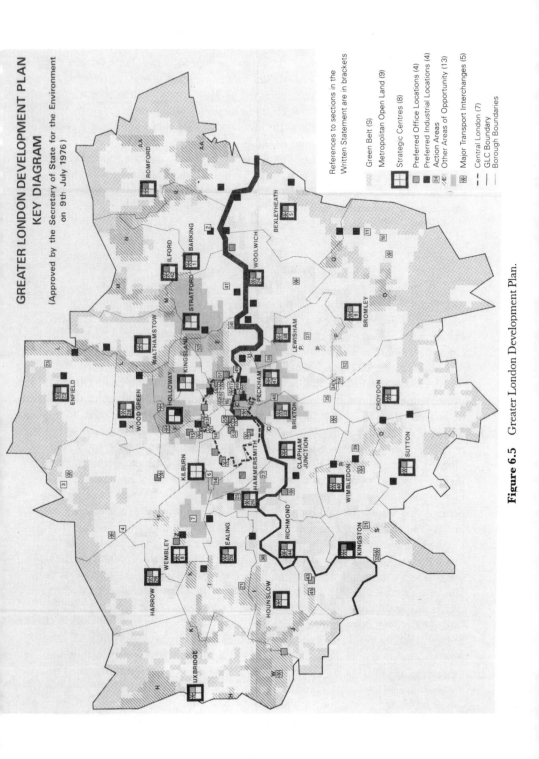

Figure 6.5   Greater London Development Plan.

distinction that had been drawn between Major and other Strategic Centres, and deleted the sector shopping floor-space proposals. Several modifications were made to the Section on Open Land: Recreation and Minerals. For example, the MGB policies were tightened, a new policy for private open space was inserted, the reference to water recreation was expanded, and provisions was made for the supply and distribution of aggregates. The most surprising amendment concerned the deletion of the policy which related the provision of open space to the size and distribution of population. This long-established approach had been re-stated in the Abercrombie Plan and the IDP. The Secretary of State's decisions to delete the Metropolitan Structure Map, which had been used inappropriately as an aid to development control, and to replace the non-statutory illustrations in the draft Plan with the Urban Landscape Diagram, served advance warning of the problems that would be posed later by structure plans.

The unsuccessful attempt to amend the GLDP

Although the GLC was empowered to submit proposals for the amendment of the GLDP to the Secretary of State, under the provisions of Section 10 of the 1971 Planning Act, no enabling regulations had been issued for Greater London. The Council's attempt to amend the GLDP was hindered, and finally defeated by Ministerial obduracy, which was in marked contrast to the treatment accorded to the Greater Manchester Council. On 30th November 1982 the GLC's Chief Development Planner informed the DoE that it was essential that these enabling regulations be issued forthwith, so that the Council could submit the amended plan in the Spring of 1984. It was not until 16 June 1983, however, that the Minister agreed to include specific reference to Greater London in the Town and Country Planning (Structure and Local Plans) Regulations 1982. The subsequent announcement of the forthcoming General Election meant that the Minister was now unable to "sign" the amended regulations. Following the General Election, the Secretary of State informed the Council on 2 August that the Government proposed to introduce legislation that would abolish the GLC and the Metropolitan Councils. It was no longer deemed appropriate to issue regulations which would empower the Council to amend the GLDP. On 7 October the Council obtained leave to apply for a judicial review of the Secretary of State's refusal to issue regulations, under Sections 8(1) and 9(3)(a) of the 1971 Planning Act, covering the procedures to be followed in connection with the alteration of the structure plan for Greater London. Mr Justice Hodgson expressed the view that the Secretary of State was failing in his statutory duty by refusing to issue the requisite regulations (*GLC* vs *Secretary of State for the Environment* 1983: 29). The problems posed by this embarrassing judicial ruling were resolved in the Local Government (Interim Provisions) Act 1984, which relieved the Secretary of State of this duty to consider proposals submitted to him for the alteration of the GLDP.

The GLC had already undertaken a review of the land use and environmental components of the GLDP to determine whether the policies and proposals required amendment in the light of changing circumstances (GLC 1981). Particular concern was expressed at the marked contrast of living and environmental conditions in different areas, and at the rapid decline of manufacturing employment in the eastern corridor. A review was undertaken of the policy changes that had already taken place during the 1970s, and of the new initiatives which had been, or were about to be, introduced. It was noted that:

> In recent years, planning policies for London have been radically changed through various policy statements (e.g. the Annual Budget Plan and the Transport Policies and Programmes), through policy reports (e.g. "Planned Growth Outside London", and "A Freight Strategy for London") and through specific decisions. Decentralization policies have been set aside by drastically curtailing the Expanding Towns Programme and by abandoning Part V housing development outside London (apart from seaside homes). New initiatives for tackling inner city problems have been relaxed and the Location of Offices Bureau abolished. The Council has now decided to introduce major new initiatives for regenerating the economy and improving employment prospects. These include the setting up of the Greater London Enterprise board, the preparation of the London Industrial Strategy, and the London Manpower Plan, and the adoption of an interim policy for office development in Central London . . . (GLC 1981: 3–4)

In 1982 the Council consulted the London boroughs, community groups and many other public bodies and private agencies about the need for alterations to the GLDP. An informal consultative draft was distributed in June 1983 to solicit comments and representations. A formal consultation draft was approved in early 1984, and use was made of press, radio, TV, public meetings, leaflets and posters to ensure that this second "launch" received wide publicity. There was general agreement that alterations to the GLDP were urgently needed to help the boroughs prepare local plans and set priorities for their housing, transport, employment and environmental programmes. It was envisaged that the GLDP, supported by the borough local plans, would constitute the main basis for determining some 40,000 planning applications which were made each year in Greater London. The results of this consultation exercise were incorporated in the draft plan, which was formally approved by the Council on 25th September 1984 and forwarded to the Secretary of State for the Environment.

An examination of the 1984 GLDP Written Statement confirms that the Council had formulated a strategic framework which was not only positive and relevant but also based on a sensitive appreciation of changing societal and environmental values. The GLC had formulated policies to assist those groups, such as women, ethnic minorities, the elderly and people with disabilities, who ". . . experience problems and pressures brought about either through direct discrimination, or, more often, through inconsiderate policies and decisions" (GLC 1984a: 79). This approach was extended to encompass the spatial context within which "problems" are perceived and "solutions" implemented. A series of Community Areas were defined with the specific objective of promoting developments, such as housing, community facilities and suitable jobs, to meet the needs of local residents. These Community Areas had already experienced a massive loss of population, homes and jobs, resulting in the decline of the traditional local economy and a significant change in their character (GLC 1984a: 149). The treatment of environmental considerations broke new ground in that the London boroughs would have been required to define natural habitats and biological corridors, allocate sites for the protection and enjoyment of nature, and bring forward programmes for the management of habitats, the establishment of local nature reserves, and for nature conservation in ecologically deficient areas (GLC 1984b: 45). An unconvincing attempt was also made to incorporate policies for energy conservation, notwithstanding the fact that the DoE had maintained that development plans should not address energy considerations (Owens 1986: 83). The Explanatory Memorandum confirms that the Council attached very high priority to attacking the causes of social and economic inequalities which denied ". . . many hundreds of thousands of Londoners the opportunity to live a full life, in a decent home, and in a convenient, safe and pleasant environment, and with well paid jobs available for all who need them" (GLC 1984a: ii).

Local plans adopted by the London boroughs: 1965–90

Section 25(4) of the London Government Act 1963 stipulated that each London borough should prepare a local development plan which restated the relevant provisions of the IDP, and the GLDP when it had been approved. Schedule One of the 1968 Planning Act applied this Act's development plan provisions to Greater London. It was still envisaged, however, that the London boroughs would also prepare borough structure plans once the GLDP had been approved. Although the Minister subsequently announced in 1970 that the London boroughs would not be required to prepare individual structure plans, it was not until 1974 that local plan regulations were issued for Greater London (DoE 1974). These regulations set out the procedures to be followed in connection with the preparation, submission, approval, adoption and subsequent repeal and replacement of local plans. The London boroughs were now empowered to prepare district local plans based on a comprehensive consideration of the matters affecting the development and other use of land. They were also empowered to prepare subject local plans which were based on a consideration of one type of land use or a particular development, and action area plans for those areas where comprehensive development, redevelopment or improvement could be implemented within 10 to 15 years.

The London boroughs could decide whether a local plan was needed, the type of plan to prepare and the area that it should cover. Predictably, this system gave rise to confusion and uncertainty. For example, doubts existed about the rôle, content and utility of the strategic framework that the GLC was required to prepare, the interpretation of the IDP, the need to prepare local plans, the rival merits of borough-wide and district-based approaches to policy formulation and implementation, and the desirability of preparing informal "bottom drawer" plans (Field 1983: 26; Healey & Underwood 1977: 16).

Throughout the 1960s concern was expressed about the latent planning abilities of the newly created London boroughs. This concern reflected initial doubts about the ability of the officers and local politicians who had to operate and administer the proposed new system. "The London Boroughs as constituted in 1965 initially had their own administrative and political battles to resolve. They had not had, in most cases, any real planning powers, and the basis of their development planning activities was, essentially, the experience of the new staff that had joined them" (Tapsell 1975: 1). A detailed account of the problems encountered in the London Borough of Camden during the transitional period 1964–5 is particularly revealing. In the case of some departments where the workload exceeded staff capacity ". . . the result was overwork and low morale leading to illness and resignations, with a vicious downward cycle which affected the performance of the function concerned" (Wistrich 1972: 272). A review of the arrangements that individual London boroughs made for the organization and administration of planning found that some had established separate planning departments, whereas others either combined planning with other "allied" disciplines such as architecture, or accorded planning a subordinate rôle in the borough engineer's department (Field 1979: 2). There were similar variations in the actual size and composition of the newly created planning departments which ranged from 17 to 96 professional officers (Healey & Underwood 1976: 37). Various reasons were advanced for these variations including ". . . the problems of each area, political demands, the distribution of power within the local authority and the planners' own aspirations (Healey & Underwood 1976: 10).

Progress 1965–90

Most boroughs accepted the fact that they would not be able to prepare either structure or local plans until the GLDP provided the strategic framework and objectives for Greater London. During the late 1960s several boroughs gathered and collated data about the demographic characteristics of the population, household size, employment, housing quality, journeys to work, and recreational activities. This information provided the first general view of the problems posed by individual boroughs. Inevitably this encouraged some boroughs to focus attention on the provisions of the IDP, which were to have statutory effect until replaced by adopted local plans. One borough considered that the IDP was deficient on two counts, i.e. the rigidity of the land-use zones and the uncertainty about the actual implementation of the proposed changes in land use (LB Camden 1976: para. 12).

Although the IDP's policies were still deemed to be generally valid, they did not always reflect the views of individual boroughs regarding employment and industry, the establishment of housing redevelopment programmes, the implementation of public open-space proposals, and the establishment of local planning information and aid centres. As a consequence some boroughs reviewed the IDP to determine whether it observed the political guidelines set by the newly elected councils. This resulted in proposed amendments to, and departures from, the provisions of the IDP. One writer has suggested that the boroughs should have prepared local plans which dealt with immediate issues and thus encouraged public participation in the planning of local communities (Tapsell 1975: 1).

One noteworthy trend, which was subsequently to influence plan-making and the rôle of plans, was the advocacy of corporate planning in the Maud Report (1967) and the Bains Report (1972). The corporate approach is predicated on the belief that all departments of a local authority must work together to meet the needs of the people for which the authority is responsible. In other words, corporate planning is concerned with the formulation and implementation of realistic plans. It is concerned with general wellbeing rather than the passive provision of statutory services (City of Bradford Metropolitan Council 1976). A few boroughs prepared community plans which reviewed the provision and future development of council services (LB Lambeth 1974). By 1976 some 17 London boroughs had introduced various forms of corporate planning and management (Healey & Underwood 1976). In essence, the corporate plans dealt with short-term immediate issues, whereas the land-use plans were concerned with longer-term strategic concepts (LB Lambeth 1974: 24).

Doubts were already being expressed about the relevance of the GLDP when the Minister announced in 1970 that the London boroughs would not have to prepare structure plans. The Minister also announced that the boroughs could commence work on the preparation of local plans, provided that the plans conformed generally to the provisions of the GLDP. Some boroughs decided to adopt a do-nothing strategy, while others decided to prepare non-statutory local plans for those neighbourhoods and town centres which were either experiencing development pressure or which presented environmental problems. A few boroughs were already committed in principle to the preparation of a borough-wide plan. For example, the London Borough of Camden decided to prepare a statutory borough local plan because it would guarantee the rights of participation and objection, and it would also constitute a more secure statement of planning policy when determining planning applications and handling planning appeals (Thompson 1977: 146). These early attempts to prepare local plans were marked by uncertainty, indecision and many false starts. Several reasons have been advanced to explain why there was so much confusion. The most frequently cited reasons include the statutory duty to prepare a structure plan, the views expressed by the Layfield Panel regarding the strengths and weaknesses of the draft GLDP, the prolonged wait for the GLDP to be approved, and the belated issue of local plan regulations for Greater London in 1974 (Field 1983: 28).

In 1973 the Central London Planning Conference (CLPC), which consisted of seven London boroughs and the GLC, undertook a review of the major planning issues and problems that faced Central London. A joint team was established to

118

prepare an advisory plan for Central London. The underlying aims of this exercise were to investigate those major issues that were beyond the resources of an individual borough, to promote co-operation in the formulation and implementation of central area policies, and to enhance Central London's rôle as the national capital, the major centre of business and administration, and the country's major focus of tourism. The CLPC published an advisory plan in 1976 which attached importance to fostering important central functions, promoting "living" and "working" facilities, meeting the demands for movement of people and goods, and improving the physical environment (CLPC 1976: 7).

During the 1970s most boroughs prepared a series of discussion papers which examined the topics listed in Schedule One of the 1974 local plan regulations for Greater London (i.e. population and employment, housing, industry and commerce, transportation, shopping, education, social and community services, recreation and leisure, and conservation). The London Borough of Bexley, for example, prepared a series of "Interim Policy Statements" for transportation, offices, open lands, shopping and housing, to facilitate the subsequent preparation of a borough plan. The London Borough of Lewisham highlighted the problems posed by the data, the complexity of the issues, the conflicting views of public and private interests, and, as a first step to resolve these conflicts, prepared a comprehensive statement of the Council's current policies. This statement was accompanied by "Positional Papers" on housing, the economic and physical environment, recreation and leisure, and social welfare. The London Borough of Haringey produced twelve "Policy Option Papers" which analyzed the social, economic and physical structure of the borough. The London Borough of Lambeth produced "Topic Papers" which examined various aspects of borough life so that the public could determine their priorities for the future (LB Lambeth 1975).

A survey undertaken in 1979 found that some 22 boroughs were committed to the preparation of borough local plans (see Fig. 6.6), which in 16 cases would be supplemented by detailed plans for individual districts and neighbourhoods. These more detailed local plans comprised statutory insets (four cases), non-statutory plans (ten cases), and a combination of both approaches (two cases). A further nine boroughs were working almost exclusively at either a district or a neighbourhood scale. Five of these boroughs were committed to the preparation of statutory plans which would ultimately result in borough-wide coverage. Similar variations were found in the level of commitment to the preparation of action area plans, notwithstanding the fact that there was a statutory duty to prepare plans for the 50 borough action areas identified in the GLDP. Work was proceeding only on the preparation of 13 borough action area plans, while some 25 proposed action areas had either been quietly abandoned or subsumed within borough plans (Field 1983: 32–4). Only two borough plans (Camden and Waltham Forest) and four district plans (Brent, Lambeth, Newham and Redbridge) were formally adopted during the period 1965–80. The transfer of additional development-control powers from the GLC to the London boroughs in 1980 (DoE 1980), however, highlighted the importance that would now be accorded to adopted local plans.

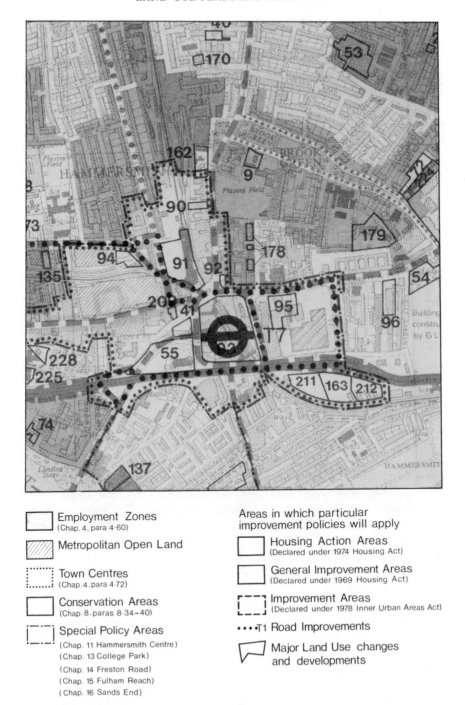

Figure 6.6 Extract from Hammersmith and Fulham Borough Local Plan.

Figure 6.7 Adopted local plans in Greater London, 1977–90.

There was a marked improvement in the adoption rate during the next five years when a further 13 borough plans and 20 district plans were formally adopted. By 1990, when the last local plan was adopted in Greater London, some 23 boroughs were wholly covered by adopted local plans (see Fig. 6.7). A further nine boroughs were partly covered by adopted district plans, while the London Borough of Barnet had failed to adopt a local plan. Further information concerning the local plans prepared by the London boroughs is set out in the Table 6.4.

The local plans prepared by the London boroughs were justified in terms of the manipulation of socioeconomic data, the need to determine district priorities, the need for a framework to guide the preparation and evaluation of redevelopment proposals, and the need to generate public involvement and debate. Given the dearth of appropriate techniques for district-level planning, most boroughs adopted a rational cyclical plan-making model whereby alternatives were quickly generated and evaluated and then subjected to public scrutiny and debate. In the case of Camden the alternatives were presented to the members and other officers for their immediate reactions (Thompson 1977: 147). Planning in Inner London during this period was effective, albeit in different ways and to different degrees.

121

Table 6.4 Adopted local plans, 1977–90.

Type of plan	Number adopted
Borough	23
District	25
Action Area	10*
TOTAL	58

Source: DoE Progress Lists, September 1990 and 1992.
* *NB:* includes one plan adopted by the GLC.

Because of political factors, and the pre-eminence of private sector development, the positive implementation of policies tended to be small-scale and intermittent. The local plans rarely commanded the political support that was needed to secure sufficient scarce resources and promote redevelopment. The importance of political support for local plans was highlighted in 1978 when the Wandsworth Draft Borough Plan was withdrawn by the new Conservative administration following the borough election. This plan was amended to include such controversial policies as the sale of council houses and the proposed transfer of control over borough schools from the Inner London Education Authority (ILEA) to the Council.

Procedural and legal problems

The preparation and adoption of local plans in Greater London posed procedural and legal issues which highlighted the respective rôles of the Planning Inspectorate, the Secretary of State for the Environment, and the High Courts. The Planning Inspectorate still played a key rôle in resolving the objections that were lodged against these plans, notwithstanding the fact that the Inspectors' findings and recommendations were now reported to the borough concerned and not to the Secretary of State for the Environment (DoE 1983: para. 15). In the case of the public inquiry into the Wandsworth Draft Borough Plan, there were over 1,500 duly lodged objections, mostly to the overtly political nature of some key policies. The Inspector's report was highly critical of these policies, and the plan was not formally adopted until 1984, following a further local election. By way of contrast, however, in the London Borough of Hammersmith and Fulham, the Council decided to grant planning permission for the Hammersmith Broadway redevelopment proposals, notwithstanding the criticisms that were levelled at the scheme by the Inspector responsible for the local public inquiry into the borough plan, which was taking place at the same time. The Inspector's conclusions regarding the North Southwark plan, which was deposited on 12 December 1983 and attracted considerable local support, are particularly interesting given the plan's subsequent chequered history. Although the Inspector agreed that priority should be accorded to "... the problems of inadequate living conditions and high unemployment", he considered that the plan had ignored other equally important matters (Inspector's Report dated 25 April 1985). Other Inspectors criticized the planning gain policies included in the draft plans prepared by 22 London boroughs, notwithstanding the fact that the approved GLDP recommended that the location of office development should be contingent upon the attainment of specified planning advantages (GLC 1976: 30). In the case of Bromley the Inspector recommended that these policies should be modified, whereas in the case of Harrow the Inspector recommended that they should be omitted altogether.

The Secretary of State for the Environment saw fit to exercise his powers of direction in respect of the Waterloo District Plan (1977) and the North Southwark Plan (1986). In the former case he directed that Lambeth Borough Council should repeat the public consultation exercise; in the latter case he directed that the plan should not be adopted because it was in direct conflict with established national policies and was not consistent with the London Docklands Development Corporation's strategy for the regeneration of the area under its jurisdiction. Inevitably, there were occasions when the Secretary of State considered that the provisions of a local plan should not take precedence over other material considerations. For example, he granted planning permission for development of land which formed part of the proposed MGB in the Ealing Draft Borough Plan. He also refused to "call in" the Hammersmith Centre redevelopment scheme, which was in conflict with the provisions of the deposited borough plan, because these matters were deemed to be essentially of local concern and ". . . therefore matters for the local planning authority to resolve" (*Hansard* vol. 997, no. 34, 26 January 1981, Col. 340).

The High Courts were also called upon to determine the legal status of the policies and proposals contained in the local plans prepared by the GLC, the City of Westminster, and the London boroughs of Enfield and Southwark. In 1975 Enfield Borough Council unsuccessfully applied for a motion to quash the Secretary of State's decision to grant planning permission for development in the MGB on the grounds that he had failed to have due regard to the provisions of the development plan (*Enfield LB* vs *Secretary of State for the Environment* 1975). Five years later the High Court ruled that the GLC was empowered to grant planning permission for development which was not in accord with the policies and proposals contained in the Covent Garden Action Area Plan (*Covent Garden Association Ltd* vs GLC 1980). The importance of adopted local plans was confirmed in 1984 when the Court of Appeal ruled that policies governing the development and use of land should be contained in the actual statutory plan and not relegated to supplementary planning guidance (*Great Portland Estates plc* vs *City of Westminster* 1984). In 1987 the High Court rejected Southwark Borough Council's application for a judicial review of the Secretary of State's decision not to permit the formal adoption of the North Southwark Local Plan. The High Court judges ruled that the Secretary of State had acted properly in reaching his decision to call in the plan and that he had in fact considered the plan afresh before refusing permission for it to be formally adopted (LB *Southwark* vs *Secretary of State for the Environment* 1987).

Unitary development plans

The Local Government Act 1985 made provision for the abolition of the GLC and the metropolitan county councils, the transfer of planning powers and functions to the London boroughs and the metropolitan district councils, and the preparation of unitary development plans (UDPs). The Act also established the London Planning Advisory Committee (LPAC) to advise the Government on the views of the 33 London boroughs regarding the content of strategic guidance. LPAC undertakes annual reviews which ". . . assess the current situation and achievements across London, and set out further policy advice based on new information and changed circumstances" (LPAC 1992: 1). It also provides advice to boroughs about the relationship between their UDPs and the London-wide strategic framework. Particular attention is being paid to the following matters which require co-ordination: housing, economic development, retailing, green issues, transport, East London regeneration, Central London fringe and West London (Simmons 1990: 36).

The statutory arrangements for the preparation of UDPs are contained in Part II of the 1990 Planning Act. Further advice regarding the form, contents, functions and general procedures for making, adopting, altering and replacing UDPs is set out in the Town and Country Planning (Development Plan) Regulations 1991 (DoE 1991a) and in PPG 12: Development Plans and Regional Guidance (DoE 1992a). It suffices here to note that a UDP consists of two parts. Part I, which fulfils the functions of an approved structure plan, consists of a written statement of the local authority's general policies for the development and use of land, together with appropriate measures for traffic management and the improvement of the physical environment (e.g. see Fig. 6.8). These policies must have regard to current national and regional policies, to any strategic guidance issued by the Secretary of State for the Environment, to the availability of resources, and to such other matters as the Secretary of State may prescribe. The main function of Part I is to provide the context and the framework for Part II of the UDP, which fulfils the same functions as an adopted local plan. Part II consists of a written statement of the local authority's more detailed development control policies and proposals, which may include the designation of an action area. It must also include a proposals map together with a reasoned justification of the policies in Part I and the more detailed provisions of Part II. When the UDPs become operative they will supersede the GLDP, the local plans that have been adopted by the London boroughs, and those provisions of the IDP that are still operative in Greater London.

The DoE have advised that Part I of a UDP should, as appropriate, include land-use policies for the following key strategic topics: housing, green belts, rural economy, urban economy, transport, mineral working, waste treatment and disposal, tourism and energy conservation. They have also advised that the strategy, objectives and policies contained in UDPs should be presented in a unified and consistent manner; that particular attention should be paid to the linkages which can occur between these components; that full account should be taken of the social, economic and environmental effects of the policies and proposals; and that adequate

124

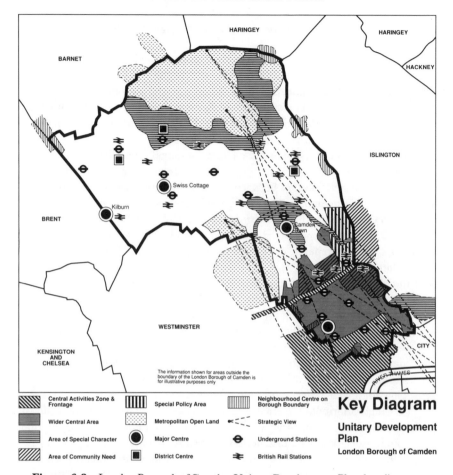

Figure 6.8   London Borough of Camden Unitary Development Plan, key diagram.

provision should be made for development over a 15-year period (DoE 1992a: para. 5.9; 1992b: 38).

Although the precise content of Part II of a UDP is left to the discretion of each borough, it is anticipated that the policies and proposals will generally follow the key strategic topics dealt with in Part I. Minerals and waste issues will also figure in Part II of a UDP. It is envisaged that the detailed development-control policies contained in Part II will seek to control particular types of development, particular aspects of development, development in specific areas, and development which adversely affects transport infrastructure.

Although environment does not figure in the list of topics, it is assumed that environmental issues will underlie consideration of all the key strategic topics. It is also anticipated that aspects of leisure and, increasingly in the future, some aspects of energy generation, will figure prominently in most UDPs (DoE 1992b: 41).

Strategic planning framework for Greater London

Between 1986 and 1988 LPAC produced draft strategic advice which was subjected to widespread consultation and then forwarded to the Secretary of State for the Environment. LPAC recommended that London required planning policies that recognized ". . . its special problems of scale, diversity, complexity and administrative fragmentation" (LPAC 1988: 1). The advice focused on seven topics (i.e. housing; economy and employment; transportation; environment, conservation and leisure; infrastructure; urban renewal; and investment). Some 33 objectives, together with 132 individual policies, were identified. The Secretary of State's attention was drawn to the interrelationships between key strategic topics, e.g. population, housing and jobs; housing and environment; transport, land use and the environment; and new development and the environment (LPAC 1988: 7–9).

In 1989 the Secretary of State issued strategic planning guidance to provide a framework for the preparation of UDPs in Greater London. The main objectives of this guidance are to:
- foster economic growth bearing in mind the importance for the national economy of London's continuing prosperity
- contribute to revitalizing the older urban areas
- facilitate the development of transport systems that are safe, efficient and have proper respect for the environment
- maintain the vitality and character of established town centres
- sustain and improve the amenity of residential districts
- allow for a wide range of housing provision
- give high priority to the environment, maintain the Green Belt and Metropolitan Open Land, preserve fine views, conservation areas, surrounding countryside and the natural heritage (DoE 1989b: para. 10).

In 1991 the Secretary of State issued further supplementary guidance on the need to protect strategic views of St Paul's Cathedral and the Palace of Westminster (DoE 1991b).

Although many of the strategic issues and policies set out in LPAC's 1988 strategic advice and the Government's guidance are still valid, changing economic and social circumstances have led LPAC to undertake a review of the content of RPG3 (see Fig. 6.9). LPAC's recently published fourfold "Visions for London" seeks to establish ". . . common values and a shared purpose: a consensus on the kind of London we want to achieve" (LPAC 1994: 1). The four elements of this vision comprise (LPAC 1994: 2):
- *A strong economy* – with a regenerated and broadened base; strengthened business, manufacturing, arts, culture and entertainment, education and tourism industries; and an efficient, high-quality, well maintained infrastructure, particularly public transport.
- *A good quality of life* – which nurtures safe and healthy communities, and a high urban quality based on conservation and improvement of its green and urban environment.

126

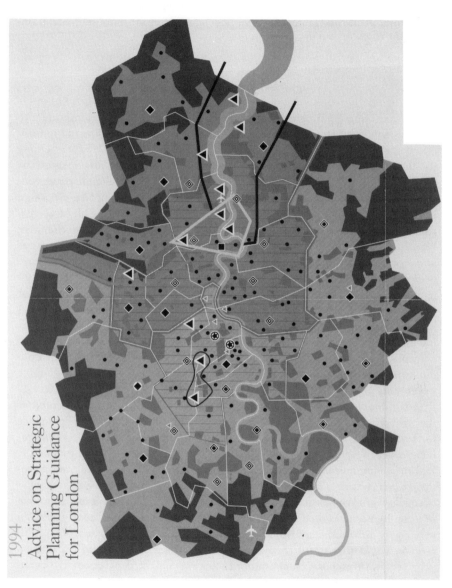

1994
Advice on Strategic
Planning Guidance
for London

Figure 6.9 LPAC strategic framework, 1994.

- *A sustainable future* – where conflicting demands for development and transport infrastructure are balanced with the need to protect and improve the environment for future generations.
- *Opportunities for all* – in a city that strives to ensure equitable access to homes, work, leisure and recreation, transport facilities, health, education and training.

Progress, problems and issues

Before reviewing the progress that has been made in London, it is important to recall that the UDP system was devised at a time when there was mounting Government criticism of the planning system. The Government White Paper "Lifting the Burden" argued that the planning system imposed unacceptable costs on the economy and constraints on enterprise (DoE 1985). A DoE consultation paper considered that structure plans were too long and detailed and contained policies that had little or nothing to do with land-use planning and improving the physical environment (DoE 1986). The Government White Paper "The Future of Development Plans" confirmed that the Government was of a mind to abolish structure plans and replace them with statements of county policy (DoE 1989a). Recent years have witnessed a remarkable change in the Government's views about the planning system. In a speech at the 1992 RTPI conference, Sir George Young, Minister for Housing and Planning, confirmed that the 1991 Planning and Compensation Act has ". . . laid the foundations for the new development plan-led system, by requiring every part of the country to have plans, providing the basis for development control within a broad strategic framework." It can be seen therefore that the London boroughs commenced work on their UDPs during a period of considerable uncertainty about the rôle and importance of development plans.

The London boroughs have responded positively to the challenge presented by the UDP system, bearing in mind that the Secretary of State's strategic guidance for London was not issued until 1989 (DoE 1989b) and that the first commencement orders were not issued until August 1989. In the case of four boroughs (i.e. Hackney, Hammersmith and Fulham, Hillingdon and Lewisham) the commencement orders were not issued until April 1990. Although the DoE envisaged that the boroughs would be able to place their UDPs on deposit within two years of the issue of a commencement order, this has not proved possible in some cases. Table 6.5 and Figure 6.10 provide further information about the preparation of UDPs in Greater London. Various reasons have been advanced to explain the uneven progress of UDP preparation in Greater London. Staff cuts, departmental reorganization and changes in political power have sometimes been responsible for the slow progress of individual boroughs. In some cases protracted negotiations on, or the prolonged wait for the outcome of public inquiries into, major development proposals with a bearing on the content of the plan have also led to delays. One commentator has concluded that ". . . neither the political complexion of a bor-

Table 6.5   Preparation of UDPs in Greater London, 1989–94.*

Stage reached	Number of plans
Adopted	6
Post public local inquiry	13
Public local inquiry	11
On deposit	3
TOTAL	33

Source: DOE/LPAC annual returns.   * As at 31 March 1994.

ough council, nor its location in Inner or Outer London, seem to have had a bear-ing on its record" (Dolphin 1992: 16).

Problems have arisen because the DoE considers that some boroughs are not fully observing the regulations and national planning guidance. To some extent this concern reflects the increased importance that is now attached to development plans by virtue of Section 54A of the 1990 Planning Act (inserted by Section 26 of the 1991 Planning and Compensation Act) which states that: "Where, in making any determination under the Planning Acts, regard is had to the development plan, the determination shall be made in accordance with the plan unless material

deposit

inquiry

post-inquiry

adoption

1 0 1 2 3 4 5 6 7 kilometres

Figure 6.10   Status of UDPs, 22 February 1994.

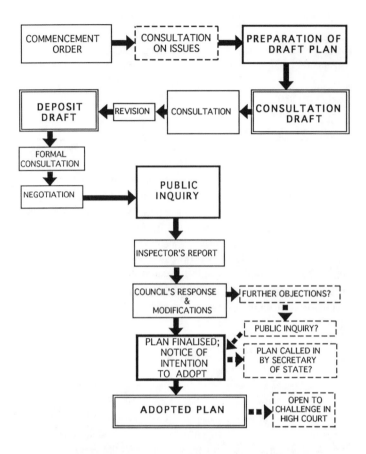

Figure 6.11 The unitary development plan process.

considerations indicate otherwise." The DoE anticipates that some London boroughs will be directed to amend their plans to avoid being too prescriptive (*Planning
in London* 1993a: 5). Three types of objection are now being lodged by the DoE, viz.:
"where policies are couched in very rigid, prescriptive terms; where non-land-use
policies are being used; and over the relationship between standards, supplementary planning guidance and the contents of appendices" (McCormack 1993: 2).
Concern has also been expressed at the attempts of some boroughs to mix and
combine Parts I and II of their UDPs (*The Planner* 1992: 17–18). It is significant that
the London Borough of Redbridge may refuse to adopt its own UDP in an attempt
to avoid the modifications that the DoE has prescribed (*Planning in London* 1993b: 3).

The preparation of UDPs in Greater London has raised strategic issues and local
technical problems, and it is subject to procedural complexity. For example, the
UDP plan-making process is still convoluted and time-consuming (see Fig. 6.11).
"Given the novelty of the strategic planning framework for London, it is perhaps

not surprising that the strongest criticism of the 16 full and partial consultation draft UDPs so far focuses on their approach to co-ordinational and integrative themes, and the ways in which they respond to the question of what Boroughs can do for London rather than resist what London does to them" (LPAC 1990: 4). For example, it has proved difficult to establish a metropolitan consensus on key strategic topics such as growth points, the treatment of strategic centres, business and office development in Central London, shopping policy and waste disposal. "In translating London-wide concerns into UDP policy, the main weakness is that an overall strategic direction, particularly about the need to sustain London's world city and metropolitan rôles, is not emerging properly in the plans" (LPAC 1994: ix). At a more mundane level there are significant variations in the level of detail of the UDPs. In some cases the proposals maps are almost land-use zoning plans, whereas in other cases they provide little information about the proposed land-use structure. Similar variations occur in respect of the treatment of the MGB, metropolitan open land, green chains and corridors, and areas of environmental importance. There is no consistent approach to the designation of open land in the Lee Valley, whereas the southeast London boroughs have adopted a coherent approach to the designation and proposed treatment of their green corridors and chains. Problems have even arisen regarding the designation of what are currently termed Areas of Special Character in the GLDP. These areas are now referred to as Areas of Special Metropolitan Character, or Areas of Metropolitan Significance, or Areas of Landscape Quality. A similar problem has arisen in respect of the treatment of Urban Development Areas which were viewed initially by the DoE as "black holes" in the UDP proposals maps. These problems and variations reflect the lack of an agreed notation for growth points, roads, industrial land, nature conservation sites, open space and other special policy areas. In some cases shopping-centre catchment areas and strategic view vectors stop abruptly at the borough boundaries (LPAC 1990: 4). Inevitably, the cartographic quality of the proposals maps leaves a great deal to be desired. It is hardly surprising therefore that it has sometimes proved difficult to secure the active involvement of community groups, let alone the public, in the consultation exercises that have been launched to promote the "new style" UDPs. Finally, most boroughs are concerned at the cost of preparing and printing their UDPs, and at the length and cost of the public local inquiries required to consider the merits of duly lodged objections.

Policy content of the London boroughs' UDPs

A cursory review of the form and content of Part I of the UDPs prepared by the London boroughs confirms that they are somewhat descriptive, repetitive, vague and not particularly user friendly. Predictably, the boroughs are at pains to demonstrate the importance that they have attached to established national and regional policies. Although it is accepted that national policy will take precedence in those cases which pose environmental issues and problems, there is growing recognition of the fact that the European Union's (EU) economic, environmental and social policies may also be a material consideration. However, the references in Part I to the national, regional and metropolitan context set by Strategic Guidance and Advice are not always translated into appropriate local policies, proposals and action in Part II of some UDPs (LPAC 1990: 4). In the case of some boroughs, the treatment of key strategic issues constitutes little more than an introduction to the plan (LPAC 1991: 7). It is worth recalling that this dichotomy between metropolitan structure and local detail has a long pedigree which can be traced back to the 1965 Report of the Planning Advisory Group (Williams et al. 1992: 115).

The UDP Part I's set out the boroughs' general approach to London's metropolitan structure, related strategic issues and the priority that will be attached to a wide range of local issues. Particular importance is attached to some or all of the following objectives:

- developing, enhancing and protecting the existing land-use structure
- maintaining and improving the built environment
- creating a safe crime-free environment
- satisfying community needs
- improving access to facilities and services
- providing a safe and efficient transport system
- promoting town centre vitality and viability
- improving the quality of life
- creating job opportunities for all, and
- enhancing open spaces and the natural environment.

A variety of other issues in respect of housing, employment and transport are also addressed, including the need to secure additional resources and private sector investment. One common policy issue reflects a general concern about equality of opportunity and related issues. Most boroughs confirm that every effort will be made to meet the needs of all residents, regardless of age, sex, religion and disability, and so on. For example, the London Borough of Greenwich will ensure that its development policies ". . . reflect the needs of all the Borough residents, especially the priority needs of the most disadvantaged individuals, communities and neighbourhoods" (LB Greenwich UDP 1991: 15). Some boroughs advocate positive discrimination and there are frequent references to the provisions of the Race Relations Act 1976. It is recognized, however, that the boroughs are essentially enablers, because they are reliant largely upon government finance, EU grants, and partnerships with private businesses and community groups.

The Local Government Act 1985 stipulates that Part II of a UDP must incorporate any local plans in force for the area in question at the time the UDP is prepared; an initial review of the UDP Part IIs so far prepared by the London boroughs confirms that they often bear a close resemblance to the borough local plans that they will replace (see Fig. 6.12). Separate chapters are devoted to housing, employment, transport, shopping, services, townscape and the built environment, leisure, recreation and tourism, open land and conservation. In some cases additional environmental planning performance standards and related development-

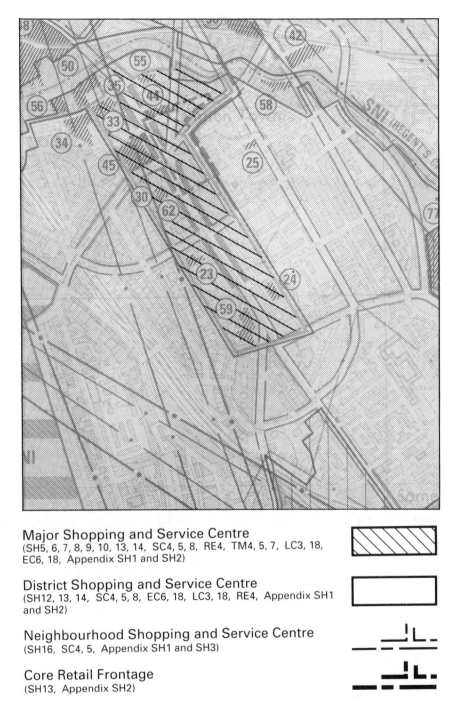

Major Shopping and Service Centre
(SH5, 6, 7, 8, 9, 10, 13, 14, SC4, 5, 8, RE4, TM4, 5, 7, LC3, 18, EC6, 18, Appendix SH1 and SH2)

District Shopping and Service Centre
(SH12, 13, 14, SC4, 5, 8, EC6, 18, LC3, 18, RE4, Appendix SH1 and SH2)

Neighbourhood Shopping and Service Centre
(SH16, SC4, 5, Appendix SH1 and SH3)

Core Retail Frontage
(SH13, Appendix SH2)

Figure 6.12 Extract from London Borough of Camden Unitary Development Plan.

control design criteria are set out in the form of supplementary planning guidance (LB Camden 1992). Inevitably this approach to UDP preparation places a premium on integration, because the individual chapters are relatively self-contained. LPAC has drawn attention to the strategic weaknesses and structural implications of this approach (LPAC 1991: 6–21). It has already been argued earlier in this book that the linkages between housing, transport and employment require special treatment, including stable and co-ordinated programmes of investment and a closer partnership between the public and private sectors. Once again this highlights the important rôle that the UDPs should play in providing the land-use framework and policies that are required to secure both public and private sector investment. The treatment accorded to housing, transport, employment and the environment is reviewed briefly in the following paragraphs.

There is general agreement about both the severity and range of London's housing problems, which include the increased number of inadequately housed people, the spread of homelessness, and the workings of the regional and local housing markets. In some boroughs these problems are exacerbated by the sharp fall in the supply of social housing and by the prevalence of unemployment and low incomes, which make it impossible for residents to participate in local, let alone regional, housing markets. As a consequence, attention is focused on the issue of special housing needs, particularly in relation to the disabled. Most boroughs are responding to a variety of strategic and structural housing issues, including the changing patterns of investment, the critical relationship between housing, transport and employment, the alternative commercial pressures on potential housing sites, and the need for a major review of the current system of housing finance. Increased importance is attached to partnerships with the private sector in an attempt to augment the supply of affordable housing, because few boroughs believe that housing associations can provide sufficient accommodation to meet local needs. The inclusion of quota policies, whereby private developers are required to allocate upwards of 25% of the units to low-income households, does not find favour in the eyes of the government. Several boroughs (e.g. Hackney, Hammersmith & Fulham, Lewisham and Tower Hamlets) have criticized the financial underpinnings of government housing policy, notably the right-to-buy scheme and the failure to release the proceeds from the sales of council housing stock. There is increased concern about the unrealistic nature of the housing targets that have been set for each borough by the DoE. These targets represent the contribution that each borough is expected to make to the complex metropolitan housing market as a whole, rather than a concerted effort to resolve the housing problems of each borough. The House Builders Federation (HBF) intends to demonstrate at UDP inquiries that the targets for Inner London boroughs represent an over-estimate of capacity and argues that the outer boroughs should be encouraged to make good the predicted shortfall.

There is general agreement about the transport problems that currently beset London. For example, most boroughs have expressed concern at the levels of congestion, the health and safety problems posed by through-traffic, the establishment of "rat-runs" through residential areas, and the indiscriminate parking of vehicles. As a consequence, the treatment accorded to transport is wide-ranging and it reflects the traditional powers, responsibilities and concerns of the boroughs (LPAC 1990: 61). Attention is focused on the likely outcomes of the strategic decisions which have either been taken recently or are about to be taken by the government in respect of Heathrow, the North London CrossRail Link, the Channel Tunnel London rail terminus, and the extension of the Jubilee Underground line. Although most boroughs pay lip-service to the concept of an integrated metropolitan transport strategy, such as that adopted in several European cities, there are differences of opinion about the CrossRail link and the desirability of bus deregulation and road pricing measures. Even when there is a broad level of agreement, as is the case with bus priority schemes, the multiplicity of agencies gives rise to problems. "The funding and co-ordination of the implementation of bus priority is increasingly becoming a greater problem in introducing schemes than their technical and policy justification" (LPAC 1991: 62). Similar problems are also likely to arise in respect of the enforcement of parking regulations. Although some boroughs have not defined comprehensive road networks and hierarchies, they are all seeking to strike a balance between the needs of essential road users. The success of this approach is largely dependent on government policy for bus deregulation, public transport investment, rail privatization and road pricing.

Although the depth of treatment accorded to economic and employment issues varies considerably, there is general agreement about the need to address the mismatch between available jobs and local skills, to encourage the employment of more women, to promote equal employment opportunities, to encourage all types of economic activity, and to ensure that new developments do not result in a loss of amenity in residential areas. There is also broad support for the provision of child-minding facilities in the workplace, the launching of training schemes, the creation of small businesses and the promotion of "environmentally friendly" development.

The provision of sites for small businesses and industrial firms is a key feature of the employment strategies adopted by most boroughs, and there is strong support for measures that will improve the employment of local people. For example, the London Borough of Southwark council will endeavour ". . . to improve the range of jobs available to local people and to make employment opportunities more accessible to people who suffer disadvantage and discrimination in the labour market, particularly the disabled, women and people from black and ethnic communities" (LB Southwark 1991: 114). Several boroughs will attempt to secure planning gains in the form of suitable public, social, environmental and transport facilities (e.g. LB Greenwich, City of Westminster), whereas others will seek the provision of nursery facilities and training programmes (LB Hammersmith & Fulham), and programmes of effective local recruitment and training (LB Islington). Inevitably the boroughs have been obliged to adopt an essentially local approach to economic and employment issues. Doubts have already been expressed about the likely effectiveness of these disjointed approaches to both the complexities of the metropolitan labour market and the enhancement of London's rôle as a world city centre of finance and commerce (LPAC 1991: 22; LPAC 1994: ix).

There are also considerable variations in the extent and depth of treatment of environmental issues (LPAC 1990: 50). An initial review of UDP Part IIs confirms that there is widespread concern about the natural and built environment, and that most boroughs are promoting measures to protect the environment. In the case of the natural environment, the boroughs have formulated policies that will encourage the protection of open space, the making good of any open-space deficiency, and improving access to, and the quality of, existing open spaces. The justification for these policies, however, focuses on the recreational, and to a lesser extent ecological, rôles of open space instead of ". . . balancing these with its structural amenity and other functions" (LPAC 1991: 40). There is also general agreement about the need to safeguard and improve the quality of London's built environment.

In designated conservation areas strict control will be exercised over proposed new development and extensions to existing buildings. There is a general presumption against demolition in these areas, and attempts will be made to secure the enhancement of buildings of architectural and historic interest. Most boroughs have prepared detailed guidelines for the protection of local views, the control of advertisements and satellite dishes, the design of shop fronts and access for the disabled. Policies for the arts, culture and entertainment, however, focus on the service these provide for local residents rather than the contribution they can make to consolidating or regenerating town and strategic centres (LPAC 1991: 40). The most striking omission is the absence of policies on energy and related issues. According to LPAC there is a need for a more co-ordinated approach to the supply of aggregates and the use of void spaces for waste disposal, and to the provision of waste incinerators and recycling plants (LPAC 1991: 40).

The Planning Inspectorate will continue to play a key rôle in evaluating the policies, proposals and planning standards in these draft UDPs. For example, an inspector has criticized the Wandsworth UDP for failing to make a real commitment to the provision of affordable housing for people on low incomes (*The Independent* 1994). In the case of the City of London UDP, the inspector has recommended that plot ratio should no longer be used to determine whether proposed developments are acceptable or not. Plot ratio was first introduced by the LCC in 1951, and it ". . . has been such a well known control in the City and other boroughs that its demise is bound to arouse great interest" (*Planning in London* 1994: 10). The next two years will almost certainly witness many disagreements about the proposed policy content of some of the UDPs. Although in most cases the inspectors' recommendations will be accepted, either in whole or in part, the Secretary of State may feel obliged to intervene to ensure that individual London boroughs observe the planning guidance set out in the RPGs and the PPGs. If this occurs, the High Courts will almost certainly be called upon to determine the legality and validity of the Secretary of State's actions.

References and further reading

Abercrombie, P. 1945. *Greater London Plan 1944*. London: HMSO.

Bains Report 1972. *The new local authorities: management and structure*. London: HMSO.

Barlow Report 1940. *Report of the Royal Commission on the Distribution of Industrial Population*. Cmnd 6153. London: HMSO.

Bressey, Sir Charles & Sir Edwin Lutyens 1938. *Highway development survey 1937 (Greater London)*. London: HMSO.

Buckinghamshire County Council 1951. *County Development Plan, county map – report and analysis of the survey*. Aylesbury: Buckinghamshire County Council.

Burns, W. 1973. *Towards an urban policy?* Occasional Papers in Estate Management 4, College of Estate Management, University of Reading.

City of Bradford Metropolitan Council 1976. *Metplan: progress report*. Bradford: Bradford Metropolitan District Council.

CLPC 1976. *Advisory plan for Central London*. London: Central London Planning Conference

Crawley, I. 1991. Some reflections on planning and politics in Inner London. In *Dilemmas of Planning Practice*, H. Thomas & P. Healey (eds), 101–14. Aldershot: Avebury.

DoE (Department of the Environment) 1970a. *Strategic plan for the South East*. Report by the South East Joint Planning Team. London: HMSO.

—1970b. *Development plans: a manual on form and content*.

—1974. *The Town and Country Planning (Local Planning Authorities in Greater London) Regulations*. SI 1481.

—1977a. *Unequal city*. Final report of the Birmingham Inner Area Study.

—1977b. *Inner London: policies for dispersal and balance*. Final report of the Lambeth Inner Area Study.

—1977c. *Change or decay*. Final report of the Liverpool Inner Area Study.

—1980. *The Town and Country Planning (Local Planning Authorities in Greater London) Regulations*. SI 443.

—1982. *The Town and Country Planning (Structure and Local Plans) Regulations*. SI 555.

—1983. *The Town and Country Planning (Local Plans for Greater London) Regulations*, SI 1190.

—1985. *Lifting the burden*. Cmnd 9571.

—1986. *The future of development plans*. Consultation Paper. London: DoE.

—1988. *Green belts*. PPG2.

—1989a. *The future of development plans*. Cmnd 569.

—1989b. *Strategic guidance for London*. RPG3.

—1990. *This common inheritance*. Cmnd 1200.

—1991a. *The Town and Country Planning (Development Plan) Regulations*. SI 2794.

—1991b. *Supplementary guidance for London on the protection of strategic views*. RPG3 Annex A.

—1992a. *Development plans and regional guidance*, PPG12.

—1992b. *Development plans: a good practice guide*.

—1992c. *Land use change in England, no. 7*, DoE Statistical Bulletin (92)4, London: DoE.

—1994. *Regional planning: guidance for the South East*. RPG9.

Dolphin, G. 1992. Analysing form in the UDP Handicap. *Planning in London* 1, 16–7.

Donnison, D. V. & D. E. Eversley (eds) 1973. *Urban patterns, problems and policies*. London: Heinemann.

Elson, M. J. 1986. *Green belts*. London: Heinemann.

Eversley, D. E. C. 1973. *The planner in society*. London: Faber & Faber.

Field, B. G. 1979. *Local planning in London: a survey*. Occasional Paper 1/79, Faculty of the Built Environment, Polytechnic of the South Bank.

—1983. Local plans and local planning in Greater London. *Town Planning Review* **54**(1), 24–40.

Foley, D. L. 1963. *Controlling London's growth*. Berkeley: University of California Press.

Forshaw, J. H. & P. Abercrombie 1943. *County of London Plan*. London: Macmillan.

GLC 1969. *Greater London Development Plan statement*. London: Greater London Council.

—1976. *Notice of approval: written statement, proposals map, key diagram and urban landscape diagram*.

—1981. *Planning policies for London: appraisal*. Report P124.

—1984a. *Alterations to the Greater London Development Plan: explanatory memorandum*.

—1984b. *Alterations to the Greater London Development Plan: revised plan incorporating the alterations*.

Hall, P. 1970. Transportation. *In London under stress*. London: Town and Country Planning Association.

—1989. *Cities of tomorrow: an intellectual history of urban planning and design in the twentieth century*. Oxford: Basil Blackwell.

Hart, D. A. 1976. *Strategic planning in London: the rise and fall of the primary road network*. Oxford: Pergamon.

Healey, P. & J. Underwood 1977. *The organisation and work of planning departments in the London boroughs*. Conference Paper 18, Centre for Environmental Studies, London.

Herbert Report 1960. *Royal Commission on Local Government in Greater London 1957–60*. Cmnd 1164, London: HMSO.

Holden, C. F. & W. G. Holford 1944. *Reconstruction of the City of London*. London: Batsford.

House of Commons 1977. *Planning procedures, vol. 1*. Eighth Report from the Expenditure Committee. HC 395-I, 466. London: HMSO.

Hughes, M. R. (ed.) 1971. *The letters of Lewis Mumford and Frederic J. Osborn*. Bath: Adams & Dart.

The Independent 1994. Inspector says Wandsworth housing policy inadequate. (20 January)

Layfield Report 1973. *Greater London Development Plan: report of the Panel of Inquiry*. London: HMSO.

Ling, A. 1955. The minister approves the County of London Development Plan. *Journal of the Town Planning Institute* **XLI**, 126–8.

London Borough of Camden 1976. *A plan for Camden: written statement – the reason why*. London: London Borough of Camden.

—1992. *Unitary Development Plan: Consultation Draft*.

LB of Greenwich 1991. *Unitary Development Plan: Deposit Edition*. London: London Borough of Greenwich.

LB of Lambeth 1974. *Lambeth Community Plan 1975–79*, vols 1–7. London: London Borough of Lambeth.

—1975. *Policy Topic Paper: Population and Housing*.

LB of Southwark 1991. *Unitary Development Plan: Deposit Edition*. London: London Borough of Southwark.

London County Council 1951. *Administrative County of London Development Plan statement*. London: LCC.

—1960. *Administrative County of London Development Plan, first review: County Planning Report*. London: LCC.

LPAC 1988. *Strategic Planning Advice for London: Policies for the 1990s*. Romford: London Planning Advisory Committee.

—1990. *Strategic Trends and Policy: 1990 Annual Review*.

—1991. *Strategic Trends and Policy: 1991 Annual Review*.

—1992. *Strategic Trends and Policy: 1992 Annual Review*.

—1994. *Advice on Strategic Planning Guidance for London*.

Maud Report 1967. *Report of the Committee on the Management of Local Government*. London: HMSO.

McCormack, S. 1993. The UDP Earthquake – London Calling. RTPI, *London Branch Summer Newsletter*, 2.

MHLG (Ministry of Housing and Local Government) 1944. *The control of land use*. Cmnd 6537, London: HMSO.

—1951. *Town and Country Planning 1943–1951*. Progress Report, Cmnd 8204.

—1955. *Report of the MHLG for the period 1950/1–1954*. Cmnd 9559.

—1956. *Report of the MHLG for the Year 1955*. Cmnd 9876.

—1957. *Report of the MHLG for the Year 1957*. Cmnd 193.

—1961. *Report of the MHLG for the Year 1960*. Cmnd 1435.

—1964. *The South East Study 1961–81*.

—1966. *Town and Country Planning (Development Plans for Greater London) Regulations*. SI 48.

—1967. *A strategy for the South East*. 1st Report by the South East Economic Planning Council.

—1968. *Town and Country Planning (Development Plans for Greater London) (Amendment) Regulations*. SI 815.

Owens, S. 1986. Strategic planning and energy conservation. *Town Planning Review* **57**, 69–86.

The Planner 1992. (11 May) 17–18.

Planning 1992. Regeneration agency to resolve control of power. (**978**: 1).

Planning Advisory Group 1965. *The future of development plans*. London: HMSO.

Planning in London 1993a. DoE warning on inflexible UDP policies. (Issue 5: 5).

—1993b. Redbridge snubs DoE over UDP adoption. (Issue 6: 3).

—1994. Plot ratio abandoned in the model City. (Issue 9: 10)

Porter, S. 1990. *A minister for London: a capital concept*. London: FPL Financial Limited.

Pryce, G. 1981. Strategic planning and the London boroughs. In *The future of the Greater London Development Plan*, B. Field (ed.), Conference Paper 15, Department of Town Planning, Polytechnic of the South Bank.

Redcliffe-Maud Report 1969. *Royal Commission on Local Government in England 1966–1969*. Vol. 1, Report, Cmnd 4040. London: HMSO.

Rodwin, L. 1956. *The British New Towns policy: problems and implications*. Cambridge, Mass.: Harvard University Press.

Royal Town Planning Institute 1990. Development plans: UDPs and district-wide plans – which way forward? *The Planner* (11 May), 17–8.

—1992. *Planning in London – ten years on*. London: London Branch of the RTPI.

Scott Report 1942. *Land utilisation in rural areas*. Cmnd 6378. London: HMSO.

Self, P. 1971. *Metropolitan planning: the planning system of Greater London*. London: Weidenfeld & Nicolson.

Sharp, E. 1969. *The Ministry of Housing and Local Government*. London: Allen & Unwin.

Simmons, M. 1990. London through the eyes of LPAC. *The Planner* (14 December), 36–40.

Stirling, P. 1952. A twenty-year plan for London. *Journal of Planning Law*, 6–12.

Tapsell, M. 1975. Making local planning work – the London experience. Paper presented at the PTR Summer Annual Meeting, University of Warwick. London: PIRC.

Thompson, J. M. 1969. *Motorways in London: a report of a working party*. London: Duckworth.

Thompson, R. 1977. Camden's local plan: a district-wide approach. *The Planner* (September), 145–7.

Thorburn, A. 1970. A strategy for London. In *London under stress: a study of the planning policies proposed for London and its region*. Welwyn Garden City: Broadwater Press.

Town and Country Planning Association 1971. *Region in crisis: an independent view of the Greater London Development Plan*. London: Charles Knight.

TPI 1956. *Report on planning in the London region*. London: Town Planning Institute.

Tripp, Sir Alker 1942. *Town planning and traffic*. London: Edward Arnold.

Uthwatt Report 1942. *Export Committee on Compensation and Betterment*. Cmnd 6386. London: HMSO.

Williams, G., M. Strange, M. Bentley, R. Bristow 1992. *Metropolitan planning in the 1990s: the rôle of unitary development plans*. Occasional Paper 34, Department of Planning and Landscape, University of Manchester.

Wistrich, E. 1972. *Local government reorganisation: the first years of Camden.* London: London Borough of Camden.

Young, K. & P. L. Garside 1982. *Metropolitan London: politics and urban change 1837–1981.* London: Edward Arnold.

CHAPTER SEVEN

Effectiveness and outcomes of land-use planning in Greater London

Michael Collins

The dramatic environmental and societal changes that have taken place since the planning system was devised in 1947, and then reformed in 1968, have focused attention increasingly upon the achievements and future rôle of land-use planning. For example, growing public concern at the environmental consequences (including health and safety implications) of global warming, increased levels of atmospheric and water pollution, and the destruction of wildlife habitats has demonstrated the need for effective systems of land-use planning and environmental protection. The government has confirmed that the main function of the planning systems is to provide:

> *guidance*, to help people plan the use of their land confidently and sensibly, and to help planning authorities to interpret the public interest wisely and consistently; *incentive*, in that by designating land in their statutory plans for particular types of development, local authorities can stimulate such development; and *control*, which ensures that developers cannot ultimately insist for private reasons on a change which would be against the wider public interest and that people affected by proposals for change can have their views and interests considered (DoE 1992a, para. 1.2).

The effectiveness and outcomes of land-use planning are largely dependent upon the actions and investment decisions of other public bodies and private agencies. For example, the powers conferred upon LPAs are constrained by several factors, including the financial controls exercised by central government, and ". . . the incredible complexities of attempting to impose a 'rational' form of planning on a mixed economy wedded to the principle of an individualistic system of land ownership . . ." (Cullingworth 1975: xi). A recent study commissioned by the DoE defined effectiveness as ". . . the extent to which development takes place or is

141

prevented" (PIEDA plc 1992: iii). This study conceded, however, that:

> While control over the use and development of land might appear a rela-
> tively blunt instrument, bearing in mind the range and complexity of cir-
> cumstances to which it is applied, in practice planning is just one of the
> armoury of weapons used to achieve public policy objectives in the field of
> economic development and environmental protection. (PIEDA plc 1992: 4)

The regional dimension

Although successive governments have favoured an advisory model of regional
planning, whereby LPAs collaborate and allocate scarce resources for strategic
activities and projects, it is generally agreed that regional planning has helped to
shape the geography of London and the South East of England. The Greater London Plan 1944, which was predicated on the principles set out in the Barlow
Report, provided clear and positive guidance about the rôle of the metropolis, the
interplay of town and country, the redevelopment of Inner London, the need for
new towns, and the establishment of a green belt to restrain the peripheral growth
of London. Many of the plan's proposals were subsequently incorporated in the
development plans prepared by LPAs in the LMR and parts of RoSE. These development plans provided the framework for the exercise of planning control over
new development. By 1951 some eight New Town projects were launched in the
South East region to take people and industry from London. Many existing towns
had also been selected for large-scale expansion to accommodate the outward
movement of industries and people from London (MHLG 1951: 74–5). These new
and expanded towns (Fig. 7.1) demonstrated that good living conditions and a better environment could be achieved by careful land-use planning (DoE 1976: 37).
Likewise, the establishment of the MGB confirmed that it was *possible* to restrict the
growth of London.

Throughout the 1950s LPAs in the LMR considered that there was no reason
why the policies in the Greater London Plan could not, or should not, continue.
The Royal Commission on Local Government in Greater London, however, concluded that these policies required early reconsideration (Herbert Report 1960:
83). The fact that this plan had provided relevant regional and local planning guidance for over 16 years testifies to its innate quality. It also demonstrated that
regional planning objectives could be successfully achieved without the creation of
an elected regional authority. All that was needed was government belief in, and
support for, the policies and proposals set out in the regional plan. However, subsequent national and regional trends in population growth during the 1960s and
1970s gave cause for public concern and, as noted in Chapter 6, this led to the
preparation of several regional studies for the South East. Although these studies
did not receive the unqualified support that had been accorded the Greater London Plan, they nevertheless influenced key decisions about the location and scale
of new urban development. During the 1970s the structure plans prepared by LPAs

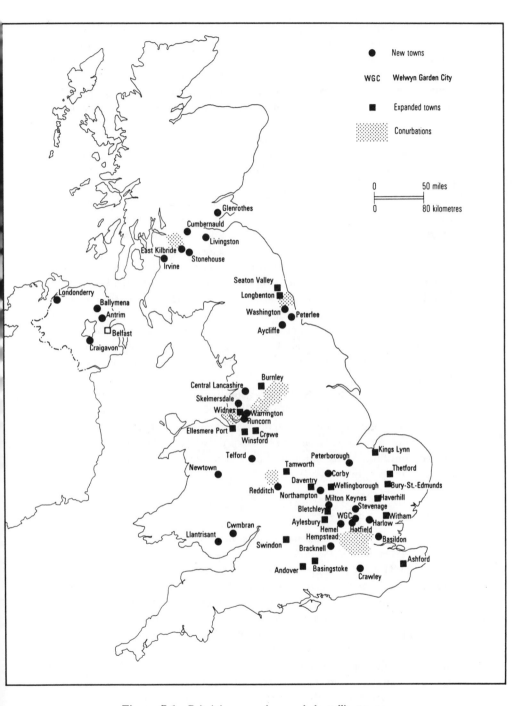

Figure 7.1 Britain's new and expanded satellite towns.

had to observe the policies set out in these regional studies. The inherent problems posed by the hierarchy of regional, structure and local plans were reviewed by the Expenditure Committee of the House of Commons in 1976–7. Concern was expressed at the lack of statutory provision for public participation in regional planning, now that much of the content of structure plans was increasingly determined by the regional studies. The Expenditure Committee concluded that regional planning should not be developed at the expense of structure planning. They preferred to see *ad hoc* regional or subregional plans ". . . dealing with specific issues where the need for such a plan is clearly established and where the interests of two or more structure planning authorities clearly overlap" (HC 395-I, 466 1977: XL).

SERPLAN continued to play, and still plays, an important rôle in the formulation of regional strategies for transport, the location of new housing, employment, mineral extraction and the treatment and disposal of waste (Fig. 7.2). In the case of housing, for example, SERPLAN attempted to determine the appropriate levels of housing provision, and then monitored the actual provision made in structure and local plans. Particular importance has been accorded to housing land supply and prices, housing development in the MGB, new settlement proposals and, more recently, to the provision of affordable housing. In the case of the Channel Tunnel SERPLAN has been ". . . effective in securing positive changes in the policies of the government and British Rail" (SERPLAN 1992: 66). Perhaps SERPLAN's greatest achievement to date has been the very survival of regional planning at a time when the government showed little interest in it. The European Union now presents a major challenge for SERPLAN, because the South East is an integral and important part of the emerging Europe. SERPLAN will participate in attempts to devise ". . . new ways of developing and managing a sustainable environment" (SERPLAN 1992: 75). The Secretary of State has confirmed that ". . . SERPLAN, assisted by its constituent authorities, has an important rôle to play and is well established in monitoring the progress of development and planning policies in the region" (DoE 1994: para. 8.5).

The metropolitan dimension

Although the Greater London Plan provided a strategic land-use framework for the future development and redevelopment of the metropolis, which the ten constituent LPAs had to observe, problems arose because of this fragmented system of local government and town planning. In 1949 the London Planning Administration Committee recommended that some kind of regional body was needed, with powers of direction, finance and supervision, to carry out the Greater London Plan. This recommendation was rejected by the LPAs, who preferred to leave this task to the Minister. Co-ordination of the ten development plans that covered Greater London was complicated by the fact that over four years elapsed between the approval of the first plan in 1954 and the last plan in 1958. Inevitably this

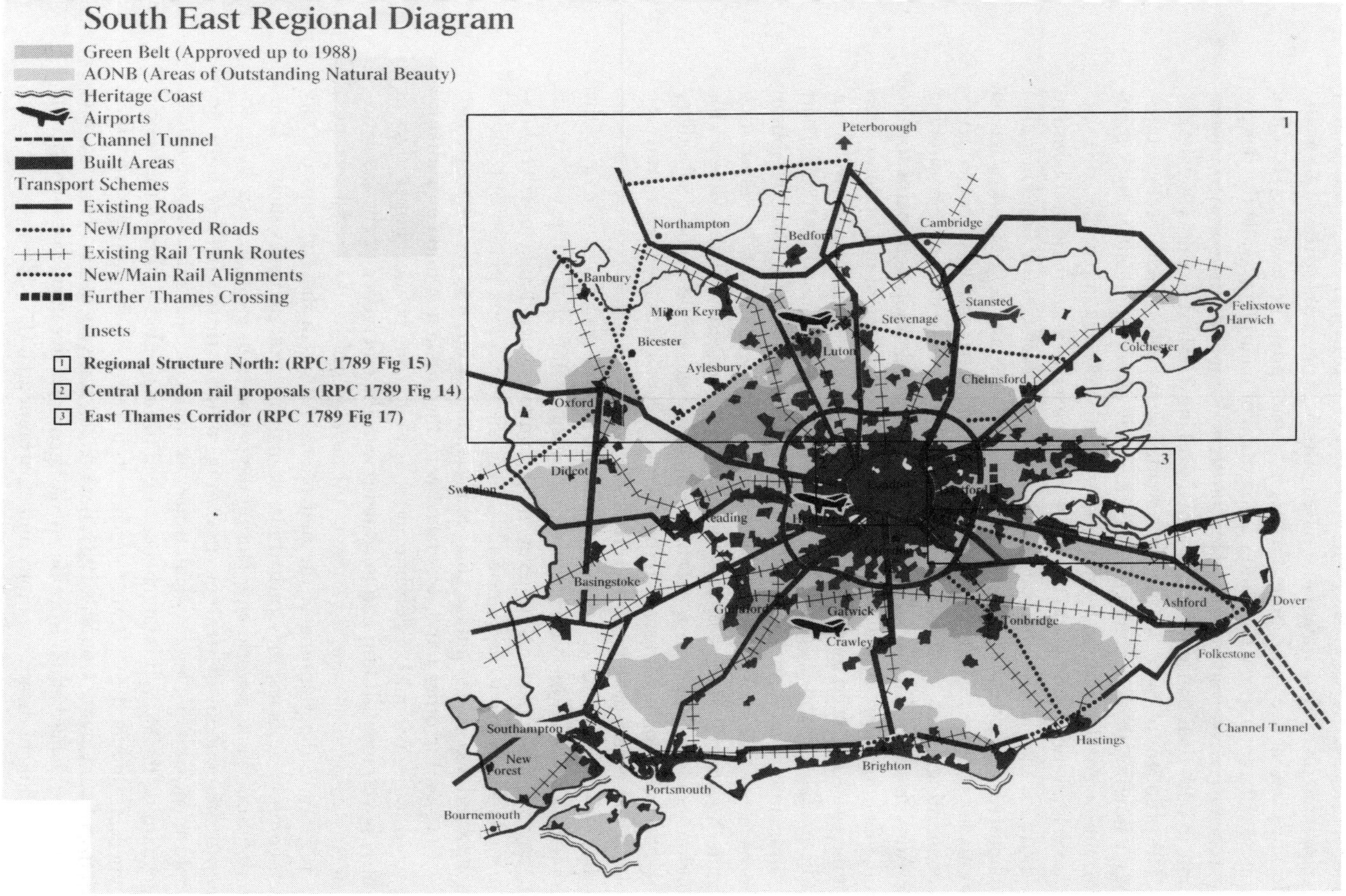
South East Regional Diagram
Green Belt (Approved up to 1988)
AONB (Areas of Outstanding Natural Beauty)
Heritage Coast
Airports
Channel Tunnel
Built Areas
Transport Schemes
Existing Roads
New/Improved Roads
Existing Rail Trunk Routes
New/Main Rail Alignments
Further Thames Crossing
Insets
1 Regional Structure North: (RPC 1789 Fig 15)
2 Central London rail proposals (RPC 1789 Fig 14)
3 East Thames Corridor (RPC 1789 Fig 17)
1
3
Peterborough
Northampton
Bedford
Cambridge
Banbury
Stansted
Stevenage
Felixstowe
Harwich
Bicester
Luton
Colchester
Aylesbury
Chelmsford
Oxford
Didcot
Basingstoke
Gatwick
Crawley
Tonbridge
Ashford
Dover
Folkestone
Channel Tunnel
Hastings
Brighton
Southampton
Portsmouth
Bournemouth

Figure 7.2 South East Regional Diagram

"time lag" became even greater when the ten LPAs reviewed and updated their development plans. This meant that the Minister was never able to examine all the relevant plans at the same time. Further problems arose because the LPAs had adopted different approaches to the preparation of their plans, while the delegation schemes introduced in Essex, Hertfordshire, Kent and Surrey varied considerably in both their conception and actual working (Herbert Report 1960: 81).

The problems of co-ordination were made increasingly difficult because questions of housing, the location of industry, highway construction and railway modernization were determined by different ministries. For example, the "divorce" between land-use planning and transport planning led to an increase in congestion on the roads and railways. Although the siting of offices in Central London and of the houses for office workers were now subject to planning control, no provision was made to ensure that the transport system could cope with the increased levels of commuting. These problems were particularly acute in the area surrounding the Administrative County of London, because the development plans for the Home Counties were based on the principle that employment in London would not increase. The need for a strategic (i.e. metropolitan) authority responsible for traffic management throughout Greater London was identified by the Herbert Commission. The Commission also highlighted the need for a metropolitan approach to housing problems and provision in Greater London. It is interesting to note, however, that the Commission rejected the suggestion that a Minister for London should be appointed, because local authorities would become subsidiary and subservient to the Minister (Herbert Report 1960: 92). Some readers may well feel that these fears have since been realized.

The creation of the GLC in 1965 appeared to provide the answer to many of the problems examined by the Herbert Commission. But, as noted previously in Chapter 5 of this book, the GLC never enjoyed unquestioned dominance over London's affairs. Its predecessor, the LCC, had enjoyed a long period of political stability and was able to pursue consistent planning strategies over a long period. The GLC, on the other hand, was faced with the conflicting and contradictory demands of individual London boroughs, as well as the political imperatives of central government. It also had to contend with the emergence of civic societies, residents' associations and a variety of pressure groups, who were all seeking a greater say in the planning of the metropolis. Although these groups initially focused on local issues, they turned increasingly to strategic issues such as London's future rôle as a world city. During the period of its existence, the GLC pioneered the concept of strategic planning, notably in the field of housing, employment, and to a lesser extent, transport; and it also played an active rôle in safeguarding the MGB. It is largely because of the concerted actions of the county councils, including the GLC, that green belts have survived relatively unscathed (Metropolitan County Councils 1984, para. 2.28). It is very much to the credit of the GLC that the last administration encouraged the active participation of people in the planning of their community and environment (RTPI 1992: 6).

It was noted previously that the proposed amendments to the GLDP sought to restrict the further growth of offices and hotels in Central London, and that increased importance would have been accorded to the adjacent community areas where planning policies would focus on the needs of local residents. Subsequent events in Greater London, notably the advent of UDPs, have highlighted the need for effective advice and guidance to ensure that the strategic needs of the metropolis are properly addressed in the plans now being prepared by the City of London and the 32 London boroughs (LPAC 1994: ix). The Secretary of State for the Environment has advised that London must develop its rôle as a financial, commercial, tourist and cultural centre, broaden its economic base, and encourage high-quality development at locations served by public transport (DoE 1994: para. 2.2). The evidence to hand, however, raises doubts about the ability and willingness of some boroughs to meet this challenge.

The local dimension

1947–65

The "old development plans" prepared by the ten LPAs in Greater London provided a framework against which day-to-day development proposals could be considered. It was always envisaged, however, that these plans would be simple, flexible and realistic, and that they would concentrate on what really needed doing and what stood a realistic change of being implemented within a 20-year period. The effectiveness of these plans can be assessed first in terms of their general impact upon the geography of the South East as a whole, notably the distribution of population and employment, and secondly in terms of their ability to control and promote development. The evidence to hand confirms that these plans played a key rôle in controlling the location, scale, servicing and general quality of new development in London and the South East region. It was now possible to designate green belts which checked the sprawl of towns and severely restricted the sporadic unplanned development in the countryside. This ensured that the amount of land converted from rural to urban use was both minimized and compacted; in other words urban growth was successfully contained (Hall et al. 1973: 393). The containment of urban growth can be regarded as an outstanding success for the planning system in terms of its own objectives, because the outcome accorded with the ideologies of the early post-war period. It also reflected both the power of the agricultural and rural preservation interest groups, as well as the reluctance of urban authorities to lose population. On the debit side, however, urban containment led to the suburbanization of large areas, the transfer of population and employment to free-standing towns beyond the MGB, the growing separation of residential areas from the main centres of employment and services, the adoption of higher residential densities than might otherwise have occurred, and the inflation of land and property prices.

It was now also possible to identify, designate and comprehensively plan the sites for New Towns, and to make provision for the planned expansion of existing towns, to facilitate the decentralization of population and employment from London. The "old development plans" provided the land-use framework that was needed to co-ordinate and integrate these proposals. They also provided the means whereby designated sites could be safeguarded from premature and inappropriate development. In the South East, by the end of 1963, over 84,000 houses and 17.6 million square feet of industrial floor-space had been completed in the eight designated New Towns. An additional 12,687 houses (out of a projected total of 54,451) and 5.4 million square feet of industrial floor-space had been provided in nineteen Town Expansion Schemes. The success of the Town Expansion Schemes owed much to the patient negotiations, generous financial contributions and technical expertise of the LCC.

Another measure of the effectiveness of the "old development plans" was their ability to promote development and redevelopment. It suffices here to note that the 1947 Planning Act empowered LPAs to acquire land compulsorily either to secure its comprehensive development or redevelopment, or to ensure that a particular site was developed for a purpose specified in the plan. The use that was made of these powers reflected the political philosophy of the government in power, the state of the national economy, and the political stance of individual LPAs. In essence, LPAs were – and still are – providers of ". . . social service facilities, some transport services and utilities, some housing and occasional involvement in town centre development or cultural or recreational provision" (Solesbury 1974: 38). This promotional rôle frequently entailed the use of financial incentives in the form of grants and the use of local knowledge about past, present and future situations. The LCC, for example, designated thirteen Comprehensive Development Areas (CDAs) covering an area of over 1,200 acres, and then sought authority to acquire compulsorily most of the land to facilitate and expedite the proposed redevelopment of these areas. By 1960 considerable progress had been made in securing the redevelopment of these CDAs. Although this form of comprehensive planning had not altered the quantity of rebuilding, nor did it add to the total cost of rebuilding, it did secure ". . . economies to the community and greater efficiency, and it has sought to make redevelopment coherent in terms of London as a whole" (LCC 1960: 160).

A final measure of the effectiveness of "old development plans" was their ability to facilitate the exercise of control and influence over development. LPAs were expected to provide clear and precise statements about the type and amount of development that would be permitted in urban and rural areas. It was envisaged that development plans would provide a degree of certainty as to what types of development would and would not be permitted, thus encouraging developers to prepare feasibility schemes because of the presumption that planning permission would be forthcoming if the scheme conformed to the provisions of the plan. Between 1947 and 1965 over 172,000 planning applications were determined each year by LPAs in Greater London and the South East. Over 93% of these applications were approved, thus disproving the claim that planning existed to prevent development. In the majority of cases, LPAs ensured that the development conformed with the general policies and zoning proposals in the development plans. They also ensured that the proposed development complied with the relevant environmental planning standards governing the number, size, layout, siting, design and external appearance, landscaping and proposed means of access. This approach sought to improve the general quality of development, while also securing economy, efficiency and amenity in the use of land and buildings. The following evaluation of the achievements of the British land-use planning system also holds true for London:

> . . . immense strides have been made in planning and controlling the use of land. Green belts have checked the sprawl of towns; much of the new building needed has been sited in new towns or in extensions of existing smaller towns; public services have been planned ahead of development and provision made for them; new industries have been largely sited in estates designed for the purpose; most of the more attractive countryside and the better agricultural land has been preserved from building despite often intense pressure; the layout of housing estates has, in general, been improved out of knowledge; rundown or congested areas of old towns are being redesigned; many fine old buildings have been saved from spoiling or destruction. It is always much easier to see the failures of planning – or what are thought to be its failures – than its successes; so many of the successes lie in the things that have been prevented. The failures, or the supposed failures, are all too evident: the inability of some of the great cities, hemmed in by green belts, to open up their crowded areas or meet their housing needs; the failure to anticipate the growth of car traffic or, even now, to see how to handle it; the amount of ugly, badly sited, badly laid out building that has taken place; mistakes that have been made when short-term pressures have dictated decisions that proved wrong. Many developments are attributed to planning failure which in fact were unavoidable; the result of industrial needs or of population increase. Some people seem to think of planning simply as a means of preservation; and to them the planning failures are all too numerous. It is a sad fact too that control, even when intelligently exercised, cannot force good development; it can only prevent bad. Nevertheless both the practice and the techniques of planning have come a long way since 1947; and take it all in all an enormous amount has been achieved. (Sharp 1969: 142–3)

1965–89

It is difficult to measure the effectiveness of the local plans prepared and adopted by the London boroughs, because of the external changes that occurred in respect of the operational context governing their observance and implementation. For example, this period witnessed political controversy about the government and planning of London. There were major disagreements between the government and the GLC, between the government and individual boroughs, and between the

GLC and individual boroughs. It was noted previously in Chapter 5 that the advent of the anti-motorway box movement in 1969 led to other political challenges to the established planning policies for London. These problems were compounded in the 1970s by growing doubts about the relevance of the GLDP. The 1980s witnessed growing uncertainty about the future of structure plans and even the need for, and future rôle of, land-use planning. Privatization, deregulation and private–public sector partnerships were now very much to the fore. Recognition of the fact that the implementation of local plans depended, in the main, upon private sector finance and initiatives led to the emergence of an "appeal-led" system of planning. This change in emphasis represented a "... shift from 'positive' planning to a more 'negative' style in which local government regulates development initiated by the private sector in response to market forces" (Davies & Bishop 1989: iii).

The 1970s and 1980s also witnessed the imposition, by Labour and Conservative governments, of increasingly tighter controls over local authority expenditure. Inevitably, individual London boroughs looked very closely at the resource implications of preparing and adopting a local plan. Although most boroughs were dissatisfied with the out-of-date provisions of the IDP, this did not, of itself, persuade some boroughs to embark upon the preparation of local plans. Even the transfer of additional development control powers from the GLC to the London boroughs, which highlighted the need for relevant up-to-date planning policies, did not result in total local plan coverage of Greater London (see Fig. 6.7). The diminished importance that the government attached to adopted local plans during the 1980s may well have led some boroughs to conclude that the expense of preparing and adopting a local plan was not justified.

The impact of the planning system, including the effectiveness of local plans, can be measured by examining the development control outcomes that resulted during this period. Between 1966 and 1991 over 82% of the 1.2 million planning applications determined by the 33 London boroughs were approved. Although it is difficult to determine the precise land-use implications of these decisions, because of the lack of accurate time-series data, it is possible to gain some impressions of the patterns of land-use change that resulted. Between 1966 and 1971, for example, there were increases in the amount of land given over to educational, residential, office and shop uses, and decreases in the amount of land given over to industry, commerce, public buildings and health. There was also a large decrease in the amount of open land. Further information is set out in Table 7.1.

Recourse to the net annual land-use changes which occurred during this period in the portion of the MGB located within Greater London provides further evidence of the effectiveness of the planning system. It can be seen from Table 7.2 that there were significant increases in the use of land for educational and other public purposes. These categories of development, which tend to retain the open nature of the land in question, accord with the general advice and guidance issued by the DoE (PPG2, Green Belts, January 1988).

Recent statistics issued by the DoE confirm that 80% of new development in Greater London took place on land that had previously been developed for urban

Table 7.1 Greater London land-use change, 1966–71 (hectares).

Land use	1966	1971	1966–71
Residential	53,844	54,122	+278
Industry	3,140	2,844	−296
Commerce	3,068	2,917	−151
Offices	1,524	1,567	+43
Shops	1,220	1,226	+6
Health	1,602	1,586	−16
Public buildings	3,641	3,369	−272
Education	5,618	6,018	+400
Open areas	46,169	45,367	−802

Source: 1978/9 *Annual abstract of Greater London statistics*, pp. 109–11.

Table 7.2 Greater London land-use change in the MGB, 1966–71.

Land use	1966	1971	1966–71
Residential	1,121	1,139	+18
Industry	72	79	+7
Commerce	72	92	+20
Offices	62	62	–
Shops	28	28	–
Health	378	356	−22
Public buildings	647	705	+58
Education	771	891	+120
Open areas	26,463	26,145	−318
Minerals	697	568	−129

Source: 1978/9 *Annual abstract of Greater London statistics*, p. 112.

uses. Over 32% of residential development in Greater London in 1987 had likewise taken place on land that had previously been used for residential purposes. Only 13% of the land developed for urban purposes in Greater London had previously been used for agriculture (4%) and other rural uses (9%) prior to 1987 (DoE, June 1992b: 5 and 8).

An independent study undertaken in 1986–7 concluded that the development plan system was working reasonably well in Inner London:

Unwanted development is controlled where there are up-to-date statutory plans or more recent supporting policies and development/planning briefs based on a consultation process; but the system of appeals does incrementally undermine some local planning policies. Furthermore the less than fully integrated way that public resources are bid for in some boroughs, and allocation priorities are decided upon at local and central government levels, militates against the full potential of the positive implementation rôles of the planning system. It is the case that planning in Inner London is mostly about the management of change; but such change is not all small-scale – least of all in the City of London and in the LDDC territory of North Southwark – and it is in these areas where the demands on the local planning system may pose the greatest challenges. In other parts of Inner London the greatest challenges are, first, the continued pressure for commercial development, including that related to tourism; and, second, the lack of adequate private sector or public sector investment to maintain or to increase those land uses and activities which create employment for the unskilled and adequate housing for those whose low incomes exclude them from access to the housing market. (Collins & McConnell 1988: 83)

1989–93

It is difficult at this juncture to reach any firm conclusions about the merits, let alone the effectiveness, of the UDPs that are currently being prepared and adopted by the London boroughs. The limited evidence to hand suggests that those boroughs with an established tradition of local plan adoption have built upon this foundation and incorporated, albeit suitably amended and updated, the key features of their local plans. The main advantages of UDPs compared to the previous system of structure and local plans are deemed to be local autonomy, the speed of preparation, the importance that is now attached to comprehensiveness, and better co-operation between neighbouring authorities (Carter et al. 1990). On the debit side, however, it should be noted that concern has been expressed about the limited importance that is attached to London-wide strategic issues and problems, the difficulty of co-ordinating some 33 separate UDPs, and the lack of local specificity of some plans. As a consequence it is sometimes difficult for local firms and residents to relate to the broad-brush approach to land-use planning that characterizes some UDPs. It is to be hoped that the boroughs will be both able and willing to prepare more detailed supplementary plans which can provide the positive land-use framework that is needed to generate local confidence and stimulate investment in the future of run-down and blighted localities. The recent City Challenge submissions from London and other parts of the country have highlighted the need for a fresh look at the relationship between land-use planning and urban regeneration. When he announced the winners of the 1992 City Challenge Competition, the Secretary of State for the Environment, Mr Michael Howard, said that:

> Unsuccessful authorities will naturally be disappointed. But the map-plans they have drawn up will provide a focus for future development of their areas, and may be used as a basis to make progress through private and public funding of some initiatives. (*Planning* 1992: 1)

Although the UDPs will no doubt be able to provide the guidance and control advocated in para 1.2 of PPG 12, it is less certain that they will be able to provide sufficient incentive to stimulate private sector development. The Confederation of British Industry (CBI) considers that the development of major sites in London is being delayed due to the lack of economic and planning policy. They recommend that a London Development Agency should be established to provide a London-wide perspective. This agency would be empowered to assemble sites (either by agreement or compulsorily) and to enter into agreements with private and public sector bodies, thus facilitating ". . . development to the benefit and enhancement of London's economy" (CBI 1991: 6). Clearly, there is also a need for more detailed land-use plans, such as those that formed an important and integral part of local authority submissions for the City Challenge Competition. Perhaps the final word should be left to another former Secretary of State for the Environment, Christopher Patten, who considered that:

> The planning system is in many ways the most effective tool of environmental management available to us. It offers us choices. It is important that local communities are given the maximum opportunity to make these choices for themselves; and that we exercise choice in the interests of quality – environmental quality, landscape quality, and quality of design. This is the best way of meeting the challenges that face us (Patten, 4th October 1989).

References and further reading

Carter, N, T. Brown, T. Abbott 1990. UDPs: style or substance? *Planning* **892**, 24–5.

CBI 1991. *A London development agency: optimising the capital's assets* (London Region Discussion Paper). London: Confederation of British Industry.

Collins, M. & S. McConnell 1988. *The use of local plans for effective town and country planning*. Town Planning Discussion Paper 48, Bartlett School of Planning, University College London.

Cullingworth, J. B. 1975. *Environmental planning 1939–1969*, vol. 1: *Reconstruction and land use planning 1939–1947*. London: HMSO.

Davies, H. W. E. & K. Bishop 1989. *Dacorum Hertfordshire: land use planning and the management of land use change*. Department of Land Management and Development, University of Reading.

DoE (Department of the Environment)

—1976. *Planning in the United Kingdom* (National report for Habitat Vancouver).

—1992a. *Development plans and regional guidance*, PPG12.

—1992b. Land use change in England, no. 7. *Statistical Bulletin* **92**, 4

Hall, P. 1973. *The containment of urban England*, vol. 1: *Urban and metropolitan growth processes*; vol. 2: *The planning system*. London: Allen & Unwin.

Herbert Report 1960. *Royal Commission on Local Government in Greater London 1957–60* (Cmnd 1164). London: HMSO.

LPAC 1994. *Advice on Strategic Planning Guidance for London*. Romford: London Planning Advisory Committee.

LCC 1960. *Administrative County of London Development Plan first review: County Planning Report*. London: London County Council.

Metropolitan County Councils 1984. *Town and country planning: The case for metropolitan councils*. London: Metropolitan CCs.

MHLG (Ministry of Housing and Local Government) 1951. *Town and country planning, 1943–1951* (progress report). Cmnd 8204.

Patten, C. 1989. "Planning and land use change." Statement issued by the Rt Hon Chris Patten MP, Secretary of State for the Environment. London: DoE.

PIEDA plc 1992. *Evaluating the effectiveness of land use planning*. London: HMSO.

Planning 1992. Regeneration agency to resolve control of power. (**978**, 1).

RTPI 1992. *Planning in London – ten years on*. London: Royal Town Planning Institute

(London Branch).

SERPLAN 1992. *Thirty years of regional planning 1962–1992* (RPC 2000). London: South East Regional Planning Conference.

Sharp, E. 1969. *The Ministry of Housing and Local Government.* London: Allen & Unwin.

Solesbury, W. 1974. *Policy in urban planning.* Oxford: Pergamon.

CHAPTER EIGHT

Planning implications of London's world-city characteristics

James Simmie

Introduction

This chapter takes up two of the main themes of this book and analyzes their implications for London in the context of its status as a "world city". The two themes are, first, the issue of the geographical definition of London and how this affects the scales of planning that are required to deal with London as a whole and, secondly, the paradoxical arguments that, on the one hand, everything is interconnected with everything else in London but, on the other hand, there are high degrees of structural differentiation and segmentation in both labour and housing markets.

Both themes are discussed in terms of the extent and power of the primarily economic structures and connections that make London one of a small handful of world cities. Here it is shown that, while London's population has been declining both absolutely and, in international terms, relative to other large cities, the economic power wielded from it has been growing.

Secondly, the economic effects of these changes are described. It will be seen that one of the major effects of the rôle that London plays in the global economy is to change the structure of its economy in such a way as to increase service employment and decrease local manufacturing jobs. These two sectors are highly segmented from one another, so that increases in service employment do not generally re-employ those workers who are losing their jobs as a result of local manufacturing decline.

Thirdly, these economic changes have interconnected social implications. As the job structure of London has changed, so has the social structure based on that employment. Some of the results include increasing social polarization between the insiders who derive economic benefits from London's world-city activities and the outsiders who bear many of the costs in terms of poor housing conditions and unemployment. It is argued that there is also an ethnic dimension that overlays this basic distinction.

Fourthly, the combination of London's world-city characteristics and their economic and social consequences are shown to have important spatial effects which confront land-use planners with special problems. These derive from the ways in which world cities and their major economic organizations structure their divisions of labour in space.

Fifthly, these interconnected problems are examined in terms of their main implications for planning. In this section it is argued that the definitions of issues and problems depends on whose interests are at stake and where they are located in space. Thus, what constitutes a planning problem for world-city insiders will not necessarily be top of the planning priorities of world-city outsiders. As they tend to live and work in different parts of London, this will also mean that the same general characteristic, namely London's world-city status, throws up different planning issues and problems in different parts of the city.

A concluding section draws these various discussions together. It makes the general point that planning London as a whole is indeed a very complex problem.

London as a world city

It is important to have a clear and precise definition of what is meant by the description "world city". As with the definition of London, "common sense" is not necessarily the best guide to which cities should be defined as truly world cities. Common sense, for example, might suggest that population size could define world cities. Those with the largest populations qualifying as world cities; increasingly this would confine cities defined in this way to the Third World where urbanization is rapid and giant cities are being created. Since 1950, for example, cities such as Mexico City, São Paulo, Shanghai, Calcutta, Buenos Aires, Rio de Janeiro, Bombay and Seoul have all overtaken London in terms of population. Figure 8.1 also shows that Tokyo and New York are significantly larger than London in terms of population. Nevertheless, simple population numbers are not, by themselves, sufficient to confer world-city status.

The idea of world cities originated with Patrick Geddes. In 1915 he published a seminal book called *Cities in evolution*. In it he described world cities as "those in which in which quite a disproportionate part of the world's most important business is conducted". This idea was taken up and elaborated more recently by Cohen (1981), Friedmann & Wolff (1982), Ross & Trachte (1983), and summarized by King (1991).

The two main arguments developed in this more recent work are:
- that, since the 1950s, a global market economy has been developing in which national markets are becoming linked through the growth of giant transnational corporations (TNCs) many of which have internal economies greater than those of all but a handful of nation states;

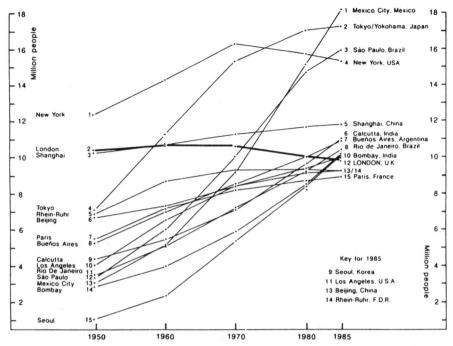

Figure 8.1 Growth and world ranking of the London metropolitan area, 1950–85. (*Source:* UN Department of International Economic and Social Affairs data tabulated in World Resources Institute, *World resources 1986*, table 3.3 (New York: Basic Books, 1986)).

– since about the early 1970s, the cities which have concentrations of the headquarters of these TNCs together with supporting producer services have developed into specialized world cities.

In such world cities are "the headquarters of the great banks and multinational corporations. From these headquarters radiate a web of electronic communications and air-travel corridors along which capital is deployed and redeployed, and through which the fundamental decisions about the structure of the world economy are sent" (Ross & Trachte 1983: 393).

A first approximation of which cities qualify as world cities on the basis of this definition can be gained by comparing the numbers of headquarters of TNCs in particular cities. Table 8.1 shows the cities with more than 10 such headquarters in 1984. On this basis New York, London, Tokyo and Paris stand out as world cities.

Cohen (1981) has refined such basic information and included banking as part of a statistical definition of world cities. He constructed two international indexes of business and banking. When combined, they indicate two main levels of world city. These are named in Table 8.2.

The concentration of economic power in London at the beginning of the 1990s is confirmed by Table 8.3. It shows the concentration of the headquarters of the largest 1,000 companies in Britain in the London region. It may be seen that

Table 8.1   Cities with more than 10 TNC headquarters, 1984.

City	No. of headquarters
New York	59
London	37
Tokyo	34
Paris	26
Chicago	18
Essen	18
Osaka	15
Los Angeles	14
Houston	11
Pittsburgh	10
Hamburg	10
TOTAL	252
WORLD TOTAL	398

Source: Smith & Fagin (1987), p. 6–7.
Note: Banks are excluded from this data source.

Table 8.2   World cities in the mid-1970s.

First rank	Second rank
New York	Osaka
Tokyo	Rhine–Ruhr
London	Chicago
	Paris
	Frankfurt
	Zurich

Source: Cohen (1981), p. 307–308.

around half of all the headquarters of these companies were located within the area covered by Greater London and the outer metropolitan area (OMA). It is this spatial concentration of economic decision-making power that defines London as a world city.

Economy

According to Friedmann & Wolff, "A primary fact about emerging world cities is the impact which the incipient shifts in the structure of their employment will have on the economy and on the social composition of their population" (Friedmann & Wolff 1982). The concentration, or, as economists like to call it, "agglomeration", of headquarters functions means that "The dynamism of the world-city economy results chiefly from the growth of a primary cluster of high-level business services which employs a high number of professionals – the transnational elite – and ancillary staffs of clerical personnel. The activities are those which are coming to define the chief economic functions of the world city; management, banking and finance,

Table 8.3 Spatial distribution of the headquarters of the largest 1,000 "industrial" firms located in the London region.

	Sectors			
	Manufacturing		Services[a]	
	Total	Foreign	Total	Foreign
London zones				
Central London	146		164	
Rest of London	58		44	
Greater London		73		44
OMA	85		45	
Outer South East	35		22	
Rest of South East		63		17
TOTALS	324	136	275	61

Source: adapted from "A new geography of London's manufacturing" by F. E. I. Hamilton, in *London: a new metropolitan geography*, K. Hoggart & D. R. Green (eds), tables 4.1 and 4.2, pp. 56–8 (London: Edward Arnold, 1992).

a. Excluding financial and legal.

legal services, accounting, technical consulting, telecommunications and computing, international transportation, research and higher education" (Friedmann & Wolff 1982).Table 8.4 shows the structure of employment in London in 1989. It shows that industry groups 8 and 9, (banking, finance, insurance, business services, leasing, public administration and other services), are the largest groups of employment in London. They provide some 2,897,000 jobs out of a total of 5,936,000 in the LMR as a whole. This constitutes nearly half of the total workforce. Public administration within this group is concerned, among other things, "with the maintenance and reproduction of the world city, as well as the provision of certain items of collective consumption: the planning and regulation of urban land use and expansion; the provision of public housing . . . transportation services; the maintenance of public order; education; business regulation; urban parks . . . and public welfare for the destitute" (Friedmann & Wolff 1982).

A second major group of world-city employment mainly serves this first group of relatively well paid and secure employees. Its demand is largely derived, and it employs proportionately a much smaller number of professionals: real estate, construction activities, hotel services, restaurants, luxury shopping, entertainment, private police and domestic services. A more varied mix than the primary cluster, its fortunes are closely tied to it" (Friedmann & Wolff 1982). Table 8.4 shows that this group of employees, construction, distribution, hotels, catering and repairs, constituted some 1,962,000 jobs, or approximately one third of the total workforce in the London Metropolitan Region (LMR) in 1989.

Not all of the employment in this group is as secure or well paid as that in the

Table 8.4 Employment by industry groups, 1989 (000s).

	Zones of London		
Industry groups	Greater London	OMA	London region
Agriculture, forestry and fishing	0	36	36
Energy and water supply	42	36	78
Manufacturing	442	521	963
Construction, distribution, hotels, catering and repairs	1,125	837	1,962
Banking, finance, insurance, business services, leasing	1,866	1,031	2,897
Public administration, and other services			
TOTAL	3,475	2,461	5,936

Source: Central Statistical Office (1991), p. 36.

first group. Much of the labouring employment in construction, for example, is seasonal and cyclical. Many hotel and restaurant jobs are both insecure and poorly paid. This is also true of culture and entertainment. Despite this, the London Planning Advisory Committee (LPAC 1991) study of London as a world city points to the much underrated importance of this employment. The cultural sector within the London core turns over some £7,500,000,000 per annum. It grew by some 20% during the 1980s to employ about 214,500 people directly. Its products attract national and international tourists to the capital.

These are catered for by a third cluster of employment in world cities identified by Friedmann & Wolff (1982). This cluster of jobs services international tourism. According to King (1991), tourist expenditure contributes some 8% of the core of London's gross domestic product (GDP). It supports about a quarter of a million jobs of which around a quarter are in hotels. As with the second cluster of service employment, some of these jobs are secure and well paid. Many, however, are part-time, casual and non-unionized. The net result of these latter characteristics is that hotel and catering is among the ten lowest-paid industrial sectors in Britain (King 1991).

A fourth cluster of employment in world cities is manufacturing. London is distinguished, along with New York, by a particularly marked decline in manufacturing and growth in financial services. Table 8.4 shows that manufacturing employment (industrial divisions 2–4) has now fallen to 963,000, or 16% of the total. There is also a preponderance of manufacturing production in the OMA (521,000 jobs), as opposed to the core of the metropolis which contained some 442,000 manufacturing jobs in 1989. Such manufacturing industry that remains in the London core is a mixture of high-technology (office machinery and electronic data-processing equipment), craft-based industry (e.g. leather goods) and information processing and dissemination (printing and publishing).

The decline of well paid, skilled and often unionized jobs in the middle of London's employment and income structure has contributed to income polarization. The growth of highly paid business and service occupations at the top, combined with the increase of low-paid, part-time temporary or casual work at the bottom, has increased both the high- and low-paid ends of the job structure while, at the same time numbers in the middle have declined. This has important social implications that will be examined in the following section.

A final cluster of situations in world cities is "the informal, floating or street economy which ranges from the casual services of day labourers and shoeshine boys to fruit vendors, glaziers, rug dealers and modest artisans" (Friedmann & Wolff 1982). Much of this is referred to as the "black economy" in Britain.

In addition to those in work, there are also the unemployed. These make up a large and varied group who have become marginalized from the sources of wealth creation in London. Accurate estimates of their numbers are hard to come by. Nevertheless, the House of Commons Library has analyzed the 1991 Census returns to show that, among the 100 wards in England with unemployment rates of 25% or above, 13 were in Inner London. These were mostly concentrated in the boroughs of Tower Hamlets, Southwark, Newham, Hackney, Lewisham and Lambeth. The rate was up to 33.9% in the Spitalfields ward of Tower Hamlets (House of Commons Library, Statistical Section, Research Division 1993; personal communication from Frank Field).

By 1992, unemployment had reached 10.6% or 418,100 in the London core (Employment Intelligence Unit, April 1992). It was generally higher around the Thames estuary and lower in the rest of the OMA. Within the London core itself, Table 8.5 shows that the highest levels of unemployment are recorded in Inner London. It is at its numerically highest levels mostly in a crescent of boroughs surrounding Westminster and the City of London to the north, east and south.

Table 8.5 London boroughs with the highest unemployment, 1992.

Borough	Number unemployed
Lambeth	23,910
Southwark	20,334
Hackney	19,698
Haringey	19,322
Lewisham	19,180
Brent	18,931
Newham	18,296
Wandsworth	16,928
Islington	16,031
Tower Hamlets	15,610

Source: Employment and Intelligence Unit (1992).

In 1988, *Regional trends*, showed that the crescent of boroughs around the east of Central London had both the same population and the same unemployment as Merseyside. Statistics such as these led to parts of London being placed on the new Assisted Areas Map which came into force in August 1993. They included the London boroughs of Newham, Enfield, Hackney, Waltham Forest and Tower Hamlets.

Thus, London's economy is marked by both great private affluence and extreme poverty. These contrasts are both a common characteristic and exaggerated by the economic conflicts located within world cities.

Social structure

The changes in London's employment structure described above (and in Ch. 2) are a major determinant of changes in social structure. These social changes can be summarized as:

  – growth in professional and managerial secure and well paid jobs
  – underpinned by growth in supporting service employment of which a minority is secure and well paid and a majority is insecure and poorly paid
  – decline in well paid skilled manual jobs
  – increases in the black economy and the unemployed.

These changes were already under way during the 1960s and 1970s. Table 8.6 shows the main occupational changes in the London region during these decades.

Table 8.6　Changing occupational structure among economically active males.

	Change, 1961–81 (%)		
Occupational group	Greater London	Rest of South East	England and Wales
Employers, managers, intermediate and professional	11	82	48
Non-professional, self-employed and farmers	30	76	37
Skilled manual, foremen and supervisors	−43	−7	−20
Semi-skilled, personal service, junior non-manual	−37	−7	−20
Unskilled manual	−49	−30	−35

Source: adapted from "The changing socioeconomic structure of London and the South East, 1961–81", C. R. Hamnett, *Regional Studies* **20** (1986), 391–406. (Featured in *The Observer*, 3 October 1993.)

It shows small or average increases in non-manual employment in Greater London and a much larger increase in these kinds of occupations in the rest of the South East. Conversely it shows very heavy falls in manual jobs in Greater London. In the case of unskilled manual occupations this decline amounted to nearly half the total jobs that were available in 1961.

This social restructuring in London, in common with other world cities, may be summarized as growth at the top the occupational structures combined with decline among middle-income blue-collar workers, and rising unemployment at the bottom; this is leading to social polarization. This is the most fundamental change taking place in the social structure of world cities. Increasingly, they are becoming cities for transnational elites and national professionals, declining numbers of middle-income manual workers, and a growing underclass consisting of the poorly paid, unemployed and/or ethnic minorities.

Some politicians have suggested that raising the incomes of the insider elites will lead to employment generation and a trickle-down effect of income to other social classes. But, Newman & Thornley (1992) assert that the trickle-down effect does not work. Reports by the Institute of Fiscal Studies and a government report itself support their view. They showed "that since 1979, tax and benefit changes gave an average £87 a week to the richest 10%, while the poorest 10% lost £1 a week. A government survey, *Households below average incomes*, stated in 1990 that from 1981 to 1987 average incomes rose ten times as fast as the incomes of the poorest 10% (*The Observer*, 3 May 1992: 20). Figures such as these underpin the argument that both economic and social polarization are increasing phenomena. They are at their most extreme in world cities such as London.

The operation of the original Abercrombie plan for Greater London (1945) encouraged and assisted many of the members of the skilled manual class to move out of London to jobs and homes in the new and, later, expanding towns. Those that remained have also been relatively successful in gaining access first to council housing and subsequently to private ownership.

Nevertheless, in London the decline of these classes is combined with poor education and training provision. This not only makes it difficult for existing skilled manual workers to retrain for the main groups of such jobs in high-technology (office machinery and electronic data-processing equipment), craft-based industry (e.g. leather goods) and information processing and dissemination (printing and publishing), but also reduces the chances of upward social mobility among the underclass.

The underclasses in London are a growing collection of outsiders. Most of them are unable to compete successfully in the labour and housing markets. They are also unable to participate effectively in the city's political and social framework. Many of them are brought up in one-parent families. According to the 1991 census, 17% of all children in Britain came from single-parent families; about 2 million dependent children are in 1.25 million one-parent families. The proportion for greater London was 22.6%, rising to 32.6% for Inner London, 41.6% in Lambeth and 60.1% in Lambeth's Prince's ward." (*The Observer*, 3 October 1993: 13).

Overlaying the underclass issue is that of race. The LMR has around 60% of the numbers of economically active persons from ethnic minority groups. It contains two thirds of those of West Indian and Guyanese origin. The latter group, age-for-age and qualification-for-qualification, has double the national unemployment rates (SERPLAN 1989: 3).

A recent study for the Royal Town Planning Institute (RTPI) by Thomas & Krishnarayan showed, in one unpublished paper, that "Over 25% of the population of Inner London is non-white, and Inner London contains the largest concentrations of 'Black Caribbean' (7.1%) 'Black African' (4.4%) and 'Black Other' (2.0%) in the UK. Outer London's population is 17% non-white and has important Indian settlements . . . It is clear, too, that the growing divide between rich and poor in this global city is, in general, creating more disadvantage for the black population than it is creating opportunities for advancement".

It may be concluded from this discussion that the social changes associated with London's development as a world city affect different social classes differently. On the one hand, there has been some growth in non-manual occupations; some of these are well paid and secure. On the other hand, many of the least skilled manual jobs have disappeared, leaving large numbers and concentrations of the unemployed. Combinations of unemployment, single-parent families and racial characteristics are developing a permanently excluded underclass in London.

Land-use structure

Demands for land uses are driven by the kinds of economic and social change outlined above. They are mitigated by existing uses and political decisions transferred through the land-use planning system. World cities such as London have some land-use demands which are either different from, or of a different order of magnitude from, other cities. This section will focus on these distinguishing land uses in London. They may be summarized as:

- in recent decades economic forces have led to the expansion of financial, business and producer services in the centre of London;
- economic forces have also driven the decline of industrial activities in an arc around the centre to the north, east and south; these boroughs have become areas of economic depression and social deprivation;
- this arc of economic and social depression around Central London has a handle that stretches out along the Thames estuary;
- new "sunrise" industries have developed in an arc further out in the OMA to the north, west and south of London's core.

As a result of these changes, London has now become a polycentric region containing over twenty separate travel-to-work-areas (TTWAs). Among the more important of these are Heathrow and Crawley, in which are located two of London's major airports, Heathrow and Gatwick. At the core of this region is Central London, comprising mainly the borough of Westminster and the City of London. It is this area that contains most of the activities that make London a world city. They are summarized in Table 8.7 At the moment, locating all these activities together

Table 8.7   Central London core activities.

Central London activities are defined as including those of national, international or regional importance, mainly depending for their efficient and convenient conduct on face-to-face contacts at the highest level, as well as housing for existing communities. A comprehensive list is impracticable, but by way of illustration they include the following:

The State: Royal palaces, Parliament, the Law Courts and Government departments

Overseas representations: embassies, high commissions and agencies

Finance: the Stock Exchange, central administrative offices of the Bank of England, clearing banks, overseas banks, merchant banks, discount houses, and insurances

Professional headquarters: headquarters of institutes or associations, and offices for regional and nationwide practice

Other headquarters: of other national associations and institutions

Communications: national press, publishing, advertising, radio, television and telecommunications

Shopping: a wide range, from those meeting day-to-day needs of residents and the workforce, to facilities of regional, national and international importance, such as specialist shops and showrooms

Religion: cathedrals and other national and religious centres

National collections: museums, art galleries, libraries, and other collections

Entertainment: concert halls, theatres and cinemas

Tourism: hotels and conference centres

Housing: provision for all income groups

Education: universities

Supporting activities are defined as those that provide essential support for the activities referred to above. They are vital to the functioning of the central area, although not necessarily located within it, and they include the following:

Transport: British Rail's Central London termini and other stations, London Regional Transport's services, and provision for taxis and essential car parking and servicing.

Local services: police, local government, banking, professional and local business offices, local churches, mosques, temples, synagogues, local press, community facilities, health facilities, shops, clubs, local cinemas and other entertainments, and schools for people living and working in the central activities zone.

Industry: industrial uses, many of which have important linkages with Central London activities, which help to widen the range of available jobs.

---

in Central London generates agglomeration economies. It provides opportunities for elite decision-makers to have face-to-face meetings. This is combined with close networking of supply, subcontracting, intermediate services and production. In addition, affordable offices in appropriate locations, a large and diverse pool of labour skills, and world class communications, all taken together form the bases of agglomeration economies.

Offices are the buildings in which most of these activities take place. The development and redevelopment of offices is one of the major concerns of land-use planning and as such is of particular concern here. London is well provided with office space. Table 8.8 shows the total office floor-space in different parts of London in 1991. At the time of writing, vacancy rates are up to 20% in these prime locations. This combined with the overall cost of living, personal taxes, office overheads, property and direct employment costs make London a cheaper office location than its main European competitors, Paris and Frankfurt (LPAC 1991: 59).

Despite these cost advantages a growing number of firms are moving their headquarters out of Central London for other reasons. A study by property devel-

Table 8.8   Central London office space, 1991.

Location	m^2 (million)
West End	7.0
City of London	4.3
Holborn	1.7
Other	1.1
In the pipeline:	
Docklands	2.0
Elsewhere	4.0
TOTAL	20.1

Source: LPAC (1991), p. 147–8.

oper Markheath (1992) found that 15% of London's thousand largest companies were contemplating leaving Central London within the next three years. Many have already departed (King 1991: 103). The reasons why firms are beginning to move their headquarters out of Central London are a complex combination of congestion and environmental costs (also of particular interest to land-use planning), together with the location of the homes of key decision-makers. One may speculate that the spread and development of new high-technology communications will enable this process to accelerate in the future.

At the same time that these processes are working out in Central London, the surrounding boroughs, particularly in an arc north, east and south of the core, have become areas of economic depression and social deprivation. The contrasts are so stark that some commentators have likened them to the differences between First and Third World cities (King 1991: 123).

In these Inner London boroughs "the polarization of high pay / high skill and low pay / low skill employment is reflected in an increasing spatial separation of residential space according to occupation, race, ethnicity and income. The degree of "ghettoization has greatly increased" (King 1991: 28). This arc of economic and social depression around Central London has a handle that stretches out along the Thames estuary. Here industries have declined and unemployment rates are up to 12.8% in Sittingbourne and Sheerness, compared with 9.1% for the South East Region (Employment and Intelligence Unit 1992).

In contrast to these areas of depression, technopoles – large concentrations of high-technology industries combined with research and development establishments and higher-education institutes – have developed focused on Berkshire and Hertfordshire in the OMA. These form the centres of the so-called Western Crescent of "sunrise" growth industries around the western periphery of London. These areas are responsible for much of the growth in employment in the OMA shown in Table 8.4.

These major world-city land-use phenomena are separated spatially from one another over the full scale of the London city region. The size of this functional region is significantly extended by the existence of the planned MGB. It is physically linked together by a transportation network that focuses mainly on the edges of the central area. The main exceptions to this arrangement are the North and South Circular roads and the M25. For those whose employers pay their transportation costs or who can afford to pay for themselves, this transportation network is just about adequate to make much of London one large labour market in which they can work. For the rest, it effectively cuts off those who live within one transportation corridor from looking for work in another. This segments London for its poorer residents, who are most in need of employment, into many separate local labour markets. This is particularly severe for those living to the east of Central London, where employment is scarce and unemployment high along the length of the transportation radials. CrossRail may improve this situation if it is ever built. Other European cities, such as Paris, already have such a system in place.

Planning issues and problems

In Chapter 1 the "real" London was defined on the basis of the extent of its daily, local economic linkages. In this chapter the special characteristics that differentiate it as a world city from other cities were also identified. The most important of these are its economic command and control functions. This section identifies the main planning problems that these urban results give rise to, which of them land-use planning can attempt to deal with, and the conflicts that influence its success.

What constitutes a planning problem depends, to a large extent, on who you are and what your interests in a particular issue are. World cities such as London contain major divisions of interest. The divisions that are focused on here are those between the organizations and social classes who may be described as world-city insiders and other citizens of London, many of whom are outsiders with respect to world-city activities. It is argued that where there is some connection between these two groups of interests in both intangible and spatial ways, then there is likely to be some agreement on the need for planning action. Where these interests do not overlap in economic or social terms or spatially, then it is likely that there will be conflicts over planning actions or inaction. Table 8.9 illustrates the perception of planning problems in London according to these major divisions.

Surveys of world-city insiders were conducted as the bases of the LPAC (1991) London World City report. From their points of view the most important attributes of a world city were wealth creation based on business and trade, combined with its global promotion, and the infrastructure of transport and communications that supports it. World-city functions are in competition with those in other world cities. There is therefore continuing pressure to remove obstacles to competition which are imposed by the central government. This process has made the City more of an unregulated enterprise zone than that in Docklands. This brings it into conflict with other citizens as physical expansion takes precedence over local housing, employment and environmental needs.

Table 8.9   Perceived planning problems in London, by interests.

World-city insiders	Outsider London citizens
Wealth creation Business and trade International rôle and global promotion Transport and communications	Transport
Business accommodation	Affordable housing
Innovation and enterprise	
Labour shortages	Employment opportunities Education and training Economic polarization Unemployment
Personal safety Congestion Environmental quality Pollution	Personal safety Congestion Environmental quality Pollution

Sources: LPAC (1988, 1991), SERPLAN (1989).

Despite this, wealth creation is significant for both insiders and other citizens. Differences of interest arise over the question of its distribution. The regressive distributions of wealth and income during the 1980s mean that, the further down the social structure, the less is the interest or benefit from wealth creation. Physical transport is of interest to both groups either to carry workers to work or to widen the effective labour markets for citizens. One would therefore expect considerable agreement between the two groups on the need for an adequate transportation system, but some conflict over its costs and who should bear them.

When the objective of wealth creation is translated into demands for buildings in which to conduct wealth-creating business, this contributes to high land prices and therefore increases the difficulties of producing affordable housing for other London citizens. Incomes and housing costs in London are such that the provision of new dwellings for one group in one part of London does not trickle-down benefits to other groups lower on the income scale. Development and redevelopment in London's core tends to intensify the crisis in housing. New developments in one place tend to be accompanied by accelerating decay elsewhere.

This conflict is made more severe by the stringent MGB policy which sharply reduces the supply of building land nearer to Central London and therefore increases its price by up to 40% (DoE 1992). High house prices serve to make the MGB a cordon sanitaire for world-city insiders who, paradoxically, tend to have their main homes outside the core and in the MGB. Very little of it is open to the public. In contrast, Paris, which has no green belt, has many acres of public forests interspersed by urban development. Some areas of the MGB land are derelict, polluted or inaccessible. The conflict between business uses and the need for affordable accommodation is seen most sharply in and around London's Docklands.

Innovation and enterprise are essential to the continual regeneration of wealth-creating economic activities. This may or may not be significant for ordinary citizens, depending on whether or not they are enabled to participate in the new forms of employment that result from innovation. At the moment, London's performance is poor both in encouraging innovation and in educating and training its citizens to participate in what innovation there is. Financial and business institutions have been criticized for their short-term attitudes to manufacturing, research and development and training.

This is in marked contrast to both Tokyo and Paris, both of which have developed large technopoles, new universities and training to staff them. In London similar developments centred in Berkshire and Hertfordshire have grown up in an *ad hoc* fashion, often restricted rather than assisted by planning policies.

A fourth group of planning problems that arise in London result from its rapidly changing world-city employment structure. On the one hand insiders experience labour shortages in skilled support services, such as computer programmers. On the other hand, many citizens whose jobs have gone, or those joining local labour markets, find that they do not have access to education or training that would equip them either to become insiders or to compete for insider support jobs. As a result, many citizens are finding themselves at the bottom of the polarized employment structure or, worse still, unemployed.

Economic and social conflicts such as these were a major factor in the 1970s crisis in New York which led to the flight of headquarters from the city. They were also a factor in the largest urban riots in the USA in South Central Los Angeles in 1992. If ignored on a permanent basis, they have the potential to undermine the incentives for world-city insiders to remain in Central London.

A final major group of planning problems concern what economists call public goods. These are goods, services or conditions that affect all individuals regardless of whether they are insiders or outsiders. For example, everyone has to breath polluted air. The special characteristics of public goods are that they are responses to collective problems that are very difficult to solve using normal market mechanisms. This usually means that a public organization, like a planning authority, is given the responsibility of solving those problems.

Differences of interest arise over who pays these public authorities to solve the problem. TNCs in particular are interested in having governments take on as much financial and organizational responsibility as possible for the costs of production, education and training, and the maintenance of law and order.

At the same time, multinational institutions and banks are also capable of undermining public policies. For example, much traffic congestion is caused by employers choosing to locate in particular areas and encouraging their employees to travel to and from work by car. Much of this congestion and its associated pollution could be avoided if the employers contributed capital to the public transport system and subsidized the use of it by their employees. At the moment, despite huge collective costs of congestion, they are usually unwilling to pay such costs.

Conclusions

The planning problems and conflicts facing planners in London are formidable. These conclusions discuss whether they have the tools for the job. First, the scope of planning action is summarized. This is much more limited than the extent of London's problems. Secondly, the appropriateness of the structure of planning in London will be discussed. Finally, the significance of politics and distribution with respect to planning London will be introduced.

Even focusing primarily on planning problems and conflicts in London throws up many issues that extend across the breadth of urban policy and cannot be dealt with by land-use planning in isolation from other policy fields. Therefore, it is appropriate at this point to summarize the limited scope of planning. In the first place, the statutory and legal powers of the planning system depend on the socio-political system in which it operates. Thus, for example, the legal powers of planners are different in more market-driven political economies such as the USA, and different again in what used to be collective political economies in such countries as the former Yugoslavia.

Secondly, within these political limitations, the planner in Britain "can to some extent influence the size and distribution of centres for office employment, shopping and services. In several ways – both by land-use controls and by the provision of vital infrastructure – he can influence the provision of, location, size, shape and density of new residential areas. He can also help shape the distribution of open space. He can try to affect the shape and mode of the transportation network that ties these various land uses and activities together" (Hall 1977: 251). Increasingly planners have also become interested in influencing employment structures in local economies. But they can do only what the statutory powers permit.

The powers that planners are permitted by central government have to be exercised within the local government structures established at different times by those same politicians. These structures changed radically in 1965 with the establishment of two-tier government in London's core, and again in 1986 with the abolition of the GLC. The result of all these changes is that there is no strategic planning authority for the whole of London.

In view of the complexity of London's interconnected planning problems and the lack of any unified mechanisms for dealing with them, it is difficult to see how its continued downward drift can be arrested. Some of the flavour of the magnitude of the task to be done was captured by the London Planning Advisory Committee in their strategic advice to the Secretary of State when they said that "The world-city aim will have to be pursued as much through macro-economic and other national policies as through planning activities. Equally, though, boroughs will need to reflect this larger-scale rôle as well as London's local needs when they come to review UDP policies" (*Planning*, 9 July 1993: 19).

References and further reading

Central Statistical Office 1991. *Regional trends 26*. London: HMSO.

Cohen, R. B. 1981. The new international division of labour, multinational corporations and urban hierarchy. In *Urbanization and urban planning in capitalist society*, M. Dear & A. J. Scott (eds), 287–315 London: Methuen.

DoE (Department of the Environment) 1992. *The relationship between house prices and land supply*. London: HMSO.

Dicken, P. 1986. *Global shift: industrial change in a turbulent world*. London: Harper & Row.

Dicken P. & P. E. Lloyd 1981. *Modern Western society: a geographical perspective on work, home and wellbeing*. London, Harper & Row.

Employment Intelligence Unit 1992. Press notice (May). London: EIU.

Friedmann, J. & G. Wolff 1982. World city formation: an agenda for research and action. *International Journal of Urban and Regional Research* **6**, 309–344.

Geddes, P. 1915 (1968). *Cities in evolution: an introduction to the town planning movement and to the study of civics*. London: Williams & Norgate (1968 edn, London: Benn).

Hall, P. 1977. *The world cities*, 2nd edn. London: Weidenfeld & Nicolson.

Hall, P. & D. Hay 1980. *Growth centres in the European urban system*. London: Heinemann.

King, A. D. 1991. *Global cities: post-imperialism and the internationalization of London*. London: Routledge.

LPAC 1988. *Strategic planning advice for London: policies for the 1990s*. London: LPAC.

LPAC 1991. London: world city moving into the 21st century. London: HMSO.

Markheath 1992. *Moving out – relocation trends among London's 1,000 largest companies*. London: Markheath.

Newman P. & A. Thornley 1992. Londoners lose out in world city stakes. *Planning* **961** (March), 6–7.

Portes, A. & J. Walton 1981. *Labour, class and the international system*. London: Academic Press.

Ross, R. & K. Trachte 1983. Global cities and global classes. The peripheralization of labour in New York City. *Review* **6**(3), 393–431.

Sassen-Koob, S. 1984. The new labour demand in global cities. In *Cities in transformation*, M. P. Smith (ed.), 139–172. London: Sage.

Singh, A. 1977. UK industry and the world-economy: a case of deindustrialization? *Cambridge Journal of Economics* **1**, 113–36.

Smith, M. P. & J. R. Feagin 1987. *The capitalist city*. Oxford: Basil Blackwell.

SERPLAN 1989. *Into the next century: review of the South East Regional Strategy*. (Consultation paper RPC 1500) London: SERPLAN.

Thrift, N. J. 1986. The internalization of producer services and the integration of the Pacific Basin property market. In *Multinationals and the restructuring of the world economy*, M. J. Taylor & N. J. Thrift (eds), 142–92. London: Croom Helm.

Townsend, P. 1987. *Poverty and labour in London*. London: Low Pay Unit.

CHAPTER NINE

London 1994:
retrospect and prospect

Peter Hall

The reader, having persevered so far, knows even better what he or she probably knew well enough before: that London is a fearsomely complex place, for which there are no neat and agreed prescriptions. Already in Chapter 1, there was the nagging and insoluble problem of definition: James Simmie argued convincingly that London could no longer be neatly bounded by the limits of the old Greater London Council or by the M25. It now meant something much larger; how much larger was and is open to argument. The fact is that London's influence extends far out along the lines of transportation and communication into the Rest of the South East (RoSE) and even beyond it, into the neighbouring parts of the South West, West Midlands, East Midlands and East Anglia regions, to constitute a Greater South East (Hall 1989). At this huge scale, however, the individual parts may be relatively self-contained in important respects, networked into a larger regional entity in other respects.

Places such as Bournemouth–Poole, Swindon, Milton Keynes–Northampton, Cambridge–Huntingdon–Peterborough and Ipswich, to take only a few of the more obvious examples, are important in their own right and are largely self-contained in terms of daily movements of people to work or to shop; but they exchange information with London, both in the form of movements of business and professional people, and of flows over electronic networks. Their dynamic growth in the 1980s is clearly related to their geographical position, but it is something more complex and more subtle than simply an outwash of people and jobs from London: although some people have migrated from the capital, others have migrated from other parts of the country; much of the employment growth is indigenously generated. So we are dealing here with a huge and complex metropolitan region, one of the largest in the world, the dynamics of which we still understand very imperfectly.

The contributors who follow Simmie have refused to be led down that treacherous road: they limit their London and thereby their problem, but by the same token they limit the depth of their analysis and the validity of their prescriptions. Within that more restricted and more familiar London, these contributions make clear that employment, housing and transport form a crucial planning triangle – crucial anywhere at any time, but more so in London because of the intensity and complexity of its problems.

The problem is that these problems simultaneously have an objective existence, but also come to be viewed according to what kind of a Londoner you are, in terms both of your ideology and (not unrelatedly) of your position in society. No one who has sought to live in London for a week, let alone a year, would seriously doubt these propositions: London's economy generates plenty of good well-paying jobs but also a host of poor-paying jobs and no jobs at all for a substantial minority of its population; Londoners pay more for their housing, and get less for their money, than other British people; London's road network is more congested than any other British city, its public transport system is more complex and more vital to its functioning than anywhere else, and as a result Londoners are more obsessed by transport problems than any other group in the country.

Yet, at the same time, as a Londoner your view of these problems will differ hugely, depending on who you are. You might be a fervent, unreconstructed true believer in planning; you might be an equally unreconstructed free marketeer for whom London society, like any other society, did not exist. Or you might, most likely, occupy a slightly sceptical position some way in between.

You might for instance be a single mother on a council estate in Hackney, widely perceived as not exactly a great place to live if you could help it, where your neighbours are nearly all other single mothers because the council had put you all there and everyone else had got out, trying to live on just over £100 a week and plagued by attempted break-ins and drug dealing on the deck outside. You might have little chance of a job because you left school at 16 and, well, your GCSEs are almost non-existent, and in any case there is the child care problem. Your mother, who is also living alone, is on the other side of London and getting to see her is a hassle, so there is not much support there either.

You might, on the other hand, be a champagne socialist in the leafier bits of Hampstead, chiefly concerned about the services (or lack thereof) provided by the local council to various deserving minority groups; your own job is in the media down in the West End, and it pays well enough except that the paper is losing circulation and there are rumours of a collapse and/or takeover by a rival, which causes some sleepless moments. The Northern Line is a mess and you think the government is cynically irresponsible in first promising money for modernization before the election, only to withdraw it afterwards. You would drive your car to work, but parking now costs £20 a day and the paper won't subsidize you, since your job does not involve unsocial hours. Your other worry is the local State school, and whether you can take the morally unacceptable step of removing your kids to the nice private school down the road, where their middle-class friends already go.

Or you might be an Indian shopkeeper in Wembley, worried mainly about reports in the local paper about racist attacks, and likewise concerned to get your children into the voluntary sector school which has such a good reputation. Or you might be a merchant banker commuting from the City to a large house on the edge of Wimbledon Common, who is delighted by his local council's record on the community charge and thinks that almost every other London borough is a quagmire of chronic mismanagement and fiscal recklessness. You have given up the District Line because your bank will pay for your parking, and the main bane of your life is the Wandsworth one-way system; you enthusiastically support the idea of road pricing because you suspect that you will be more than willing to pay the cost and that a goodly proportion of your fellow-commuters won't. You care not one whit about the schools, because both your boys are at Eton.

Those different backgrounds are not exactly reflected in the chapters that follow Simmie's. The reader should be warned (and, doubtless, by now, has perceived) that they represent a vigorous defence of what could be called the classical planning prescription. Their authors reflect a fairly consistent philosophy and view of the world: if not champagne socialism, then Sainsbury's Soave socialism. They are not people, you will have gathered, who are exactly ecstatic about Thatcherism and its successor.

That should be expected, because after all socialism was historically about planning, and planning historically grew up as part of the same reformist movement as did social democracy; as Michael Collins shows in his long historical account, it essentially started life as part of the post-war Welfare State. Thatcherism, as it set out to dismantle large parts of that structure, gave itself a mission of trimming the planners down to size, if not shrinking them into insignificance. So this collection of chapters represents a vigorous defence of the fundamental virtues of the planning approach, and – thus, almost inevitably – a counter-attack on the philosophies and politics of the governments of the post-1979 era. Fervently, their authors argue their message: we need a structured, hierarchical system of planning, in which strategic plans provide the framework for the detailed control of land use.

Those other Londoners, I think it fair to assume, would not be listening very attentively. For the odd fact is that not all, perhaps not any, of those Londoners would put planning anywhere near the top of their list of pressing concerns. They would be apt to care much more about immediate matters: getting and keeping a job, the arrival of the Giro cheque if the job is lacking, the traffic jams, the trains that fail to arrive or are run down when they do, the car radios that disappear in the middle of the night. Insofar as they think about planning at all, they are likely to side with Prince Charles and think that "the planners" are nerdy people who stop you putting in efficient double-glazed aluminium windows while licensing yet new high-rise speculative excrescencies. And that might equally go for Clapton mums, fashionable Hampsteadian media folk, Wembley shopkeepers or striped-shirters from Wimbledon village.

Most of these people will see planning the way Prince Charles sees it: in strictly physical terms, in brick and concrete manifestations. So the planners get blamed for the excesses of the architects, which is part unfair because (as the planners will tell you) they have been told not to worry too much about aesthetics, partly fair because when they did worry they were not much good at it, because rather remarkably they had never been trained for that job. But planning means something else, something deeper and therefore more significant, which is what this book's contributors are bothered about: the planning *style*. They argue, and their argument is worth hearing, that you cannot get cities right by allowing the market simply to let rip; that first you must provide a framework, within which separate decisions (by individual people, and individual organizations) can be better related to each other. That way, the planners' self-defence runs, everyone will finally be better off – even though some people will kick when the resulting decisions seem to go against them individually.

There is a textbook example: traffic congestion. As each person joins the morning traffic queue on all the main radial roads into London, all these drivers consider only the individual consequences, not the effect on all the rest of the drivers. As a result, all of them are worse off. There are two ways out: either regulate to push some of the drivers off the road (by parking restrictions, for instance), or price them off (by parking meters or permits). In effect, in London and all the other cities of the world we have done a bit of both, but not enough, and not consistently. We may take a further massive bite at the problem, through pay-as-you-go road pricing; but still, we would probably require co-ordination in other areas, such as Red Routes to keep traffic moving along main arteries, and provision of alternative public transport, probably with built-in priority. In fact, that is just the bundle of policies that the Government is at present working on.

This is just one obvious example; there are scores of others. The economy, for instance: firms, especially the more dynamic ones in areas such as high-tech manufacturing and business services, have preferred to locate west of London because there they get a good environment, the right kind of labour force that can pay to live in that good environment, and access to Heathrow. Especially in boom times, the west of London has overheated (for proof, look at the M25, any morning or evening) while the east has languished. We could try to deal with this by a differential tax on firms in the west, or by tough planning controls there, or by trying to make the east more attractive. Over the past fifty years we have avoided the tax answer, used the control solution intermittently, and are now just starting on the third solution through the East Thames Corridor strategy.

The big argument of the contributors to the middle part of this book is this: that, quite contrary to the style of the early 1980s, strategic planning is far from dead. Only by setting a broad framework for the orderly development of London, and then translating that framework into local plans, will we avoid chaos and muddle. That argument, it could fairly be said, is now generally accepted: we are a long way beyond the attempt to set the people free from the planners. During the late 1980s and early 1990s, successive (Tory) governments have firmly set in place a coherent system, whereby designated local authority associations – the London Planning Advisory Committee (LPAC) within London and the Standing Conference for South East Regional Planning (SERPLAN) for the whole area of the South East – proffer official advice to government, and government responds by issuing regional guidance, which provides firm guidance to the local planning authorities in drawing up their own plans. So maybe no one is arguing about planning very much any more. Or maybe they are: as so often, in political polemics we stress the differences. The main point of difference is about public spending: the contributors are essentially saying that we need to spend much more on job creation, on public transport, on affordable housing. That is a legitimate political stance, although in practice any government, however inclined to spend, would find that it depended on the state of the public finances. Extending regional aid to parts of London, as the Government did in 1993, can encourage employers to locate there. Major new public transport links, such as the Jubilee Line extension through Docklands, and maybe CrossRail if it proves affordable, could improve access to those same areas. The East Thames Corridor offers a unique potential for building affordable housing on brownfield sites, if only the money can be found from English Partnerships, the English urban regeneration agency, to clean them up first.

Before we return to these basic questions of 1993, though, it is helpful to step back and up. How is it that the image of planning became so discredited? Why has it become so much an object of interest or derision? How could a professional movement become so fundamentally politicized? The answer is to be found over the history of the past 50 years, and in particular of the past 30.

Planning in London: how we got from there to here

For it was not always thus. The world has hugely changed since 1943–4, when Abercrombie and his minuscule team braved the buzz bombs to produce their two momentous plans, and when a popular Penguin version sold in its tens of thousands to the troops. It has changed a great deal even since 1969–70, when two considerably larger teams produced the logical successors to Abercrombie: the Greater London Development Plan and the Strategic Plan for the South East, and when interest was such that the London plan attracted 28,000 objections. The changes can be summed up under these heads: a weakening belief in the efficacy of planning, but above all of large-scale strategic planning; correspondingly, a new division of powers between central and local government; a new emphasis on large-scale project planning, or mega-developments, with associated infrastructure; a shift of focus from New Town building to inner urban regeneration and, for the future, corridor approaches; finally, greater stress on efficiency aspects, and above all on London's competitive position *vis-à-vis* its global competitors, especially on the nearby European mainland, and less stress on equity aspects.

The death of strategic planning?

The demise of strategic planning seemed to have definitively taken place in 1983, when a government White Paper declared that the Greater London Council (and the six Metropolitan County Councils in the conurbations of provincial England) had been set up during "the heyday of a certain fashion for strategic planning, the confidence in which now appears exaggerated" (Secretary of State 1983: 2); they had been engaged in "a natural search for a "strategic" rôle which may have little basis in real needs" (ibid.: 3). But the reports of its death may have been exaggerated. A decade later, as already noticed, there is still in place a formal – indeed, strengthened – mechanism for strategic planning, through shared responsibility between central and local government.

What has gone is the Greater London Council, set up in 1963–5 with the specific aim of providing a framework of strategic land-use and transport planning for the whole of the continuously built-up conurbation. But there are strong doubts, in retrospect, whether the GLC ever performed that rôle effectively, or indeed at all. If it was to have done that, it would have to have had some overriding powers over the 32 boroughs, as well as direct powers in road-building, public transport investment and management, and traffic control. It did some of these things not at all, because it was not given no powers or inadequate powers (over public transport for instance) or because it abdicated its rôle (in road-building for instance) or because it lost power steadily to the boroughs (as over land-use planning).

The experience with land-useplanning is particularly instructive. Here, the GLC acquired considerable powers from the old London County Council in the 117 square mile Inner London area; outside it, where the previous history was extremely complex, it never exercised the same authority. Its Greater London Development Plan was supposed to produce clear and binding guidelines for the boroughs, and in the case of major developments crossing borough boundaries (as in Covent Garden, or Docklands) it was specifically given a direct co-partnership rôle. But the boroughs, which built up well staffed planning offices from the start, were jealous of their powers and they resented GLC interference; in practice, it always seemed to be the GLC that beat a retreat. Because of the inordinate time that passed in the early years – four years to write the GLDP, three more for a huge public inquiry, yet another four before government approval was forthcoming – it was over a decade, almost half the GLC's life, before the guidelines were forthcoming. From then on, used to going it alone, the boroughs tended to fight the GLC every inch of the way. And the issues over which they fought were major, like the GLC's attempts to develop large-scale public housing enclaves in outer boroughs.

So, it could be argued in retrospect, the GLC represented a "flawed design" (Flynn 1985: 64–5): a slim strategic authority could never work, because it lacked the critical powers of implementation. This short and tragic history thus provides a warning: it was not so much that strategic planning was inherently unnecessary, undesirable or impossible to achieve; it was that in practice, the GLC almost managed to make it look all three.

But that was compounded by the fact that political control tended to change hands at every election, so that eventually every issue became bitterly politicized. Perhaps, it can be argued, that reflected the uniquely confrontational political style of the late 1970s and early 1980s, and so provides little guidance for policy in the 1990s. But in Chapter 4 of this book John Gyford stresses a different explanation: the nature of London politics was changing, even before Thatcher arrived in 1979. London, he argues, last enjoyed any kind of political stability under the old London County Council, before 1963. Thereafter, the entire GLC era was character-ized by political instability, coupled with fighting between the boroughs, and by the emergence of a new kind of neighbourhood politics, especially on the Labour side. In a sense, then, Thatcherism exploited this instability by promising to end it. It seemed that this was successful – but the emergence of a particularly vicious neighbourhood politics, in Tower Hamlets in summer 1993, may signal that the era of instability is not yet over.

The new division of powers

The point about the GLC's abolition is that, logically, its formal powers (as distinct from what was happening in reality) were redistributed both downwards and upwards. Most planning powers were transferred to the City and the 32 boroughs, which were given the responsibility of producing unitary plans as well as powers over 825 miles of highway. But in both planning and transport, central govern-ment acquired wide powers of direction; while responsibility for London Trans-port went to the Department of Transport. However, to return to the critical point, in late 1993 strategic planning is far from dead: the London Planning Advi-sory Committee in London, the South East Regional Planning Conference within the wider region, produce regional advice, to which the Department of the Envi-ronment responds with regional guidance. In effect, there is a new official prescrip-tion, formalizing arrangements which – in the case of SERPLAN – go a long way back: strategic regional planning results from a process of negotiation between local authority planning associations and a small central planning team in the Department of the Environment, in both cases mediated politically.

Powerful (and reasonably un-ideological) voices have been raised in favour of something stronger (Dahrendorf et al. 1992). London, it is argued, is weakened internationally by being the only major city in the world without a defined urban authority or a recognizable political leader. However, this argument contains two rather different strands. One is that on the grounds of protocol there may well be a case for an office, and an individual, to represent London in international gath-erings and negotiations. But this is not the same thing at all as the other argument, which is that London needs a strategic planning authority. With the GLC firmly abolished, and a new set of machinery in its place, the case for a strategic authority really needs to be made *ab initio*. In particular, its protagonists would need to show precisely, first, how such an authority would avoid falling into the same trap as the GLC and, secondly, how it would perform better than the slimline LPAC–SERPLAN–

DoE triangular structure that has taken the GLC's place. It might well be possible to make such a case; but it does not yet seem to have been made.

The age of the mega-project

There is however an important sense in which strategic planning, if not deceased, is at least enfeebled. It is that the strategic planning *style* no longer dominates. Instead, the 1980s and 1990s have seen a new emphasis – not merely in Britain, but worldwide – on the planning of large-scale individual projects. Of course, such an emphasis is not new: the 1950s and 1960s saw the construction of the Mark One New Towns and the reconstruction of the Barbican and East End, the 1970s that of the Mark Two New Towns, while in Europe major projects such as Hötorget in Stockholm, or La Défense in Paris, really set the tone for subsequent mega-projects elsewhere. But there were distinctively new features of the major projects of the 1980s, which in some ways set them distinctively apart.

The first was their scale. There really was no precedent for the reconstruction of London Docklands, although the Glasgow Eastern Area Renewal of the 1970s was perhaps the nearest. For this there was a simple reason: it was the unprecedented scale of the opportunity represented by the sudden collapse of the traditional inner-city economic base of manufacturing and warehousing, almost contingently associated with the new demands of the informational and image-building sectors of the economy. That these would coincide was not evident to anyone in the early 1980s, certainly not to the entrepreneur-planners of the London Docklands Development Corporation who allowed almost anything to happen on the Isle of Dogs. It took the consequences of the Big Bang in the City, coupled with that entrepreneurial approach and the vision of transatlantic property developers, to make it happen.

When however it did, it began apparently to illustrate a new principle: not merely could very large tracts of urban land be recycled from one use to another, but also that in the process the entire image of an area could be transformed, from totally derelict and undesirable to super-glitzy. So spectacular was this transformation, that by the end of the 1980s one influential school of academic interpretation was suggesting that this constituted a major structural shift in the nature of our consciousness of the world: this was the beginning of the age of postmodernity, an age in which the image progressively overwhelmed reality.

Be that as it may, the new approach did transform the image, although, as detailed in Chapter 5, the job was left only half-way finished when the great recession of the 1990s descended on the development and construction industries. The central question, sharply brought into focus by that recession, concerned the economic base of the entire recycling operation. It was evident enough what it was recycling *from*: older workshop manufacturing, port and warehouse activities, associated maritime industries. For a time in the 1980s, it also seemed evident what it was recycling *to*: a range of housing that catered for the new socioeconomic groups, from starter homes in Beckton up to luxury penthouses in the old wharves;

homes for the relocated information industries, especially newspapers and TV studios; finally, large-scale office redevelopment for the financial services and headquarters offices, that constitute another part of the informational sector of the economy. In other words, Docklands was logically responding to the great structural change in advanced economies during that decade: the transition from the manufacturing and goods-handling to the informational economy.

But by 1994, with a huge overhang of unlet offices on offer at fiercely competitive rents, and the first faint stirrings of renewed interest restricted to a few prime City sites, the last of these did not seem an immediate realistic prospect. So it appeared clear that completion of the Docklands project would have to depend on new kinds of activity: leisure, entertainment, culture, education, all the "cultural industries" that have represented, together with the informational sector, the other half of the great economic transition of the late 20th century.

That was a major question mark, because by then the Docklands project, vast as it had been, was giving way to something much larger: the East Thames Corridor project, which would involve the recycling of land and the restructuring of the economy over a much larger area, on both sides of the lower Thames, from the Royal Docks and the Greenwich peninsula all the way down to Tilbury–Gravesend and the Medway Towns. Blessed by then Environment Secretary Michael Heseltine in a statement in March 1991, this project was under intense study during 1992–3; in March 1993 it was put into the hands of a Department of the Environment Task Force, which reported early in 1994. The entire project had received a major boost in October 1991 from the Government announcement that the Channel Tunnel rail route would be routed through the corridor, thus offering the prospect that new stations could be created as a basis for activities requiring fast access to the European mainland.

Bold as was the original Docklands project, East Thames in a sense is even bolder, because it can no longer depend on the advantage of proximity to the Central London core; it must succeed as a project for a new kind of linear, polycentric urban structure, with dense urban subcentres resembling the "Edge Cities" that have proliferated in the United States in recent years. But, unlike most of those, the new centres would be strung along a new public transportation spine; the nearest parallel would be with major developments in Paris, such as La Défense, the Charles de Gaulle Aerogare, Eurodisney or Massy–Palaiseau.

There is a deeper parallel here. In the mid-1960s, as Britain planned the three Mark Two New Towns for London (Milton Keynes, Northampton and Peterborough), France planned a series of new towns (eight, later collapsed to five) around Paris. Over the intervening quarter-century, both countries completed their plans. When it came time for the French to produce another 25-year plan, the resulting blueprint contained no further proposals for new towns: instead, all the stress was on new commercial cores within the existing urban fabric, linked by new and highly ambitious public transport proposals (completion and extension of the RER; the TGV interconnection through the eastern and southern suburbs; the ORBITALE and LUTECE schemes to provide two new public transport rings around Paris).

Although London has produced no such blueprint (strategic planning may not be dead, but it is low-key), the stress here too has changed, in exactly the same way. The Mark Two New Towns are essentially complete; proposals for privately financed new communities, encouraged by the Thatcher administrations in the early 1980s, mostly died in the face of local opposition; essentially, East Thames is supposed at least in part to take their place, by providing land for affordable housing on a large scale. But more importantly still, the Parisian growth poles and East Thames represent the new spirit of planning in the 1990s: based on very large projects with a strong economic emphasis, especially directed at the informational and cultural sectors, and dependent on new forms of public–private sector co-operation.

The new global competition between cities

Most fundamentally of all, the very large projects are now seen as central elements of global competitive strategies for entire cities. As James Simmie shows in Chapter 8, a major new feature of the 1980s is the globalization of a wide range of economic activities, not merely manufacturing but also services, and the growth of a relatively few major cities worldwide, as control and command centres for the international economy. The result is intense and increasing competition between cities, internationally, in order to maintain and enhance their relative position.

The French, in their 1991 plan for Paris, have been quite specific about this: in the very words of the plan's title, this is a charter at the hour of the opening-up of Europe; the aim is quite consciously to make Paris the economic and cultural capital of the continent, and the different elements – the investment in transportation and communication infrastructure, the direct linkage to the creation of new commercial poles, the great cultural projects – are all designed, equally consciously, to that end (Anon 1991). Key decision-makers and opinion-formers in London are acutely aware of this challenge, which became the central theme of a major conference convened by the London Planning Advisory Committee in November 1991.

It centred on three main themes. First, planning, where the main topic was the need to improve mobility, above all through better public transport. The aim had to be to restructure London, like Paris, around strong activity points at major public transport interchanges. On quality of life, the consultants to the conference found a mixture: London scored moderately on air quality, high on open space, fairly high on freedom from crime, and very high on cultural provision. On education and training, the consultants painted a critical picture: fewer London workers received academic or professional education, compared with other world cities; Londoners were not being educated for the new jobs being created in London, which were filled by long-distance commuters, while Londoners remained unemployed. One particularly telling statistic: not a single Bengali inhabitant of Spitalfields was found to be working in the City of London a few hundred yards

181

away. But there was a brighter picture under the heading of innovation, enterprise and the rôle of culture. There is huge potential here to capitalize on British creativity, and on the fact that English is the new universal language.

Thirdly, promotion. Here, unhappily, was a tale of missed opportunities: the 1996 Olympics, the lack of a World's Fair, the fact that even the idea of a Eurodisney is received with horror in some circles. The consultants proposed a promotional and protocol agency to represent the capital: a London Partnership, which would perform the rôle, yet would not create the threat of a huge new level of government.

The Government responded with the London Forum, to act as a kind of gingergroup lobbying organization; and the private sector responded with London First, as a promotional agency. Then, in autumn 1993, it announced that to simplify matters and avoid confusion, the two would be merged. It would have been surprising if the challenge from the mainland – most dramatically illustrated by Frankfurt's victory in the battle over the location of the agency that will logically become the European Central Bank, if and when monetary union is achieved – did not remain a major theme in London planning for the remainder of the 1990s, or at least as long as the European project remains alive.

But this concern represents a deeper shift of emphasis. During the 1980s, social concerns clearly took second place behind wealth creation as the first priority of politics. Although one might argue that this reflected a political priority of successive Thatcher governments, it clearly reflected (or, perhaps, led) a similar groundswell throughout the advanced world, as evident in democratic Socialist countries such as France and Spain as in countries with right-wing governments. It was, fairly clearly, a reaction to the great restructuring crisis of the late 1970s and early 1980s, and to the opportunities presented by globalization and structural economic change in the half-decade that followed. The recession of the early 1990s is bound to shift those priorities somewhat, but perhaps not as much as might at first be supposed: worldwide, there appears to be a new and non-traditional politics of interest, in which lower-middle income groups are often aligned against the politics of welfare. Certainly, in Britain in the autumn of 1993, all three major political parties seemed to be edging themselves, with varying degrees of caution, to align with the middle class on this issue.

Emerging questions for the 1990s

Life moves on; and planning, like the political process of which it is a part, adjusts to face new issues and new problems. There appear to be at least four of these, which may come to dominate the urban and regional agendas in London (and indeed in Paris, New York and Tokyo) in the mid-1990s.

New sources of economic growth

The first is how soon and in what way the urban economy will resume its upward growth trajectory. Like so many other cities, but more radically and more spectacularly than most, London restructured its economy during the 1980s, out of the production and exchange of goods, and into the production and transmission of information. But in the global recession of the late 1980s and early 1990s, that process came almost to a grinding halt – as witness the huge backlog of unlet office space all over London, but above all in the centre and Docklands. By all accounts, even if developers again begin to develop offices, they will be on prime sites, and much of the unlet space will take a long time to clear; so development on peripheral sites may take a long time to resume. And meanwhile, large parts of London – mainly but not exclusively in the east and inner south – are faced with a new situation: that they are actually performing below national norms in terms of basic economic indicators such as employment. In 1993, for the first time in the history of regional assistance in Britain, substantial areas of London found themselves included in the redrawn map of the assisted areas.

That being so, we may be faced with the need to rethink the rôle of some key areas, such as the still-undeveloped parts of Docklands. Perhaps the newer, softer informational sectors – culture, the arts, entertainment, education – may provide the basis, as already anticipated in LDDC's brief for the Royal Docks. Perhaps, as many suggest, we should exploit the opportunity to develop more housing closer to the centre of London, and to the jobs already created in Docklands, thus satisfying the insistent demands for sustainable urban development.

Sustainable urban development

Sustainable development seems likely to continue to be a major theme, not only because of the impact of all the directives flooding out from Brussels, but also because British policy is becoming a lot more prescriptive in the field. (Consider for instance the Department of the Environment Planning Guidance note PPG-13, a notable policy milestone which reverses many trends, including the development of out-of-town shopping centres). There is a paradox, though: research from Michael Breheny has used DoE-sponsored research (from ECOTEC) to conclude that over the past 30 years, population trends in this country have taken us steadily away from a sustainable form of urban development (Breheny & Rookwood 1993). (Put simply, fewer people are now living in places that are economical in resource use, more of them in extravagant places). The only relief is that the overall effect on energy consumption is not that huge.

The clear implication is that, if possible, we should seek to slow and even to reverse the steady outflow of people and jobs from London (and indeed the other conurbations). How to achieve this, in a democratic and market-driven society, is not easy, particularly since we do not know enough: we need much better understanding of the precise impact of different patterns of living and working on total energy use and on pollution. Are compact cities and higher densities really to be preferred? Or would we do better to encourage people to move out into new Milton Keyneses? The ECOTEC research does not give us the whole answer: its data are presented in rather large geographical units (such as Inner and Outer London) and we need something finer-grained.

Properly designed, with a good admixture of homes and job opportunities, the East Thames Corridor could make a powerful contribution to sustainable urbanism. So, perhaps – depending on further research – would reasonably compact extensions of existing medium-sized cities and towns in the rest of the South East, grouped in clusters to maximize short-distance employment and service access. So, within limits, would be further development in London itself, especially close to public transport. All three policies could help at least to slow down and even halt the trend away from sustainability, even if they cannot reverse it. But more work is needed.

Private–public partnership

The East Thames Corridor is important in another way: it is likely to become one of the first test cases in Britain of the new rules for private–public partnership in development, which were anticipated in the Chancellor of the Exchequer's Autumn Statement of 1992. The argument is simple enough: only private enterprise could and should be responsible for most of the urban development – whether of houses, factories, offices, research parks, entertainment – in the Corridor. But equally, none of this will happen without a public contribution – to clear and prepare the land, to provide basic services, and to build roads. The new urban regeneration agency, English Partnerships, just beginning its work in the autumn of 1993 under the chairmanship of Lord Walker, will play a crucial rôle. But it will have to understand what the private sector might commit.

The same applies to a crucial piece of infrastructure associated with the Corridor, indeed underpinning it: the high-speed rail line from the Channel Tunnel to London. The Government has stated that it wants to see the private sector involved. Meanwhile, the planning work is in the hands of a public sector subsidiary, Union Railways (part of BR). What is to be the exact rôle of the public and private sectors here? And beyond that, the same kinds of question are involved in the construction of CrossRail, the major east–west express line under Central London, which would also provide commuter services to and from the Corridor.

The Government's position, which emerged in the course of a year since the original announcement, was that the private sector could come and talk. They have, but there have been few firm agreements. This is new and uncharted territory, certainly in Britain, perhaps anywhere. It may take time. In late 1993, the Government set up a new high-powered advisory group, chaired by Sir Alistair Morton (Chairman of Eurotunnel) to make recommendations on how to achieve it. Meanwhile, critical developments – such as East Thames – turn in considerable measure on the success of the negotiations.

184

Polarization and the urban underclass

There has been concern that in British cities we are seeing the emerging problem of an urban underclass – variously symbolized by homelessness, vagrancy, travelling populations, poor single-parent households, long-term unemployment, drug dependence, and a high incidence of mainly petty crime – side by side with the social mainstream, but often evoking little sympathy from it, particularly in battles over resource allocation. But, insofar as the underclass is truly an urban and above all a big-city phenomenon – a proposition that might of course be challenged – the politics of welfare are bound to loom at least as large in London, and above all in certain parts of London, as anywhere else. There is a real question as to whether London is becoming polarized in the same way as allegedly has occurred in New York, with an affluent population living cheek-by-jowl with an urban underclass, and with a disappearing middle as lower-middle income groups leave the city. On that, there is so far no firm statistical evidence, though doubtless analysts will comb the 1991 census results for it.

One comfortable view is that it is all a matter of the macro-management of the economy: a rising tide will float all boats, even those that now appear well and truly sunk. But, given the scale of the huge structural adjustments in economies everywhere (not just in Britain), this is beginning to look over-sanguine: the educational and skill demands of the new information economy, the evident failure of a part of the young population to meet these, the mounting evidence of serious social malaise in the form of crime, drugs and family breakup – all these suggest that much longer-term social forces are in motion.

The interesting fact is that there is little specific attention, on anyone's part, to the spatial policy implications of the underclass debate. For instance, it is not clear whether and how far poverty and social malaise are spatially concentrated, or if indeed their spatial incidence coincides. This stands in sharp contrast to the United States, where a vast amount of work has been done on such questions in recent years. From this, it follows that it is virtually impossible to derive any well based policy conclusions. Would it be right, as Victorian reformers thought one hundred years ago, to try to break up spatial concentrations of poverty by planned dispersal to suburbs or new communities? Or should attempts be made at dispersal within London, so as to maintain contacts with employment, family and social networks? Quite apart from the fact that such policies are currently out of fashion (and would be politically difficult, if not explosive), we do not have the database to begin to answer the questions.

The rôle of planning

This list is far from exclusive. Others would frame it differently, with different emphases and other items: affordable housing, modernizing the infrastructure, developing a jobs strategy (to quote again those prescriptions from Ch. 3). Employment, housing and transport constitute a kind of holy trinity of urban and regional planning, and all those who practice it return to these three, at whatever angle they do so.

But the angle is important: it depends on the shifts of popular and media and political perception, which constitute a kind of conceptual scanning device, colouring and emphasizing the image now this way, now that. There can be little doubt that British preconceptions of the 1990s are different from those of the 1960s or the 1930s, which so powerfully shaped the planning system and its thoughtways; among the most important current concerns are the overwhelming importance of wealth creation through market mechanisms; consequently, the rollback of the Welfare State and the injection of the market into areas from which it has been excluded, with all the consequent problems of developing new kinds of management of quasi-public, quasi-market services; and the concern with social breakdown and the need to reassert the moral basis of the social order. These are concerns that at first sight appear traditionally Tory ones, but are now shared by all parties; they seem to represent some kind of sea-change in British politics. Nor do they simply represent the triumph of the free-market policies of the early 1980s. There are the beginnings of a fundamental debate on the nature of the British economy and society in the 21st century, whose outlines are as yet dimly perceived.

Where will planning stand in all this? It is too well established a British institution, after nearly half a century of life, simply to wither away; it has a very powerful political constituency, broadly based right across the fundamental party lines; it withstood the ideological assaults of the early 1980s, which more or less proved its immortality. But it will need to learn to adjust to a subtly different socioeconomic system; it may well need to become yet more entrepreneurial, yet more responsive to change.

The problem is that, in strict statutory terms, planning has a definite and a limited remit – far more limited, indeed, than most people would credit. Essentially, ever since the historic 1947 Act, it has been concerned with making plans and enforcing development control. Since the 1990 and 1991 Acts, it has been in a sense both more focused and more rigid: the plan is now the definitive document to which reference must now be made, first and foremost, in determining whether a development should be permitted or not. The problem is that, in terms of what actually happens to any area, other policies and other considerations may loom much larger than the development plan: investments by the Department of Transport in road and rail, the regeneration programme of English Partnerships and the DoE's urban programmes, the designation of heritage and nature protection and their enforcement through the European courts. In many of these fields, both the DoE and the local authorities will play rôles; but invariably these rôles will be played by other officials, working in other directorates or divisions or departments, than those in which planning is housed.

The result is that there is a vital need for integration of these activities at some higher level, in fact the highest level. Integration of this kind within the DoE, for instance, could be achieved only at the level of the Secretary of State and the Permanent Secretary, for they are the only people who sit above the structure of Directorates. Similarly, within a local authority, only the Leader of the Council and the Chief Executive could perform the rôle, for only they sit above the structure of committees and departments. But to achieve this would seem to require some degree of backup in the form of a top-level policy or strategic planning division.

It will also raise the question of bureaucratic style and approach. Planning has its own style of procedure, based on regulation of land-use through the development plan. Other parts of government work with different styles, different approaches, different instruments: subsidies and grants, environmental assessments, pricing. They will need to be brought into some kind of common strategic framework. A common argument against planning, especially in the 1980s, was that it was anti-market, that it took no account of economic realities, and that it stifled economic growth. Planners are reacting to that in the 1990s with counter-arguments, not least that a good physical environment may actually encourage growth by attracting inward investment (as counties such as Surrey, Berkshire and Buckinghamshire testify). But more will be needed to satisfy the critics, who tend to argue in hard pounds and pence; they would like to see a cost–benefit analysis of planning, although they will be unlikely to get it.

So planning is far from dead: it is alive and well, in London as elsewhere. But it is going to have to be integrated into a much wider framework of urban and regional developmental and environmental policies, and in the process a way will need to be found of integrating its basic regulatory style with the styles of these other, related policies. Together with the rest of the agenda, it means that planners will have plenty to occupy them for the rest of the 1990s.

References and further reading

Anon 1991. *The Ile-de-France planning strategy: our ambition as Europe opens up* (summary of the project presented by the Regional Executive). Paris: Conseil Régional Ile-de-France.

Breheny, M. & R. Rookwood 1993. Planning the sustainable city region. In *Planning for a sustainable environment*, A. Blowers (ed.), 150–89. London: Earthscan.

Dahrendorf, R., A. Greengross, F. Layfield, M. Stonefrost, J. C. Swaffield 1992. *A fresh start for London: an open letter to the Prime Minister.* London: Institute for Metropolitan Studies.

Flynn, N., S. Leach, C. Vielba 1985. *Abolition or reform?: The GLC and the metropolitan county councils.* London: Allen & Unwin.

Hall, P. 1988 *London 2001.* London: Unwin Hyman.

Secretary of State for the Environment 1983. *Streamlining the cities: government proposals for re-organising local government in Greater London and the metropolitan counties* (Cmnd 9063). London: HMSO.

Index